BUCKNELL REVIEW

Culture and Education in Victorian England

STATEMENT OF POLICY

BUCKNELL REVIEW is a scholarly interdisciplinary journal. Each issue is devoted to a major theme or movement in the humanities or sciences, or to two or three closely related topics. The editors invite heterodox, orthodox, and speculative ideas and welcome manuscripts from any enterprising scholar in the humanities and sciences.

This journal is a member of the Conference of Editors of Learned Journals

BUCKNELL REVIEW

A Scholarly Journal of Letters, Arts, and Sciences

Contributors should send manuscripts with a self-addressed stamped envelope to the Editors, Bucknell University, Lewisburg, Pennsylvania, 17837.

BUCKNELL REVIEW

Culture and Education in Victorian England

Edited by
PATRICK SCOTT
and
PAULINE FLETCHER

LEWISBURG
BUCKNELL UNIVERSITY PRESS
LONDON AND TORONTO: ASSOCIATED UNIVERSITY PRESSES

Associated University Presses
440 Forsgate Drive
Cranbury, NJ 08512

Associated University Presses
25 Sicilian Avenue
London WC1A 2QH, England

Associated University Presses
P.O. Box 39, Clarkson Pstl. Stn.
Mississauga, Ontario,
LSJ 3X9 Canada

The paper used in this publication meets the requirements
of the American National Standard for Permanence of Paper
for Printed Library Materials Z39.48-1984.

Library of Congress Cataloging-in-Publication Data

Culture and education in Victorian England / edited by Patrick Scott
and Pauline Fletcher.
    p. cm.—(Bucknell review ; v. 34, no. 2)
    Includes bibliographical references.
    ISBN 0-8387-5197-0 (alk. paper)
    1. Great Britain—Civilization—19th century. 2. English
literature—19th century—History and criticism. 3. Education—
Great Britain—History—19th century. 4. Education in literature.
I. Scott, Patrick Greig. II. Fletcher, Pauline, 1938–
III. Series.
AP2.B887 vol. 34. no. 2
[DA550]
051 s—dc20
[941.081]   89-46480
                                          CIP

(Volume XXXIV, Number 2)

PRINTED IN THE UNITED STATES OF AMERICA

Contents

Recent Issues of BUCKNELL REVIEW

Notes on Contributors

PATRICK BRANTLINGER is professor of English at Indiana University and editor of *Victorian Studies*. He is the author of *Spirit of Reform: British Literature and Politics 1832–67* (1977), *Bread and Circuses: Theories of Mass Culture as Social Decay* (1983), and *Rule of Darkness: British Literature and Imperialism 1830–1914* (1988).

ALISON BYERLY is an assistant professor of English at Middlebury College. She is the author of an article on George Eliot and music which appeared in *Nineteenth-Century Literature*.

BEVERLY LYON CLARK teaches at Wheaton College in Massachusetts. The author of *Lewis Carroll* and the editor of Evelyn Sharp's *The Making of a Schoolgirl*, she is now completing *Cross-Gendering a Genre: The Case of the School Story*.

MARC DEMAREST is a technical writer at Sequent Computer Systems in Beaverton, Oregon.

MICHAEL J. G. GRAY-FOW is Director of Studies, Northwestern Military Academy, Wisconsin, and Director of the Institute for Christian Studies, Episcopal Diocese of Milwaukee. He has published articles in the *Journal of Psychohistory*, *Latomus*, and *Greece and Rome*.

INDERPAL GREWAL is an assistant professor of English at George Mason University. She has written on Salman Rushdie and contemporary women writers of the diaspora and is working on a book entitled *Aesthetics and Imperialism in Nineteenth-Century English Travel*.

INA RAE HARK, professor of English at the University of South Carolina, is the author of *Edward Lear* and editor of the special issue of *Victorian Poetry* (Autumn 1988) on comic verse. In addition to her work in nineteenth-century studies, she has published several articles on American film and modern drama.

LINDA H. PETERSON is associate professor of English and Director of Expository Writing at Yale University. Her book, *Victorian Auto-*

biography: The Tradition of Self-Interpretation, discusses the dominant male tradition of autobiographical writing; she is currently at work on a book on women's autobiography called *Reclaiming the Genre: Women's Self-Writing in 19th-Century England*.

JOHN R. REED is a professor of English at Wayne State University. His books include *Victorian Conventions* (1975), *The Natural History of H. G. Wells* (1982), *Decadent Style* (1985), and *Victorian Will* (1989).

PATRICK SCOTT is professor of English at the University of South Carolina. In Victorian literature, his work includes *Tennyson's Enoch Arden: A Victorian Bestseller* (1970), *Victorian Poetry 1830–1870* (1971), *The Early Editions of Arthur Hugh Clough* (1977), and editions of Clough's *Amours de Voyage* (1974) and *The Bothie* (1976). His other areas of interest include the Scottish novel, modern African literature, and the history of rhetoric.

JUDITH STODDART is completing her doctoral dissertation at Oxford University, where she was a Rhodes Scholar. Her essay, "Swinburne and Ruskin: An Aesthetic Kinship," is forthcoming in a collection on Swinburne. She is currently working on the relation between the feminine and the popular in the nineteenth century, as found in the reception of Jean Ingelow's poetry.

MICHAEL TIMKO is professor of English at Queens College of the City University of New York and the editor of the *Carlyle Newsletter*. He is the author of *Innocent Victorian: The Satiric Poetry of Arthur Hugh Clough* and *Carlyle and Tennyson*.

MYRON TUMAN, associate professor of English at the University of Alabama, has published articles on Victorian intellectual history and contemporary writing pedagogy. He is the author of *A Preface to Literacy*, co-developer of the word processing program *Norton Textra Writer*, and editor of the forthcoming volume, *Literacy Online*.

LESLIE WILLIAMS teaches at the University of Cincinnati and the Union for Experimenting Colleges and Universities. Her article, "The Womanly Art of Breastfeeding: Art and Discourse in Nineteenth Century Britain," will appear in *Susquehanna University Studies*. She is currently writing a book on images of childhood in Regency and Victorian Britain.

Acknowledgments

Nearly half of the papers published here were first written for a conference under the same title held in October 1988 by the Victorians Institute at Columbia College and the University of South Carolina, Columbia. The editors would like to thank the original program committee who, under Patrick Scott's chairmanship, read submissions to the conference: Ina Rae Hark, Jerold J. Savory, and William B. Thesing. Thanks are also due to Vice-President Savory at Columbia College, and Dean Carol McGinnis Kay and Joel Myerson, the English Department Chair, at the University, for financial support for the conference, and to Donald Lawler, the editor of *Victorians Institute Journal*, for his cooperation in ceding to *Bucknell Review* the journal's editorial priority over key conference papers so that this volume could be developed from those initial conference discussions.

Introduction

The theme of this volume inevitably conjures up the image of
Matthew Arnold, that high priest of culture and humble foot-
soldier in the cause of education. And yet it is only fair to say
that Arnold would hardly recognize our debates on the subject.
It is no longer possible for us to think of culture purely in terms
of "sweetness and light"; we have seen something of its dark
side so that we have learned, somewhat sadly, to assert with Walter
Benjamin that every cultural document is at the same time a
record of barbarism.

Nor is it possible to think of culture as monolithic, an unbroken
line stretching back to the Greeks and the Hebrews. Nowadays
the very word is likely to provoke snarls of "Which culture?"
or "Whose culture is it anyway?" We have become aware of ethno-
centricity and phallocentricity; we cringe when we are accused
of being "elitist" and we are aware that seeming innocence may
cloak a sinister political agenda. We have moved from Arnold's
"dialogue of the mind with itself" (which begins to sound like
a very private and gentlemanly occupation, the activity of a be-
lated prince with the leisure to soliloquize) to a cacophany of
voices clamoring to be heard.

T. S. Eliot sensed the death of high culture and in terror piled
its ruined fragments against his own destruction. We, living in
an age when its ruin seems even more complete, alternately de-
plore its loss ("Why can't Johnny read?") or glory in its annihila-
tion. It is, at any rate, exhilarating to discover, even within the
narrow limits of Western culture, and within the even narrower
confines of the Victorian period, that there are many subcultures
and countercultures waiting to be explored. New voices have
joined the centuries-old conversation in the drawing room of
the Western world; some of them would like to demolish the
drawing room altogether, others are content to open a few win-
dows and let in some fresh air. In any case, we needed the new
voices; both air and conversation had become a little stale.

There is, of course, a danger, even in our present state of enlightened acceptance of the "other" and the "marginal." We may think we have escaped the complacency of Arnold's magisterial pronouncements, but we run the risk of dying smugly in the odor of our own sanctity. We need to remind ourselves that we too are provisional and contingent, firmly embedded within our own cultural context.

The essays in this volume, then, inevitably show us ourselves as well as the Victorian Age; they cover a fairly wide range of topic, focus, and attitude, and they bring together perspectives from diverse disciplines. Michael Timko, in his brief introductory essay, considers the special meanings for the nineteenth century of the words *culture* and *education*, with particular reference to the life and writings of Thomas Carlyle. This basic exploration of terms is continued by Marc Demarest, who shows how language and metaphor in Arnold's *Culture and Anarchy* define and codify culture as a social totality that is timeless and transcendent; Arnold's definition was subsequently appropriated and transformed by E. B. Tylor in *Primitive Culture*. A third Victorian sage comes under scrutiny in Judith Stoddart's paper on Ruskin, who is seen as the forerunner of such modern architects of cultural authority as Allan Bloom.

Arnold's dictum that culture can save us from anarchy is seriously questioned by Patrick Brantlinger, who explores the relationship between crime and education in Victorian England using Oliver Twist and what he read as his starting point. Does the ability to read foster virtuous behavior, or does it simply supply young minds, nurtured on "Newgate novels," with heroes and methods from the criminal underworld? Brantlinger suggests that both *Oliver Twist* and its author share some of the moral ambiguity of the whole educational process. That ambiguity is also reflected in Ina Hark's study of the use of Jewish cultural stereotypes by Edward Lear. She demonstrates that such lapses need not interfere with a general liberalism of human behavior.

Even though culture and education may not save us from anarchy or prejudice, they are nevertheless powerful instruments for transmitting values. The role of literature in the process of socializing children is explored by John Reed. Books for children attempted to teach morality by stressing the consequences of bad behavior: corporal punishment in earlier examples of the genre giving way gradually to a more enlightened and progressive emphasis on the self-destructive nature of wickedness. This triumph of more humane forms of punishment in didactic literature is paralleled by a shift in the ethic of the school story, as Beverly Clark points out. Early examples of the school story had endorsed adult authority over loyalty to peers, but during the course of the century writers increasingly adopted the child's perspective, thus creating a potentially subversive subculture.

Alison Byerly carries the discussion of contradictory impulses in Victorian culture into the world of stage and painted props. While the theater was often regarded as morally corrupting, the practice of reading aloud was sanctified both within the school-room and the confines of the domestic circle. Even when reading aloud crossed to the public stage and became increasingly dramatic, it seems to have remained untainted by the reputation of the theater; such performances, it was believed, could become an art without losing their instructional value. The connection between art and instruction was, of course, keenly felt by the Victorians, as Leslie Williams demonstrates through her analysis of Victorian genre paintings. The push toward a broad-based, literate culture during the nineteenth century provoked fears on the part of traditional Tories that working-class children were being educated above their stations, or fitted for a life of crime. Many genre painters sought to allay these fears by depicting unwilling and comically loutish children of rural laborers who would obviously never rise to challenge the squirearchy.

Not all members of the Tory establishment were reactionaries who opposed popular education. In his study of schools in a Lincolnshire village, Michael Gray-Fow reveals the degree of patronage exercised by the Wragby squires during the nineteenth century, and shows how they gradually adapted to a decline of their seigneurial authority. Victorian schools are also examined by Myron Tuman, who draws some interesting parallels and contrasts between the present-day use of graduate teaching assistants and peer tutors and the nineteenth-century adoption of student monitors and pupil teachers.

Much education took place outside the schools. Linda Peterson shows how Harriet Martineau, in her feminist revision of Hannah More's views on female education, defines the home as the most important sphere of education for both sexes. Inderpal Grewal applies a radical hermeneutic of suspicion to the education of the public through the British Museum and its guidebooks; the museum transformed objects of use into artifacts, and enshrined both aristocratic and imperial power.

Patrick Scott's reeaxmination of the Newbolt Report forms a fitting conclusion to this selection of essays since he addresses many of the concerns and issues raised by other contributors; he suggests that the Report may serve as both warning and model for cultural educators today.

PAULINE FLETCHER

BUCKNELL REVIEW

Culture and Education
in Victorian England

Thomas Carlyle and Victorian Culture

Michael Timko

Queens College, CUNY

I N his *Culture and Society: 1780–1950* Raymond Williams states that the development of the word *culture* is a "record of a number of important and continuing reactions to . . . changes in our social, economic and political life, and may be seen, in itself, as a special kind of map by means of which the nature of the changes can be explored."[1] Before I begin to review that special map, one that focuses on Thomas Carlyle, whose life and writings illustrate the significant changes taking place in the definition of these words during his lifetime, perhaps something more ought to be said about those two words that take on special meanings in the nineteenth century: *culture* and *education.*

Some years ago Robert Langbaum wrote an essay entitled "The Victorian Idea of Culture," and in that essay he emphasized the chameleonlike nature of the word and the central role it had in helping us grasp the meaning of "Victorian" life. "One has to understand," he insisted, "that the word *culture* was from the beginning charged with a world-view and a battle cry. In a revolutionary age, the word was used to define a principle of continuity underlying political, economic and even social change."[2] That principle of continuity is what I should like to emphasize, and it is that principle which many in that period saw as the chief element in the definition of the word *culture.* "It was used," states Langbaum, "to ask about the *quality* of life—especially since quality seemed to be declining. Since the economy required specialization and dehumanization, the word *culture* was invoked as an argument for the harmonious development of all our human faculties."[3] While others and I have in the past disagreed with some aspects of this definition, most, I think, would accept it as a working principle of continuity, especially in terms of its special relationship to *education*. One can note this principle most clearly in its nineteenth-century context in the career of that influential Victorian sage, Thomas Carlyle.

Carlyle's own life and writings tell us much about education and culture, at least his view of both. His emphasis always is on the self and on the cultivation of what, for want of a better word, one might call the "soul." The principle of continuity lies in the development of the human faculties, to be sure, but those faculties that remain buried deep within each individual. In Carlyle's view, one seen in his actions as well as his writings, culture and education oppose systems of any sort, anything "mechanical" and smacking of repression. It may seem contrary to our notions of Carlyle, who is often still regarded as a proto-fascist, to hear his ideas described in these terms, but the evidence supports that view, especially as regards education. One need not think only of his insistence on the cultivation of the inner spirit, pervasive in all his works, but simply look at the way he sought to gain that which we would define as education. His residence at Edinburgh as a student (1809–1814); his comments in *Sartor Resartus* (1831), in a *Fragment* (written between 1844–1851), and in his biography of John Sterling (1851); and his remarks to the students in his "Inaugural Address" as Lord Rector at his alma mater (1866) attest the consistency of his views toward education, culture, society, and the principle of continuity, at the heart of which rests his strong belief in the ability of the individual, through supreme spiritual effort, to overcome circumstance and triumph.

Carlyle entered Edinburgh at the age of thirteen, and his years there as a student were years in which he found formal learning unrewarding and turned, instead, to reading. He found most of the professors uninteresting and unhelpful, usually concerned not so much with aiding students as advancing their own careers, and he spent as much time as possible in the library. Carlyle is described by D. A. Wilson as "devouring" all the books he could get from an early age on, and certainly his years as a student at Edinburgh were spent doing just that. Wilson's account may not be absolutely reliable, but it does, I think, give the proper "flavor" concerning Carlyle's rage to learn, to secure an education in his sense of the word, one enlarged upon in his *Life of Sterling* and the "Inaugural Address." "It cannot be said," writes Wilson,

the University made reading easy. Its library was in an old building on one side of the quadrangle, not open all day, and lacking a cata-

logue. The clergyman who was "Librarian" took the pay as a perqui-
site and did nothing. A fat Highlander . . . was in command, and
considered students his natural enemies. In 1814 Tom was a six-
footer and a good witness of what used to happen as he stood in
queue at the door, and what he said he was was funny as a farce.
At the appointed hour the students began battering the door and
the Highlander opened it slowly, slowly. He could not use his feet
or his fists to show his love for his foes, but he did what he could
as they crowded in—he bent his body at the last moment to send
sprawling as many of them as possible.[4]

More reliable, perhaps, as far as Carlyle's voracious reading
and his distrust of pedagogues is concerned, are Carlyle's own
words in *Sartor*, in a fragment dealing with education only recently published, and in the "Inaugural Address." In the first,
Teufelsdröckh condemns his teachers as "hide-bound Pedants,
without knowledge of man's nature, or of boy's; or of aught save
their lexicons and quarterly account-books" and rhetorically asks:
'How can an inanimate, mechanical Gerund-grinder . . . foster
the growth of anything; much more of Mind, which grows, not
like a vegetable . . . but like a spirit'"[5]? This spirit, Teufelsdröckh
discovers, must find its nourishment elsewhere, and he concludes:
"I took less to rioting . . . than to thinking and reading, which
latter also I was free to do. Nay from the chaos of that Library,
I succeeded in fishing-up more books perhaps than had been
known to the very keepers thereof. The foundation of a Literary
Life was hereby laid: I learned . . . to read fluently in almost
all cultivated languages, on almost all subjects and sciences" (TC
1:93).
These thoughts are echoed in both the *Fragment* and in the
"Inaugural Address." In the former Carlyle, writing from the
heart, laments the methods found in the educational institutions
of his day. "Why did you bring me up (train me)," he laments,
"according to methods that were pedantic merely and not true."
He goes on:

> Methods pedantic, I say, merely bullied into you by the bowowing
> big pedants, College doctors, and which even you yourselves, for
> all the bullying of and bowowing, never could be brought to do more
> than pretend to believe? Oh Shame! Here you had a young soul
> landed with you back fresh from the hands of its Maker to love,
> and try to imitate, eager to learn whatsoever of great and wonderful
> and beautiful the Almighty Builder of the Universe, Author too of
> that young soul, had made and done. . . . What is it that I must
> learn to know, that I should learn to do?[6]

In the "Inaugural Address" Carlyle tells the students, again
with an obvious sincerity that is striking, that the true university
is, in truth, a "Collection of Books" and that they should learn
to be "good readers." He then makes his point, one that is particularly interesting in the light of his remarks in the *Fragment*:

> What the Universities can mainly do for you,—what I have found
> the University did for me, is, That it taught me to read, in various
> languages, in various sciences; so that I could go into the books which
> treated of these things, and gradually penetrate into any department
> I wanted to make myself master of, as I found it suit me. [TC
> 29:454–55]

More crucial to Carlyle for education and culture than reading
and penetration, however, was the nourishment of the spirit,
and this act involved what many, especially the university authorities, saw as the defiance of authority. One reason for Carlyle's
writing the biography of Sterling was his disagreement with Hare
over the real character of John Sterling, and a specific topic over
which they differed was Sterling's education. Carlyle, of course,
did not think much of what we might call the education that
one received at Oxbridge. "He prefers," wrote Emerson, "Cambridge to Oxford, but he thinks Oxford and Cambridge education indurates the young men, as the Styx hardened Achilles,
so that when they come forth of them, they say, 'Now we are
proof: we have gone through all the degrees, and are case-
hardened against the veracities of the Universe; nor man nor
God can penetrate us.'"[7] Hare, in his biography of Sterling, had
made clear his disapproval of Sterling's university experience:

> In the regular course of the studies at University, Sterling did not
> take much part. Of the genial young men who go to Cambridge,
> many do not. This is greatly to be regretted. For even where the
> alternative is not blank idleness, or intellectual self-indulgence and
> dissipation, it is a misfortune for a young man to lose the disciplinary
> influence of a prescribed system, and the direction and encourage-
> ment of intelligent guides. . . . If they [the students] follow any pecu-
> liar studies by themselves, they are thereby set in a kind of opposition
> to authority and established institutions, are led to look upon them
> with dislike, if not with disdain, and to feel an overweening confidence
> in their own wisdom. It is often made a matter of complaint, that
> men of the world, men who act a prominent part in public life, feel
> little affection for their University.[8]

Those familiar with Carlyle's experience at Edinburgh, his disdain for some of his professors and his dependence on reading

and self-study, will be able to sense both his great sympathy with Sterling's choice of study and "education" at Cambridge and his rejection of Hare's faith in system and authority, of established institutions, in which Carlyle would include not only education but theology as well. Carlyle, in contrast to Hare, found much to praise in Sterling's "peculiar studies" and self-indulgence. "His studies and inquiries," Carlyle writes, "were of the most discursive wide-flowing character; not steadily advancing along beaten roads towards College honours, but pulsing out with impetuous irregularity now on this tract, now on that towards whatever spiritual Delphi might promise to unfold the mystery of this world, and announce to him what was, in our new day, the authentic message of the gods." One is not surprised, either, when Carlyle states, "His speculations, reading, inferences, glances and conclusions were doubtless sufficiently encyclopedic; his grand tutors the multifarious set of Books he devoured" (TC 11:34).

Carlyle's view of education and of culture—the nourishment of the spirit—has for its basis, then, the defying of authority and established institutions and the nurturing of those individual spirits who, in fact, insist on unfolding the mystery of the world and attempt to hear the authentic message of the gods. Here is Carlyle's own view of Sterling at the university:

In short, . . . he was already . . . at all points a Radical, as the name or nickname went. In other words, a young ardent soul looking with hope and joy into a world which was infinitely beautiful to him, though overhung with falsities and foul cobwebs as world never was before; overloaded, overclouded, to the zenith and nadir of it, by incredible uncredited traditions, solemnly sordid hypocrisies, and beggerly deliriums old and new; which latter class of objects it was clearly the part of every noble heart to expend all its lightnings and energies in burning-up without delay, and sweeping into their native Chaos out of such Chaos as this. [TC 11:36–37]

The emphasis throughout Carlyle's writings and in his own life is on this kind of "radicalism," a radicalism that insists on a strong faith in the self and the destruction of falsities, hypocricies, and uncredited traditions. Carlyle's "culture" rests clearly on the harmonious development of human faculties, but it is clear, too, that the uniqueness of each individual constitutes the principle of continuity in his view of culture. If his case is an example to all others, and he clearly thinks so in his advice to the students and in his biography of Sterling, then the emphasis always is on the "I" and not the "We" or the "Institution."

The emphasis on the uniqueness of the individual explains
Carlyle's despair, one might say his grief, over the way educational
institutions in his day crushed rather than nourished the individual spirit, smothered rather than saved or solaced the soul. In
the *Fragment* he appeals to his "honoured Seniors" for direction
and guidance:

> I am poor and small and helpless, and trust wholly to you. Where
> are the [heroisms, human noblenesses, the shining vestiges of him
> that made me] . . . , —lead me, lead me! . . . . Whatsoever you teach
> me, I will learn; you may make me all things.[9]

Surely this Carlylean approach helps explain why *Sartor* remains such a moving document and probably always will. We
read it not as one person's "religious" conversion, although some
still insist on doing so. We read it instead as one person's insistence on the uniqueness of each individual's spirit and the need
to recognize the beauty and strength of that spirit. To Carlyle,
one's education is not found in "competent skill in construing
Latin, an elementary knowledge of Greek, a legible penmanship
and the copious habit of employing it in all manner of uncon-
scious English prose or verse"; it is found, rather, in learning
to read, and in that word *read* Carlyle wants us to see what he
saw. "What I have found the University did for me, is, that it
taught me to read . . . so that I could go into books which treated
of these things, and gradually penetrate into any department
I wanted to make myself master of, as I found it suit me" (TC
29: 454–55). Note the emphasis on the subjective: me, I, myself,
and the self-mastery; master of, suit me. That is why the protest
against the Everlasting No and the Baphometic Fire-Baptism in
Sartor are so moving and significant. They do not document a
religious conversion in a theological sense; they demonstrate
Carlyle's faith in what he saw as education. Here is the Radical
standing up to Institutions and Authority and Professors: "and
then it was that my whole Me stood up . . . and with emphasis
recorded its Protest. Such a Protest, the most important trans-
action in Life, may that same Indignation and Defiance, in a psychological point of view, be fitly called. The Everlasting No had
said: 'Behold, thou are fatherless, outcast, and the Universe is
mine (the Devil's)'; to which my whole Me now made answer:
'*I* am not thine, but Free, and forever hate thee!'" (TC 1:167–68).
Here is Carlyle's moving description of his realization that he
was now on the way to finding the spiritual Delphi, which would

unfold the mystery of this world, and announce to him, in the new day, the authentic message of the gods. His "speculations, reading, inferences, [encyclopedic] glances and conclusions," and his "grand tutors—the multifarious set of Books he devoured"— had finally set free his unique spirit, the spirit we today call and recognize as Carlylean.

Notes

A longer version of this paper will appear in *Victorians Institute Journal*.

1. Raymond Williams, *Culture and Society: 1780–1950* (New York: Doubleday, 1960), xv.

2. Robert Langbaum, *The Modern Spirit* (New York: Oxford University Press, 1970), 45.

3. Ibid.

4. David Alec Wilson, *Carlyle*, 6 vols. (London: Kegan, Paul, Trench, 1923–34), 1: 87–88.

5. Thomas Carlyle, *Works*, Centenary edition, ed. H. D. Traill, 30 vols. (London: Chapman & Hall, 1896–98), 1: 85–86. Hereafter TC, cited in the text.

6. Quoted in Michael Timko, "Carlyle, Sterling, and the Scavenger Age," *Studies in Scottish Literature* 20 (1986): 26–27.

7. Emerson, as quoted in Wilson, 4:43.

8. John Sterling, *Essays and Tales by John Sterling with a Memoir of His Life*, ed. J. C. Hare, 2 vols. (London: J. Parker, 1848), 1: xiii.

9. Quoted in Timko, "Carlyle," 27.

Arnold and Tylor: The Codification and Appropriation of Culture

Marc Demarest

> During the recent past some tangible changes have taken place
> in the scope of college and university teaching. These changes
> have in the main constituted a partial displacement of the
> humanities—those branches of learning which are conceived
> to make for the traditional "culture," character, tastes and
> ideals—for those more matter-of-fact branches which make
> for civic and industrial efficiency. To put the same thing in
> other words, those branches of knowledge which make for
> efficiency (ultimately, productive efficiency) have gradually
> been gaining ground against those branches which make for
> a heightened consumption . . . and for a type of character
> suited to the regime of status. . . . It is noticeable that the
> humanities, which have so reluctantly yielded ground to the
> sciences, are pretty uniformly adapted to shape the character
> of the student in accordance with a traditional self-centered
> scheme of consumption: a scheme of contemplation and en-
> joyment of the true, the beautiful and good, according to
> a conventional standard of propriety and excellence, the sali-
> ent feature of which is leisure—*otium cum dignitate*.
> —Thorsten Veblen, *The Theory of the Leisure Class* (1899)

OF the three aspects of discursive practice that Michel Foucault cites as evidence of a "system of thought,"[1] the field
of objects, particularly the central theoretical object around which
the network of metaphors[2] that sustains a systemic discourse is
built, is by far the most important. When investigating the irruption of such a system of thought as culture, we do well to begin
not with dictionaries, usage, and the renegade events that, taken
together, may well mark a shift in the structure these scattered
verbal events attack, but with codification: that localizable point

26

at which the renegade sign is taken into language as an object around which an emerging field of discursive practice may arrange itself.[3]

We are fortunate in being able to locate the codification of culture largely within the development of a single text: Matthew Arnold's *Culture and Anarchy* (1869).[4] It is safe to say that before *Culture and Anarchy* culture remained a signifying latency, operating below formal discourse in a subjective way: culture is undoubtedly widely discussed in print from the 1850s onward, but the discourse is still gathering itself around an object whose dimensions and inventory it is by no means sure about and about which it can therefore speak with impunity. *Culture and Anarchy*'s significance for the history of the metaphor of culture is that, strictly speaking, it is the text that invented culture both for the Victorians and for modernism and then delivered it unto its enemies: by speaking its name, identifying it, codifying it, and supplying an inventory of its objectives and operations within the social field—in short, by fixing it as a defined theoretical object of a critical discourse—*Culture and Anarchy* single-handedly cleared the way for culture's dispersion and appropriation in the 1870s and after.

The arguments put forth in *Culture and Anarchy* are far too well-known for summary. We should concern ourselves here with the strategies of culture as the text figures them, with the objectives it identifies for culture, and the ways in which those objectives lend themselves to appropriation for purposes at odds with the strategies of *Culture and Anarchy*. For example, the preface to *Culture and Anarchy* sums up its goal as follows:

> The whole scope of the essay is to recommend culture as the great help out of our present difficulties; culture being a pursuit of our total perfection by means of getting to know, on all matters that concern us most, the best which has been thought or said in the world; and through this knowledge, turning a stream of fresh and free thought upon our stock notions and habits, which we follow staunchly but mechanically, vainly imagining that there is a virtue in following them staunchly which makes up for the mischief of following them mechanically.[5]

In this brief passage is sketched the fundamental metaphoricity of the essay and of culture itself as it is figured in the essay. Here is the empty body of the human subject stocked with "notions and habits" which prompt it to mechanical action: the possessed body. Here also the flow: a "stream" of thought which in entering the body and playing over the "habits and notions" transforms them and the body itself.[6]

> If a man without book or reading, or reading every day nothing but his letters and the newspapers, gets nevertheless a fresh and free play of the best thoughts upon his stock notions and habits, he has got culture. He has got that for which we prize and recommend culture; he has got that which at the present moment we seek culture that it may give us. This inward operation is the very life and essence of culture, as we conceive it. [CA, 6–7]

The suggestion that culture does not reside in a historical body of knowledge is, as we know, disingenuous; finally, culture in *Culture and Anarchy* operates within what was at the time a strictly classical Oxbridge canonicity. What is important about this passage is its schematization of the position and flow of culture: culture is both within and without, something sought and, in finding, possessed, and also something operating in the body, possessing it. The body's possession by culture is initially productive: free, fresh, liberating the body from its machinic condition. The body's possession of culture, on the other hand, is fundamentally nonproductive: a shibboleth, a marking, an indication of status or identity. This double possession in which culture and the body exchange subjectivity and objectivity is an addition to culture's inventory: not a new contribution to the metaphoric field in which culture locates itself, since the two phrases "the cultured man" and "getting culture" were in exchange before any of the essays that became *Culture and Anarchy* were published, but nevertheless an important step toward culture's fragmentation into two figurative modes: one consumptive, one productive.

The desire for an epistemologically stable point of observation, which was structurally lacking in the Victorian model of society,[7] was a driving force behind the developments that led to the promulgation of culture as a program of influence designed to counteract "pernicious" influences at the discrete level of individual bodies. Diverse groups of bodies producing diverse objects within the social field also produced and laid claim to positions of epistemological surety, claiming too the right to totalize their desire as the sum of knowledge. *Culture and Anarchy* is traced with the desire to produce such a position, one from which to once and for all ascertain value: the true, the aesthetically and socially good. On misunderstandings about the uses of culture—as a word and as a program—we find:

> [O]ur usefulness depends on our being able to . . . convince those who mechanically serve some stock notion or operation, and thereby go astray, that it is not culture's work or aim to give the victory to some rival fetish, but simply to turn a free and fresh stream of thought on the whole matter [of social value] in question. . . . Culture, which is the study of perfection, leads us . . . to conceive of true human perfection as a harmonious perfection, developing all sides of our humanity; and as a general perfection, developing all parts of our society. [*CA*, 10–11]

From these assertions—or more properly, summations—one of the text's central epistemological feints is formed: culture's work is *disinterested* work, transcending the programs and desire of groups producing within the social field, operating not as the deployed agent of a particular group but at a level before and beyond groups and therefore beyond desire and cooption. Culture is the epistemologically stable—because transcendent—position from which it itself surveys its objects: human bodies on the social field. The older metaphor of culture as self-cultivation—"harmonious perfection"—is overlaid with its metaphoric twin—"general perfection, developing all parts of our society"—as a result of a collective perfection at the discrete level of subjectivity, and the image of society's members is figured not as subjectivity but as parts of a larger and more perfect unitary body.

> And because men are all members of one great whole, and the sympathy which is in human nature will not allow one member to be indifferent to the rest or to have a perfect welfare independent of the rest, the expansion of our humanity, to suit the idea of perfection which culture forms, must be a general expansion. Perfection, as culture conceives it, is not possible while the individual remains isolated. The individual is required, under pain of being stunted and enfeebled in his own development if he disobeys, to carry along others in his march towards perfection, to be continually doing all he can to enlarge and increase the volume of the human stream sweeping thitherward. [*CA*, 48]

The path of culture as an influence over *bodies*, sketched here as the "true way of salvation," is a complete acceptance of the terms of the cultural metaphor as *Culture and Anarchy* received it from the central texts of the Enlightenment. The body passes from a state of individual isolated provinciality and lack, an isolated machinic or habitual concern with the fetish of the self or group, to an integrated identification with a totality: a perfect, indeed sublime, submergence of subjectivity into the largest social grouping conceivable. The metaphoric function of this totality is clear; in eliminating the "hole and corner"[8] mentality of provincial groups, the move toward totality (as both group subject and social objective) aligns the production of all groups and individuals under culture's influence (which becomes more human than its objects as the essay progresses), thus producing epistemological stability by eliminating or effacing all difference between groups and individuals.

The question is, of course, whether for *Culture and Anarchy* this cultural totalization is a produced, and therefore social, object or an a priori state: an object each society produces for itself or a transcendent, inviolable condition to which a transcendent culture brings those subjects under its control. Since in *Culture and Anarchy* culture is a transcendent register of valued knowledge—"the best that has been thought and known in the world"— it cannot be produced or, rather, has already been produced; all that a body under the influence of culture can achieve is a full realization of its own belatedness: culture is always already there, replete in its truth and justified in its right to prevail over everything lesser than itself.

The epistemological and aesthetic problems occasioned by a diversity of movement, grouping, and social production that plagued Victorian social theory and organization are therefore solved; social alignment with and acceptance of a single object, culture, as both influence and goal (both agent within and agent without the body) allows a constant representation of culture to substitute itself for social production. By definition in *Culture and Anarchy*, culture can produce nothing more perfect, more knowing, than its own agent in a condition of complete identification with it. But the culture's production of its agents is merely the reproduction of culture in its discrete embodiment: a machine, a transitional mechanism. In a totality where all are agents and all identify completely, the social field is uniform, every group is exactly representative of every other group, and to survey and mark the extent of culture and its values—which *Culture and Anarchy* does immaculately—is therefore to survey and mark the entirety of the social field.

This, of course, undoes social production completely, and, in so doing, leads to the unraveling—within the metaphor and actually—of the very position of epistemological surety *Culture and Anarchy* wished to develop:

> The moment this view of culture is seized, the moment it is regarded not solely as the endeavour to see things as they are, to draw towards

a knowledge of the universal order which seems to be intended and aimed at in the world, and which it is a man's happiness to go along with or his misery to go counter to . . . the moment, I say, culture is considered not merely as the endeavour to see and learn this, but to make it prevail, the moral, social and beneficent character of culture becomes manifest. [*CA*, 46]

Culture's flow is, thus, from transcendence to historical embodiment back to transcendence: from a timeless tradition to "human perfection in an internal condition" to the external perfection of social totality and the individual's absorption in and identification with that totality as a representation of the timeless. But, since the process of enculturation is finite and its final object— itself—present at least to itself prior to its social realization, the only objects culture actually produces are interim objects, makeshifts: optimally full bodies, agent subjectivities, which in turn produce an optimally full and uniform social group, both of which align with, identify themselves as agents of, and empty themselves into the social totality of culture. Thus when *Culture and Anarchy* suggests that agents of culture are the "true apostles of equality," we understand the meaning: the problems of inequality (that is to say, difference) are to be resolved in the production of a perfect empty sameness.

This notion of culture as transcendence producing its own social realization leads to, as I have said, a destruction of social production itself, since a substitution of "totality" for "provinciality" is a substitution of the social realization of cultural/ transcendent objects for the diverse production of objects of desire:

"May not every man in England say what he likes?"—Mr. Roebuck perpetually asks; and that, he thinks, is quite sufficient, and when every man may say what he likes, our aspirations ought to be satisfied. But the aspirations of culture, which is the study of perfection, are not satisfied, unless what men say, when they say what they like, is worth saying—has good in it, and more good than bad. In the same way the *Times* . . . urges that the English ideal is that every one should be free to do and to look just as he likes. But culture indefatigably tries, not to make what each raw person may like, the rule by which he fashions himself; but to draw ever nearer to a sense of what is indeed beautiful, graceful and becoming, and to get the raw person to like that. [*CA*, 50]

This raw person—the body culture wishes to enter and transform into the representative of itself—is contrasted explicitly with the transcendent subjectivity of culture itself, which, as the essay progresses, takes on more and more qualities of subjectivity as it nears its own realization in the social totality. This raw body produces according to "the rule by which he fashions himself"; when culture disrupts this production, objectivizing the subject and taking subjectivity upon itself, it substitutes not another form of production, as the text alleges, but rather a rarified form of consumption: a selection from the inventory of culture of objects and values already produced and validated by history and transcendence, to be represented or consumed by a conditioned object. Production becomes the exclusive province of culture itself as the transcendent subject, and even this transcendent subject produces only representations of itself in the bodies of its objects and in their collective cultured body—the state.

As *Culture and Anarchy* progresses, the synonymity between this condition of totality and the nationalist state becomes increasingly clear, and we discover that what culture produces, aside from perfectly formed cultural agents who empty their subjectivities into culture itself, is the state, as the "real" representative or guarantor of culture, as the immediate and "real" object of desire and alignment for bodies under the influence of culture.

> Through culture seems to lie our way, not only to perfection, but even to safety . . . [f]or we have seen how much of our disorders and perplexities is due to the disbelief, among the classes and combinations of men, Barbarian or Philistine, which have hitherto governed our society, in right reason, in a paramount best self; to the inevitable break-up and decay of the organisations by which, asserting and expressing in these organisations their ordinary self only, they have so long ruled us: and to their irresolution, when the society, which their conscience tells them they have made and still manage not with right reason but with their ordinary self, is rudely shaken, in offering resistance to its subverters. But for us,—who believe in right reason, in the duty and possibility of extricating and elevating our best self, in the progress of humanity towards perfection,—for us the framework of society . . . is sacred; and whoever administers it, and however we may seek to remove them from their tenure of administration, yet, while they administer, we steadily and with undivided heart support them in repressing anarchy and disorder: because without order there can be no society, and without society there can be no human perfection. [*CA*, 202–3]

The passage is an implicit denial of *Culture and Anarchy*'s premise that culture alone can produce order out of anarchy and indeed represents a rhetorical return to the strategies of the state in the 1815–1830 period.[9] But, although the statement appears to reject the possibility of culture existing outside the control of the state, thus placing culture in a position of subservience to the state, it does not. What is deemed impossible is the influence of culture upon a collective body in complete decadence: that is to say, a society which has destroyed its state. Thus, the state serves culture and embodies it insofar as it creates the framework within which individual and collective bodies arise and become sites for culture's operations and representation. Notice that the passage's structural premise is that the social field lies within but is not controlled by the state: the state can become the victim of the society it facilitates. Notice, too, that the stability of the state and the orderliness of the social field are directly related to the proximity of the state's administrators as representatives of a class-based group to culture: Barbarians and Philistines, being by definition removed from sweetness and light, cannot create order and the preconditions for cultural perfection precisely because they are not agents of culture.

In summary, *Culture and Anarchy* transformed and systematized the early Victorian discourse on culture, producing as a result culture as a theoretical object. Culture is represented as an inventory of already produced knowledge existing outside the social field and, indeed, outside time itself. Culture begins as transcendence and embodies itself by means of influence operating within the body of its agents, which then represent culture as a social totality. By localizing and rendering finite the reproduction of transcendent culture as a social totality, individual subjectivity is emptied of productive capabilities, and those productive capabilities are vested in culture itself, which then ends its own (re)-productivity in the perfected consumption of its image by its objectified agents. Yet culture requires stability and administration or management of the social field for its successful embodiment. These are provided to the extent that the state is controlled by agents of culture in the form of representatives of "cultured" classes. In this way, an untenable connection between epistemology—and therefore evaluation—and culture is made rhetorically persuasive and, as a narrative of longing, taken up by later discourse on culture.

More important than any of these, however, is the fact that *Culture and Anarchy* provided a codified, systemic definition of culture—that it made of culture a theoretical object in an organized discourse. This contribution cannot be underestimated, for, at almost the very historical juncture when *Culture and Anarchy* put forth the first distinct and systemic definition of culture, that definition began to slip into difference, to disintegrate, to disperse and move away in diverse directions from the humanist/critical sign under which it was invoked, to be appropriated by other discourses, the aims of which were not amenable to *Culture and Anarchy*'s purposes.

"History," E. B. Tylor writes in *Primitive Culture* (1871), "is oral or written record which can be satisfactorily traced into contact with the events it describes,"[10] and, like *Culture and Anarchy*, *Primitive Culture* chooses to place the discussion of culture within the context of history:

> The philosophy of history at large, explaining the past and predicting the future phenomena of man's life in the world by reference to general laws, is a subject with which, in the present state of knowledge, even genius aided by wide research seems but hardly able to cope. Yet there are departments of it which, though difficult enough, seem comparatively accessible. If the field of enquiry be narrowed from History as a whole to that branch of it which is here called Culture, the history, not of tribes or nations, but of the condition of knowledge, religion, art, custom and the like among them, the task of investigation proves to lie within far more moderate compass. [*PC*, 1:5]

Primitive Culture, rather than *Culture and Anarchy*, is usually credited with developing the first systemic definition of culture, but this is due more to the arrogance of the history of science than to actual historical precedence. The definition springing full-grown from the first page of *Primitive Culture* clearly shares fundamental desires and objects with *Culture and Anarchy*'s definition, while simultaneously moving away from the codification of culture as transcendence toward an image of culture as inventory: a partial return to the Enlightenment in the quest for a scientific basis for the study of culture as a set of social forms.

Culture and Anarchy cast the transactions between culture and history (as the canon) as mutually supportive and reproducing; in *Primitive Culture*, too, culture figures as the embodiment of historical laws—laws both of progression and decay, laws of natural history and the history of man—but, in this text, there is a real operational distinction between culture and Culture. Culture proper, a theoretical object, is a standard produced by as-yet-undefined "general laws" or "historical laws," to be applied as a sort of observer's checklist to any and all societies as they are found. The purpose of this theoretical object is valuation: to determine which actual social forms—cultures—are Culture's representations or embodiments and therefore fit objects of a scientific study whose goal is to affirm the very "historical laws" that produced the scheme of determination initially. Thus, where *Culture and Anarchy* postulated culture as a selective historical tradition returning to itself through its agents, the images in *Primitive Culture* are of a macrocosmic history made known to itself and to its agents by a microcosmic hermeneutic applied to observable social forms. The rupture of culture as a theoretical object produced by this image is potent: culture is simultaneously transcendent—as a theoretical object served by an observer—and phenomenal in a wide variety of more or less rude "stages" that are linked to one another in series.

> Even when it comes to comparing barbarous hordes with civilised nations, the consideration thrusts itself upon our minds, how far item after item of the life of the lower races passes into analogous proceedings of the higher, in forms not too far changed to be recognised, and sometimes hardly changes at all . . . If we choose out in this way things which have altered a little in a long course of centuries, we may draw a picture where there shall be scarce a hand's breadth difference between an English ploughman and a negro of Central Africa. [*PC*, 1:7]

Culture proper (as History) thus serves as a transcendent point of origin and return; the analysis of cultures in their individual varieties, leading back, if only implicitly, to a unification of variety in the sameness of history, becomes the proper focus of cultural study. In emphasizing phenomenon over transcendence, *Primitive Culture* in effect uses *Culture and Anarchy* against itself; it successfully develops the epistemological position *Culture and Anarchy* argued was possible within a discourse on culture, a position *Culture and Anarchy* postponed until culture's totalization, by creating the ethnologist as observer, as the agent of culture tracing his own origins in "primitive" cultures outside of which he locates himself.

The creation of this position is accomplished by categorizing culture as a subset of history closely linked with, if not identical to, the social field and explicitly exclusive of the state. *Primitive Culture* appears to break *Culture and Anarchy*'s joining of the state and culture and to free culture as potentially independent social forms. This has the effect of rendering culture a scientific object, since one considers the groups, sites, and methods of production in the social field only as such and not in the context of the state. This apparent break between culture and state is, in fact, only a suspension for the duration of the agent's observation;

the gap is closed after analysis when the historical essence of the primitive culture is brought to bear, as we shall see, on the observer's own culture as social corrective.

Primitive Culture redeploys the Enlightenment's tropes of civilization as development and decay along the horizontality of the collective social body, again as science.

> The two theories which thus account for the relation of savage to cultured life may be contrasted according to their main character, as the progression-theory and degradation-theory. Yet of course the progression-theory recognises degradation, and the degradation-theory recognises progression as powerful influences in the course of culture. Under proper limitations the principles of both theories are conformable to historical knowledge, which shows us, on the one hand, that the state of the higher nations was reached by progression from a lower state, and, on the other hand, that culture gained by progression may be lost by degradation. . . . History, taken as our guide in explaining the different stages of civilisation, offers a theory based on actual experience. This is a development-theory, in which both advance and relapse have their acknowledged places. But so far as history is to be our criterion, progression is primary and degradation secondary: culture must be gained before it can be lost. [*PC*, 1:38–39]

This redeployment has the fruitful effect of intertwining a metaphoricity of *civilization*—running parallel to the emerging metaphoricity of culture in the first half of the nineteenth century—with the metaphor of culture itself, making the two terms roughly interchangeable and allowing the disabled Enlightenment metaphor to be rehabilitated as a description of the social field detached from the state (rather than as the totality of social development, as the Enlightenment conceived it), and deployed not as explicit metaphor—as a table of similitude—but as "historical law."

A corollary to this recovered historical law: given that culture must be gained before it is modified or lost, it follows that a full culture perceiving in itself the plenitude dictated by historical law is not only in the most preferable position along the horizontal continuum of collective bodies but is also occupying the epistemologically stable—the scientific—position from which a study of any culture less developed than its own is scientifically practicable.

> The educated world of Europe and America practically settles a standard simply by placing its own nations at one end of the social series

and savage tribes at the other, arranging the rest of mankind between these limits according as they correspond more closely to savage or to cultured life. The principle criteria are the absence or presence, high or low development, of the industrial arts, especially metalworking, manufacture of implements and vessels, agriculture, architecture, &c., the extent of scientific knowledge, the definiteness of moral principles, the condition of religious belief and ceremony, the degree of social and political organisation, and so forth. Thus, on a definite basis of compared fact, ethnographers are able to set up at least a rough scale of civilisation. Few would dispute that the following races are arranged rightly in order of culture: —Australian, Tahitian, *Aztec*, Chinese, Italian. [*PC*, 1:26–27]

The English ethnographer thus occupies the privileged epistemological position—the position from which he can infer and discover the action of historical laws—by virtue of his production within a highly developed culture whose historians, soldiers, scientists, and colonists make possible the discovery of the cultures he now arranges in series. Coming out of his own culture as an agent, the ethnographer stands to one side or another of the series and inventories more primitive cultures than his own, but always with a view to explaining not those cultures but the rationality of his own: culture thus produces and serves the observer in his program of knowing his own culture.

Culture and Anarchy envisions the contents of culture euphemistically; it is, after all, much more concerned with the mechanisms whereby culture triumphs over other influences within the social field. *Primitive Culture*, on the other hand, is concerned to develop, around culture as a theoretical object, a representative grouping of institutions present in European society in order to determine in primitive cultures the "presence or absence" of these institutions and their "high or low development" in those cultures. It is possible, *Primitive Culture* argues, for any given culture to be at any given state of development within one of the types of institution (moral, political, intellectual, and industrial) and at quite another level within another: for example, it is structurally possible for hunter/gatherers to produce "fine art" or to practice a recognizable form of representative government. Yet there are thresholds; a particularly low level of development at one level precludes development beyond a certain stage at another lever inasmuch as a plenitude at the lower level is a prerequisite for plenitude at the level above it. Thus, each level presupposes a sufficiency at the level beneath it; just as a culture does not lose itself without first gaining itself, a culture does not, for example, achieve highly developed political institutions without a highly developed industrial base.

I hesitate to point out the obvious—that this structure is essentially a description of the metaphor of hierarchical class structures as embodied in the self-conception of Victorian society, a reformation of *Culture and Anarchy*'s conception of a cultured elite defending culture and the state against an insurgence from below and a replication of the three-tiered metaphor of society. The structural similarities are present because in every case *Primitive Culture* is drawing its examples of highly developed cultural/institutional categories—explicitly, without apology— from England in the 1860s. What it does with these categories, however, is to superpose them upon other, less developed, cultures in the effort to discover the less-developed forms of the English institutions themselves and thus prove the accuracy of the categories as unchanging forms and their natural culmination in late Victorian culture.

The possibility of "cultural critique" arising from this operation is noted in the final chapter of *Primitive Culture*:

> It is our happiness to live in one of those eventful periods of intellectual and moral history, when the oft-closed gates of discovery and reform stand open at their widest. . . . To the promoters of what is sound and reformers of what is faulty in modern culture, ethnography has double help to give. To impress men's minds with a doctrine of development, will lead them in all honour to their ancestors to continue the progressive work of past ages, to coninue it more vigourously because light has increased in the world, and where barbaric hordes groped blindly cultured men can often move onward with a clear view. It is a harsher, and at times even painful, office of ethnography to expose the remains of crude old culture which have passed into harmful superstition, and to mark these out for destruction. . . . Thus, active at once in aiding progress and removing hindrance, the science of culture is essentially a reformer's science. [*PC*, 2:452–53]

In what ways, then, did *Primitive Culture*'s appropriation of culture produce a metaphoricity for culture different from that produced by *Culture and Anarchy*? First, and most importantly, *Primitive Culture* fixed culture (as opposed to Culture) as a scientific rather than a merely critical object. It is here and not in the texts of Spencer, then, that we ought to locate the irruption of the "two cultures" metaphor that plagues twentieth-century thought. By breaking Culture into cultures and reintroducing

similitude and the series as the basis for a comparative and, ultimately, normative inventory of cultural forms as they are found
and as they represent the shadowing forth of universal historical/
scientific laws of cultural development, *Primitive Culture* detached
the positive notion of culture as a productive force from the
metaphor of culture as consumption. Science retains the productive metaphor: culture as a theoretical object produces in its broken and wavering teleology subjectivities fit to reconstruct its own
history and, therefore, their own. But science does nothing with
the metaphor of culture as consumption; that liability is neatly
stripped away by *Primitive Culture*'s reformulation and remains
unique of *Culture and Anarcny*'s particular tropes.

Primitive Culture also refigures transcendence, casting culture
into the realm of the real, the factual: the observable. It is not
culture—as a selective subset of history—which is transcendent,
but history itself. Culture becomes a resolutely social object—as
well as a theoretical object—formed by universal laws of History,
which laws guide human development at levels other than that
of culture. As a part of this refigurement of transcendence, the
constituent elements of culture are defined at two levels: the institution as the constitutive cultural form and the organized group
as the constitutive human element. This has the effect of abolish-
ing completely the lowest layer of the three-tiered model as a
site of cultural action: the formative massing level of individual
subjectivity becomes, as we might guess, the province of another
science—psychology—which embraces the three-tiered metaphoricity as well. Ethnology simply cannot, in *Primitive Culture*,
push back the threshold below which groups and individuals sink
from the sight of institutions and groups on the social field; the
social field is, therefore, collapsed on this level, erasing it.

Primitive Culture also deproblematized the epistemology of culture by casting an observer's relation to his own culture in terms
of similitude. Standing outside the social field of other cultures
while remaining an agent of his own, the ethnographer extracts
specific evidence of social or historical laws and then, as experimenter, applies these historical laws to the culture within which
he finds himself. Although this epistemology is in fact no more
stable than that of *Culture and Anarchy*, its scientism is reassuring,
and the difficulties of placement it involves are largely ignored
by the texts that pick up this particular displacement of culture
after 1870.

Primitive Culture's particular tropes do retain certain metaphoric elements found in *Culture and Anarchy*'s figurations, how-

ever. The text retains transcendence as the ultimate motive force behind Culture: Culture is simply moved out of the sweep of history and into concrete cultures within the social field, where cultural forms function as evidence of transcendent laws rather than the totalized realization of transcendence proper. The text also retains the relationship between culture and the state and even indicates that a proper understanding of culture on the part of the educated, enlightened, ethnographically inclined few can redirect the course of civilization—a complete endorsement of the administrator-state arrangement in *Culture and Anarchy*. *Primitive Culture*'s administrators are apparently not within the state machine proper but in a parallel institution—the institution of science, to which scientists stand as school inspectors stand to the Government—from which they will, as we shall see, deploy into formation to conduct the battle over culture after 1870.

Finally, *Primitive Culture* expands upon the class-based distinctions within culture by drawing an analogy with the high and low development of cultures. Although these terms are used in an ostensibly comparative sense—to relate primitive cultures to modern ones—they form, implicitly, a set of graded distinctions to be imported into English culture, as all ethnographic research eventually returns to its culture of origin as the real object of study.

We should see, in *Primitive Culture* and *Culture and Anarchy*, two distinct kinds of discourse about a single theoretical object, discourses that occupy various social groups and are largely at odds with one another after 1870. The discourse operating in *Primitive Culture* adheres to a metaphoricity of culture that emphasizes a stable epistemological relationship between subject and object, a phenomenal, developmental, and purely social position for a multitude of cultures, and the group and the institution, respectively, as the constitutive and productive cultural units and forms. The discourse that appears in *Culture and Anarchy*, by contrast, adheres to a metaphoricity that claims an unstable or intuitive epistemological relationship between subject and object, a totalizing position for a single unitary Culture, and the individual and the group as the constitutive consumptive cultural unit and cultural form. The discourse of science is the discourse of production: in its development culture produces subjectivity according to its relative position within a broader cultural series. The higher the level of a culture's development, the more developed the consequent subjectivity within that culture until, finally, a culture produces Culture's hermeneut: the scientist, the observer, the experimenter. The discourse of the humanities, on the other hand, is a discourse of consumption: culture produces itself by curtailing production as soon as it has created subjectivity in perfect identification with itself and its objects: a subjectivity ideally suited to consume culture's now supreme body.

Notes

The author would like to acknowledge the invaluable assistantce of Barry Faulk and Jim Hipp in the preparation of the materials from which this article is excerpted.

1. Michel Foucault, "History of Systems of Thought," in *Language, Counter-memory, Practice: Selected Essays and Interviews*, ed. and trans. Donald F. Bouchard and Sherry Simon (Ithaca: Cornell University Press, 1977), 199.

2. This network of metaphors—each of which is sustained in discourse by inferred (but nonetheless present) links to its (often absent) mates—is in fact little more than a supportive structure for the metaphor or metaphors located at the center of the network, which in discourse frequently represent the entire network synecdochically: the organizational chart, as it were, of discourse. It is these differentiated and reinforcing qualities of the network to which I refer when, in this essay, I use the phrase "the metaphoricity of X," where X is a metaphoric or theoretical object.

3. In fairness to philology, a thumbnail diachronic sketch of the usage of culture up to the period under examination in this essay might be as follows: *culture*, as a term, appears in English usage after 1500 as a variant of cultivate or cultivation in their most strictly agricultural senses (thus pointing out the organic metaphor lurking conspicuously in cultural criticism). The first usage—again, in English—of the word *culture* to frame and articulate the social objects of culture proper most probably occurred sometime between 1750 and 1770, after which it appears regularly, if not often, in what we might, for lack of better words, call learned discourse. The widest and most developed—and divergent—uses of culture during the period 1750 to 1800 are to be found in the texts of the German ethnographers of the 1780s and the 1790s, from whose texts the term was disseminated throughout northern Europe and Scandinavia. Resistance to the term *culture* was encountered most strongly in France and England, where a strong oral academic tradition favored the use of *civility* and its variants over culture; thus, in England at least, culture was kept out of general usage until after 1850, when it began, gradually, to double, but not replace, *civilization* in usage. Not until the twentieth century did civilization take on its negative, Spenglerian connotations.

4. The evolution of *Culture and Anarchy* qua text is described quite succinctly by J. Dover Wilson in the introduction to his edition of *Culture and Anarchy*. The choice of Wilson's edition was merely one of convenience.

5. Matthew Arnold, *Culture and Anarchy*, ed. J. Dover Wilson (Cambridge: Cambridge University Press, 1932), 6. Hereafter *CA*, cited in the text.

6. The significance of three metaphors—the metaphor of the empty body of the savage, the full body of social man, and the flow of influences across and within these bodies—for Victorian social theories has yet to be adequately analyzed. Suffice it to say here that I do not use either body or flow in the fashion that Deleuze and Guattari do in *Anti-Oedipus*; these constructs were, for Victorian social thought, important theoretical givens.

7. As Jerome McGann has pointed out, the fact that literary critics are particularly enamored of the transcendent subjectivity proposed by Romantic theory as the epistemo-

logical center of the universe neither makes that proposal a whit more tenable nor addresses the utter repudiation of the Romantic position on epistemology by the Victorians. The instability the Victorians sensed within their own social field was linked to the body of the individual, to the dangers of "wild" undisciplined individual productivity—the very body, the very productivity the Romantics apparently sought to exalt.

8. Note the emphasis—well studied by Foucault and Lacan—on the escape of the provincial from the panoptical gaze of the state. The importance of this structure cannot be underestimated in understanding Arnold's conception of cultural light.

9. The "ordinary selves" of the framebreaker, the pamphleteer, and the unstamped pressman, producing according to their own laws, were between the Six Acts (1816) and 1848 subject to statist strategies, first of surveillance, interdiction, and suppression, and later of cooption, as part of statist efforts to minimize the damage to statist infrastructures of uncontrolled social production.

10. E. B. Tylor, *Primitive Culture: Researches into the Development of Mythology, Philosophy, Religion, Language, Art and Custom*, 2 vols. (London: Murray, 1929), 1:5. Hereafter *PC*, cited in the text.

The Formation of the Working Classes: John Ruskin's *Fors Clavigera* as a Manual of Cultural Literacy

Judith Stoddart

*F*ORS *Clavigera* has often disappointed readers who would measure John Ruskin's message to the working classes by the needs of a nineteenth-century proletariat carved out by Marxist historians. Thus, E. P. Thompson speaks of "the pitiful impracticability" of Ruskin's rhetoric in *Fors,* arguing that while he "addressed the working men, it was not with any sense of identity of interest."[1] Raymond Williams, an exemplary reader of the kind, faults the author of *Fors* for leaving his audience at a literary and political "deadlock" which was to be broken only by William Morris. The significance of Morris's continuation of Ruskin's social inquiry was, Williams says, "that he sought to attach its general values to an actual and growing social force: that of the organized working class."[2]

Morris was not the only reader to recognize Ruskin's basic failure of identification with the lower classes. In an 1880 issue of *Fors* the author confesses that he "knew scarcely anything" of the members of the trades unions whom he addressed.[3] Since its first publication in the years 1871–84, commentators have tried to characterize its audience, measuring its effect on "The Workmen and Labourers of Great Britain" who are invoked in the series' subtitle. It has been subject to the same kind of dismissive

43

reading outlined by Gareth Stedman Jones in his study of the literature of Chartism. Historians of the movement, he points out, typically construct their analysis from a given idea of class or of class consciousness, disregarding what the participants themselves actually said or wrote, or the way in which they saw themselves and their opponents.[4]

Stedman Jones's proposal for a radically different approach to political discourse suggests a productive alternative to current discussions of *Fors*. In Chartist writings, he argues, there is undoubtedly

> an intimate connection between what is said and to whom. Yet it cannot be said that such a connection can be conceived in terms of a recognition of the preexistence of the common social properties of the addressees. It should rather be thought of as the construction, successful or unsuccessful, of a possible representation of what such common properties might be. Of course, the almost definitional claim of political discourse is to be a response to a preexisting need or demand. But in fact the primary motivation is to create and then orchestrate such a demand, to change the self-identification and behaviour of those addressed. The attempted relationship is prefigurative, not reflective. [*LC*, 23–24]

Such a relationship recalls Ruskin's claims to speak not "for the men who have been produced by the instructions of Mr. John Stuart Mill," that is, those who define their demands in the language of political economy, but for readers of "a day [that] will come," a day when "we shall have men resolute to do good work" as Ruskin defines it (27:669). Just as radical voices tried to orchestrate the needs of a rising industrial class in the 1830s and 1840s, to define, as Stedman Jones argues, its opponents and posit the terms of its oppression, so Ruskin attempts in the 1870s to redefine the terms of the laborers' struggle. He speaks to his audience not in the language through which they had learned to define their position—as a socioeconomic group in the capitalist survival-of-the-fittest—but in the words of Christianity, art and myth, words with which he tries to refashion their behavior and identity.

The seeming inappropriateness of the cultural references of Ruskin's letters to his popular audience puzzled his earliest readers. A *Guardian* reviewer predicted that "the working classes will be able to make nothing" of *Fors* beyond the occasional "direct onslaught on capitalists": "The illustrations which delight the cultivated eye, will be as much *caviare* to them as the text."[5] This jouralist's division of the cultured from the uncultured and of the aesthetic from the political Ruskin is reproduced with little challenge in current criticism.

Fors Clavigera seems to me the key text by which such categories can be tested. While Ruskin's "social" writings of the 1860s have been criticized for their naïveté, *Fors* reveals a canny understanding not only of a specific historical challenge but equally of its political stakes. In the postreform struggle for the soul of the working classes, Ruskin puts the aesthetic to practical use. The materials of culture so carefully described in his earlier writings— art, architecture, myth—become the tools for shaping a working-class sensibility. He aims to replace class consciousness by cultural consensus.

Ruskin's attempt to determine the working-class agenda responded to a widespread sense of political crisis. The violence of the Paris Commune, the rapid formation in the north of England of the "Nine Hours League"—so persuasive a voice that it gained the surprising support of the conservative *Times* and *Spectator*—the escalation in trade union membership in the first half of the 1870s: all seemed to herald a new decade of working-class organization and influence. Now partly enfranchised, this political force could not be ignored, and Walter Bagehot expressed conservative concern at the consequences. "The common ordinary mind," he wrote in 1872, "is quite unfit to fix for itself what political question it shall attend to; it is as much as it can do to judge decently of the questions which drift down to it."[6] Bagehot urged statesmen to decide for themselves what the new voters *should* like, and to place leading issues in the public mind.

But it was not just conservative thinkers who questioned the working class's ability to articulate a coherent political program. The *Bee-Hive*, a weekly working-class paper, expressed its disappointment with the group from which so much had been expected after the Second Reform Bill. The laborers had, the paper charged in 1872, "no determined well-defined thought as to any necessary work; no clear conception of any principle entertained in common by them. They originate nothing; have no hearty faith in any understood policy."[7] The complaint is echoed by Thomas Wright—the "Journeyman Engineer" now remembered mainly for his working-class autobiography—who wrote in the June 1871 *Fraser's* of the laborer's reaction to the Paris Commune. Republicanism was, according to Wright, widespread among workingmen, but

If asked what was the change they desired, they would be unable to give any definite answer. They do not know, and, still worse, they scarcely care; their feeling is, that no change that would arise out of a disruption of the present state of society could be worse for them, while any such change might easily be better for them.[8]

While sympathizing with the French communists, the workers, Wright complained, understood neither the political positions of the Paris laborers nor the form of society which they advocated.

Ruskin plays on these uncertainties in the January 1872 letter of *Fors*. Were his readers sure, he asked, that to "leave voting, and come to fighting" would help them to "arrive any nearer to your object—admitting that you *have* an object, which is much to be doubted" (27:232). The radical periodical, the *Republican*, had argued that all property should be seized and put under central control, a proposal much objected to, Ruskin reminded them, when put forth by Thomas Carlyle. "You are not all agreed upon that point perhaps?" Ruskin queried. "But you are all agreed that you want a Republic" (27:233). Were they also agreed that it would be a lesser financial burden to pay for the installation of a new government rather than for the maintenance of the present queen?

Ruskin carefully and deliberately dismantles the catch phrases of popular republican rhetoric. Could the disorganized, indecisive laboring classes be "weld[ed] . . . into one compact mass" as a Liberal M. P. from Nottingham had suggested? Or would their "fusion—[their] literal con-fusion,—be as of glass only, blown thin with nitrogen, and shattered before it got cold?" (27:234, 235). Liberty or independence "you had better cease to talk of," Ruskin advised, "for you are dependent not only on every set of people whom you never heard of, who are living round you, but on every past act of what has been dust for a thousand years" (27:50). The scarcely veiled Christian subtext by which Ruskin questions such bywords—the gold tested by the fire, the sins of the fathers visited on the next generation—is central to his method in *Fors*. The givens of republicanism are refuted by the rhetoric of an authoritative moral system. One interpretation of the situation in England is replaced by another. Like Cobbett calling sides in the *Political Register* in the battle of good and evil, Ruskin renames the enemy of the English working class.

The terms are laid down in the sixth letter of *Fors*. Through a series of images, Ruskin slowly spells out the underlying cause of the current anarchy in France—and, he warns, the potential cause of anarchy in England. As he writes, he tells the reader, he looks out of his window onto the county gaol. "It is curious," Ruskin notes, "that since the English have believed (as you will find the editor of the *Liverpool Daily Post,* quoting to you from Macaulay . . .), 'the only cure for Liberty is more liberty' . . . they always make their gaols conspicuous and ornamental" (27:106–7). As in his 1864 lecture, "Traffic," where the conspicuous and ornamental Bradford Exchange becomes the repository for the values and vices of its builders, so here the county gaol is made the repository of the values of England. An idle boy with his hands in his pockets who stands in front of the structure is made the "sign-post" (27:107) by which common values can be decoded. His idleness—particularly conspicuous, as he is no boy, as Ruskin ingenuously calls him, but is, we learn, seventeen or eighteen— represents all those whose notion of "liberty" is doing less work for higher wages. His concealed hands stand for thievery, both the conspicuous thievery of the lower classes and the silent siphoning of capital by the upper. And the building looming behind him becomes the "gaol of the grave," the inferno in which the citizens of "nations under judgment" are punished (27:107).

The banner cry for liberty is graphically transformed from a prescription for modern civilization to its symptom. The enemy that the laborers are fighting is not class or oppression but a larger evil which runs through all levels of society. Ruskin turns a familiar tale of economic and political corruption into a moral one in which all the characters are equally implicated. The event which, according to Wright, so inspired the English workers, the bloody reign of the French Commune, serves as a topical example of his revisionist method. Beginning with factual accounts culled from the newspapers, Ruskin's description of the recent horrors in France evolves into a biblical vision. The blood was on all English hands, Ruskin warned:

This cruelty has been done by the kindest of us, and the most honourable; by the delicate women, by the nobly-nurtured men, who through their happy and, as they thought, holy lives, have sought, and still seek, only "the entertainment of the hour." And this robbery has been taught to the hands,—this blasphemy to the lips,—of the lost poor, by the False Prophets who have taken the name of Christ in vain, and leagued themselves with His chief enemy, "Covetousness, which is idolatry." [27:111]

The establishment which condemned in its journals the French Commune is charged with hyprocrisy. The English simply covered with respectability the crimes they so loudly denounced across the Channel.

The vice of Covetousness or Envy, the Giotto fresco of which was reproduced as the frontispiece to the original issue of this letter, becomes the symbol for the state of modern society. Its effect is diminished in the Library Edition, where it faces the page close to the end of the letter on which it is first directly mentioned. Like the rest of the plates of Giotto's virtues and vices published in the first year of *Fors*,[9] it should stand as the allegorical figurehead for the entire letter, determining the meaning of the contemporary issues which follow. Thus, the French Commune, in its acts of destruction and vengeance, is seen in letter 7 as a fallen state, bereft of the virtue of Charity. In letters 8 and 9, the theorems of political economy are judged by the standards of Justice and Injustice. Rather than exercises in art appreciation, the plates serve as graphic markers, as illustrations of the key words by which current events are to be read.

This allegorical reinterpretation of contemporary political discourse runs throughout Ruskin's writings. Often studied in the light of his evangelical upbringing, or as a means by which Ruskin explicated works of art, it is seldom considered as a deliberate rhetorical strategy.[10] In *Fors* it does more than reflect Ruskin's Calvinistic vision. It represents a possible political conversion. Seeking to displace the workers' sense of urgency from immediate social battles to a larger cosmic picture, Ruskin presents them with a moral dilemma in which they can immediately figure, in which it is their action as individuals, not as a political group, that matters. "The stuff of which the nation is made," he writes, "is developed by the effort and the fate of ages: according to that material, such and such a government becomes possible . . . a nation wholly worthless is capable of none" (27:235). Their efforts at redressing social evils had, in other words, been misdirected. Rather than demanding rights equal to those classes whose conduct they now despised, they should ask that each individual receive what he or she deserved. To seek power in the existing system would merely perpetuate its injustices. For "if you deserve anything better," Ruskin asks, "why conceal your deserving under the neutral term, 'rights'; as if you never meant to claim more than might be claimed also by entirely nugatory and worthless persons?" (27:230). Whereas Fortune, or "Fors," according to Ruskin, rewards the individual according to his real worth, "appointing measured return for every act and thought, such as men deserve" (27:231). The French of all classes, by valorizing political rather than moral power, had collectively assured the doom of an entire nation (27:105).

Ruskin's argument at times sounds rather like that of contemporary supporters of the status quo, whose Christian platitudes situated the lower orders firmly at the base of society. As a diary entry intimates, Ruskin did feel a close connection between his message in *Fors* and the preservation of social order. On 18 December 1870, while drafting the first letter of the work, he records: "Writing for workmen. Had pleasant dream of view of Lake from hill, confused with a revolution going on among Swiss."[11] In 1873 he spoke openly of his fear that a popular uprising might bring down the vision which he had so carefully constructed in *Fors*. "He thinks that in about ten years," a visitor to Brantwood reported, "there will be a revolution in England caused by the increasing power of the Trades Unions, which will destroy his Arcadia, among other things."[12] It was a concern expressed in the *Fors* of the previous month (27:661), and one which had been the obvious subtext to Ruskin's gloomy message in the work since it was voiced in the tenth letter (27:176).

Although Ruskin feared social upheaval, it was less from any support for the existing order than from a dread of what such a move by the workers represented. The selfishness of the upper classes was soundly denounced in *Fors:* their lives had become, as Ruskin put it, merely "one large Picnic Party" (27:39). While they might have taught "how, day by day, the daily bread they expected their village children to pray to God for, might be earned in accordance with the laws of God" (27:41), they instilled in fact the merits of greed and indulgence. For the laborers, the students of such a system, to gain control of industrial England meant wrenching it even further from its roots, both moral and social. With the hierarchical structure in place, there was at least a formal link with an organic, preindustrial set of values.

The growing power and influence of organized labor is thus seen not as the harbinger of a positive future state replacing the capitalist class system, but as a move to be dreaded, a further step in the ethical degradation spawned by industrialism. While despising as surely as Marx did, England's economic organization, Ruskin saw in the rise of the working class not a solution but a continuation of the old system. Workers well-drilled in capitalism had learned first to see their labor as a commodity; in their collective organizations, they had come to see themselves in terms of market value as well. Cooperation, Ruskin lamented, had come to mean not helpfulness, but "the policy of a privileged number of persons for their own advantage" (29:147). The position of laborers would be improved not according to personal worth but according to marketplace "exchange value" (27:217). Individual value and welfare had been left out of the calculation. And by this omission, society had cut itself off from "the actual life of all glorious human states in their origin," from "the eternal law of right, obeyed alike in the great times of each state, by Jew, Greek, and Roman" (27:144, 145).

For Ruskin, as for Matthew Arnold in the 1860s and 1870s, the only corrective to an impoverished culture was to restore its inheritance, to reassert the ideals or the "best self" handed down through its past.[13] It was a project on which Ruskin had been engaged since his earliest writings, but in *Fors* it acquires both a political urgency and a practical cast. If this was the moment in which the masses were to be educated, then Ruskin would, if not determine, at any rate supplement the curriculum. To the now limited focus of education he would add stories of kings and heroes and saints (27:449), the opinions of Plato, Virgil, Dante, Carpaccio, Shakespeare, and the histories of the cities in which they had lived (27:314, 143). Instruction in the three R's, or in "the shapes of letters and the tricks of numbers" as Ruskin called it, did little to form the character of the pupils, leaving them "to turn their arithmetic to roguery, and their literature to lust" (18:502). His subjects, on the other hand, would provide them with moral exemplars which would "confirm or illustrate things that are for ever true . . . so that . . . they may become to you in the strictest sense, educational" (27:250).[14]

Littered with tales and historical digressions, Ruskin's seemingly wayward discourse in *Fors* becomes, then, what one early reader called a "University Extension Course,"[15] a manual of cultural literacy. The germ of this sort of storytelling can be found in *Ethics of the Dust*, the fantastical "Lectures to Little Housewives" drawn from Ruskin's real experiences with the girls at the Winnington School. His moral minerology, as the title suggests, is as much a course in the formation of behavior as in the formation of crystals. The quarrelsome girls in the text are plainly not yet "little housewives": it is the function of Ruskin's lessons to shape them into the orderly audience suggested in the subtitle, just as he literally has them shape themselves on the playground into the orderly particles of a crystal.

In *Fors*, too, it is clear that the group singled out in the subtitle is not one to which the reader already belongs, but one which is fashioned and defined through the letters. Ruskin spoke, he said, not to the present workers but to those who would one day understand his message. At the same time, he vowed to guide his contemporary audience through the work, explaining references, revealing what was cryptic. Just as he had tried to redefine their situation, to figure them not as an economic or political unit but as individual actors in a universal crisis, so he tries to rewrite their job description, to teach them just as the national school board schools tried to teach them to be qualified and capable participants in a particular system.

The path is briefly explored in *Time and Tide,* where Ruskin had first tried to redirect the workers' campaign for a public voice. The enemy, Ruskin insisted there as in *Fors,* was not the evil of political powerbrokers, but evil itself (17:367–68). Education, he continues, repeating a formula introduced in *Unto This Last,* "consist[s] in giving habits of gentleness and justice"; that is, in modification of behavior, not in mastering data or in learning the terms by which to strike political bargains. Ruskin feared the equation of knowledge and power which radicals, liberals, and nonconformists had made the basis of their educational efforts throughout the nineteenth century. After his experience with laborers at F. D. Maurice's Working Men's College, Ruskin had testified to the Public Institutions Committee that he felt that equation could be found "at the root of the movement among the working classes, much more so than in any other" (16:478). As Mill put it in his *Principles of Political Economy,* an "increase in intelligence" would lead to a decrease in that class's willingness "to be led, and governed, and directed into the way they should go"[16]—a prediction cited and dismissed by Ruskin (27:211). Even the wisest men in previous times, Ruskin asserts, recognized both the need to be led and the superiority of moral over intellectual power: witness, he says, the behavior of the wise men who came to worship the Christ child. For true wisdom is not "knowing how big the moon is," but "knowing what you ought to do" (29:60).

The wise men become a part of Ruskin's historical catalogue of actual and mythical figures, of writers and artists who recognized what they "ought to do"—and, by contrast, those, like the residents of Dante's hell, who did what they ought not to have done. Not only are the figures themselves meant for the edification of the audience, but the very process of reading them, of learning to follow Ruskin's thinking about them, is an educational exercise. True education, according to Ruskin's use of the term in *Fors*, is not a short exchange in the classroom, but an ongoing process of moral judgment: "Nature and Heaven command you," he exclaims, "to discern worth from unworth in everything, and most of all in man" (27:247). Modern education taught that everyone and everything was equal: "and then we complain that we can no more manage our mobs!" (27:152). But a survey of the best thinkers or actors who had shaped Western history not only demonstrated that "there *can* be but one Mr. James Watt or Mr. William Shakespeare": it provided the scale by which human worth was to be measured. For, Ruskin explained,

> all noble persons hitherto existent in the world have trusted in the government of it by a supreme Spirit, and in that trust, or faith, have performed all their great actions, [so that] the history of these persons will finally mean the history of their faith; and the sum of intellectual education will be the separation of what is inhuman, in such faiths, and therefore perishing, from what is human, and, for human creatures, eternally true. [28:656]

"Separation of inhuman from human": in other words, what Ruskin describes here is education as a civilizing force, not so very different from what in Arnold's terms would be called an agent of "culture." Culture for Arnold was a means of refining human nature, of urging "the progress of humanity towards perfection."[17] For Ruskin to civilize was not so much to push forward as inward, to search not for a more complete knowledge but for a more complete understanding of the unchanging moral nature of man.

The distinction is drawn in an anecdote from his childhood. An illiterate Savoyard guide, encountering the skeptical young Ruskin, lamented that for all his knowledge the boy "ne sait pas vivre" (27:61). The best education, Ruskin concludes, is frequently that of the children of the poor who had learned to be happy as they were, who were not plagued by all that they had yet to learn. Indeed, his "beau-ideal" of the well-educated workingman is a Tyrolese peasant of the stripe he had encountered the previous summer. He was, says Ruskin,

> as round and merry a person as I ever desire to see. He was tidily dressed—not in brown rags, but in green velveteen; he wore a jaunty hat, with a feather in it, a little on one side; he was not drunk, but the effervescence of his shrewd good-humour filled the room all about him; and he could sing like a robin. [27:193]

It is a portrait which would fit neatly into William Morris's gallery of characters in *News from Nowhere*. Morris's idea of a well-rounded moral education, influenced heavily by Ruskin, turns in his novel into a society of happy workers, a society reminiscent of Ruskin's descriptions of life in the Guild of St. George.[18] For Ruskin vows in *Fors* to create an equivalent of his Tyrolese peasant in England by introducing Tyrolese principles (27:194)—nonindustrial, noncapitalistic, nonliberal—the principles which come to form, as the letters progress, the basis of the Guild.

They are notions, Ruskin admits, which are anathema to modern England. The members—or Companions, as he calls them—of this Tyrolean company would have to be reeducated according to the curriculum to be offered all children in St. George's schools. In place of the "present staples of education," which prepared the pupil for his or her "position in life" (29:484), the schools would teach "the elements of music, astronomy, botany, and zoology" (29:479), which like the minerology of *Ethics* would offer examples of orderly patterns and relations, concrete illustrations for discussions of "the laws of Honour, the habit of Truth, the Virtue of Humility, and the Happiness of Love" (29:484). Instruction in these subjects was laid out in part in Ruskin's "grammars"—*The Elements of Prosody, Proserpina, Deucalion*—but they are also explored in a less formal way—though to the same moral purpose—in *Fors*. The reader who follows the wayward course of Ruskin's letters is trained according to the curriculum necessary to the formation of a companion. He or she is fitted to become not just an English worker or laborer, but one of "*The* Workingmen and Laborers of Great Britain," the virtuous participants in the fight of St. George's Guild, "protesting, by patient, not violent, deed, and fearless . . . word, against the evil of this our day, till in its heart and force it be ended" (29:294).

Through the readership of his letters, Ruskin thus hopes to create an alternative to the workers produced by a narrow capitalism, to those whose moral judgment is dulled by "the follies of Modern Liberalism" with its "theology of universal indulgence" (27:247). His will be a work force that can knowledgeably challenge the kind of thinking

we knew from John Stuart Mill . . . [that] taught us that the only danger confronting us is being closed to the emergent, the new, the manifestations of progress. No attention had to be paid to the fundamental principles or the moral virtues that inclined men to live according to them.

Although the words quite plainly are not Ruskin's, the complaint is the same as that which forms the basis for Ruskin's revised educational program. The quote comes from Allan Bloom's controversial book, *The Closing of the American Mind*,[19] surprisingly reminiscent of Ruskin's campaign and his method in *Fors*. Like Ruskin, Bloom writes in a moment in which the instruction of the masses is being reexamined, in which the curriculum is reevaluated according to shifting political and economic conditions. Like Ruskin, Bloom opposes the growing shift toward technical and scientific knowledge, emphasizing education as moral training, insisting on the importance to that training of values handed down through Western history. And like Ruskin, Bloom creates a teaching text, one which not only poses an educational idea but puts its readers through a basic course designed to produce just that kind of moral mind Bloom holds up as virtuous and necessary to the salvation of modern society.

At stake for Bloom is the democracy failed, according to his title, by higher education. Modern education, he explains in his preface, as influenced by the liberal thinking of Mill and John Dewey, neglects "civic culture."[20] As is evident from Bloom's choice of exemplary texts in the book—Tocqueville's *Democracy in America* and Rousseau's *Social Contract*, as well as Plato's *Republic*—the goal of instruction is to literally inform the citizen, to give form to his or her conduct in relation to the state. Democracy will be served best by those who understand its principles, who are in fundamental agreement about the meaning of justice or liberty or rights. To give reign to a system of relative values— the "cultural relativism" which Bloom marks at the outset as his primary target—is to produce a democracy of no consensus, a state of anarchy.

As deliberately as Bloom, Ruskin tries to create a common consensus in *Fors* by reeducating his audience, by shaping it to become the foundation of an ideal polity. And, like Bloom, he offers them what had generally been considered an elite curriculum. For although Ruskin purports to instruct his pupils in nontraditional subjects—astronomy, geology, botany, zoology—they are, along with the stories from English and European history and classical myth, ones with which every gentleman scholar would have been familiar. His working readers are thus given access to the sources from which upper-class values and beliefs had been formed.

While Mill might see such access as the end of order—since enlightened laborers would no longer look to a cadre of leaders for guidance—for Ruskin it is the beginning of an order based on consensus, on a general will built around generally accepted principles.[21] A stable government, he says to the workers stirred by a revolutionary republicanism, "implies the considerate acceptance of a code of laws" (27:16). It is not only a warning of the impossibility of establishing in a violent moment a regime totally opposed to entrenched ways of thinking; it is a statement of what is necessary for the preservation of social stability. All classes must be agreed on the value of the laws, on the moral basis of the code, and on the role of the individual and the state. It is in this sense that although this discussion has been addressed specifically to the relation of the workers to Ruskin's text, *Fors* is, in a sense, classless. It both leads the newly enfranchised citizens to a common fund of values and understanding, and, in its admonitions and upbraidings of squires, clergy, and lords, reminds them of the importance of that fund to the polity.

Not that Ruskin believed that all those who shared in the general will were of equal status. While Ruskin challenges the ruling classes, questioning their basis of power, he does so not to dethrone them but to set them on firmer ground through the building of common understanding of the real source of that power. For education is not, as many claimed, the great leveler, but, Ruskin says in *Time and Tide,* the great distinguisher (17:456): the best will rise, with the admiration of the rest. The end of education is, thus, happiness, Ruskin states in *Fors,* for a "man's happiness consists infinitely more in admiration of the faculties of others than in confidence in his own" (27:152).

Behind such assertions in this very personal text is always the figure of Ruskin, the tutor of his readers, the elucidator of just laws for an orderly state. "Educate, or govern, they are one and the same word," he declared in *The Crown of the Wild Olive* (18:502). By reforming its view of itself, by defining its sphere of action in society, Ruskin governs his audience, becoming the protaganist of the social order which he develops in *Fors.* He steps into the position of leadership evacuated by liberal intellectuals. Given Ruskin's real distance from the working classes—he had, he admitted, had experience only with those who were relatively well educated (16:433)—it is surprising how cannily he read the needs of, if not a large number of the workers, at least a representative sample of them. A look at the roll of the St. George's Guild shows that there were numerous members of the target audience—the newly enfranchised, skilled laborers, largely from industrial centers (where access to Ruskin's works presum-

ably was made easier by workingmen's institutes and libraries)—
who were willing enough to lay down their political arms and
call him Master.

Ending on the numbers that Ruskin attracted by his work
comes too close, perhaps, to the approaches I have tried to challenge. It risks leaving *Fors Clavigera* in the ranks of "failed" reforms, like Coleridge's pantisocracy or C. R. Ashbee's handicraft
guild. Determining whether Ruskin succeeded in mustering a
new cultural consensus is less compelling in this moment in English studies than examining his approach to the formation of
cultural authority. At a time when institutional forms of power
as well as the means of perpetuating a settled cultural agenda
are at issue, *Fors* intervenes in our developing understanding of
strategies of authority. During thirteen years of broad social and
political change in England, Ruskin's letters carried on intact
a frame of thought and reference which seemed to have little
to do with an increasingly industrialized, technical society competing in a newly international market. Yet his mission was a
response to the urgency of moment, not an escape from it.

"One tries to imagine," Anthony Burgess wrote in 1968, "the
artisan slurping tea from his saucer, sympathizing with Ruskin"
as he writes letters of *Fors* "from the Baedeker spots of Europe."[22]
One takes the point of the satire on the leisurely life which Ruskin and his Baedeker represent. Yet the cultural ideals of *Fors
Clavigera* have outlasted those of the nineteenth-century artisan.
It would appear difficult to fault Ruskin with "impracticability"
when so visible a cultural arbiter as Allan Bloom can be seen
as continuing his agenda. In retrospect, Ruskin may be said to
have played a significant role in transmitting ideals which remain
challenging to those entering the social and political arena for
the first time.

Notes

1. E. P. Thompson, *William Morris: Romantic to Revolutionary*, rev. ed. (New York: Pantheon Books, 1976), 200 and 201. My argument throughout this essay attempts to refute
Thompson's contention that "isolation had made [Ruskin] indifferent to the thought
of his contemporaries," that "it was almost impossible to recognize the world of the
1870s" in *Fors* (201). Such claims, often repeated by historians of the working classes,
have led to the conclusion that Morris is somehow a perfected version of Ruskin. That
this is the result of reading backward from the proponent of socialism, and of creating
for Ruskin a goal which he himself never embraced, will, I hope, become clear in the
course of my discussion. This essay is excerpted from a larger study of *Fors Clavigera*

which firmly situates Ruskin's thought in emerging social and political currents in the 1870s, both English and continental.

2. Raymond Williams, *Culture and Society, 1780–1950* (London: Chatto & Windus, 1958), 148. In *John Ruskin's Labour: A Study of Ruskin's Social Theory* (Cambridge: Cambridge University Press, 1983), P. D. Anthony also takes on both Thompson's and Williams's negative appraisals of Ruskin's later work (199–211), although to a rather different end than that which I pursue here.

3. *The Works of John Ruskin*, ed. E. T. Cook and Alexander Wedderburn, 39 vols. (London: Allen, 1903–12), 29:399. Hereafter, cited in the text by volume and page number. This letter of *Fors* is the only one in which Ruskin makes his address more specific than the "Friends" to whom he spoke in the early numbers. "To the Trades Unions of England" was carried on the title page of the original fascicle of letter 89.

4. Gareth Stedman Jones, *Languages of Class: Studies in English Working Class History, 1832–1982* (Cambridge: Cambridge University Press, 1983), 94. Hereafter *LC,* cited in the text.

5. *The Guardian,* 16 August 1871, 995.

6. Walter Bagehot, 1872 preface to *The English Constitution,* in *The Collected Works of Walter Bagehot,* ed. Norman St. John–Stevas, 15 vols. (London: The Economist, 1965–86), 5:172.

7. *The Bee-Hive,* 4 May 1872, cited in *Labour's Formative Years: Nineteenth Century,* ed. James B. Jeffreys, 2 vols. (London: Lawrence & Wishart, 1948), 2:197.

8. Thomas Wright, *Our New Masters* (1873; reprint, New York: Kelley, 1969), 205–6.

9. The first three—Hope, Envy, and Charity—were published from May to July 1871; Injustice and Justice appeared in October and November. The titles which Ruskin added in 1882 to the intervening letters—"Not as the World Giveth" and "Honour to Whom Honour"—locate them in the same allegorical series: they act as further explorations of the plates of Charity and Justice.

10. In *Victorian Types, Victorian Shadows: Biblical Typology in Victorian Literature, Art and Thought* (London: Routledge & Kegan Paul, 1980), George Landow suggests the usefulness of such an approach through his survey of the sage's use of biblical typology to define his own status as interpreter of contemporary events. For an extensive study of allegory and art in Ruskin's writings, see Landow's *The Aesthetic and Critical Theories of John Ruskin* (Princeton: Princeton University Press, 1971), 321–457. For the connection between allegory and evangelicalism, see Jeffrey Spear, *Dreams of an English Eden: Ruskin and His Tradition in Social Criticism* (New York: Columbia University Press, 1984), 34–40.

11. Unpublished letter quoted by permission from the Ruskin Galleries, Bembridge School, Isle of Wight, Bem. MS 16, 58. The Swiss were closely linked in Ruskin's mind with the English worker: Swiss peasants were the model after which Ruskin hoped to fashion his working-class readers.

12. Unpublished letter by Juliet Tylor quoted from the Ruskin transcripts with the permission of the Bodleian Library, Oxford, Bodl. MS Eng. Lett. c.39, 335. "Arcadia" was the name Tylor often used in her letters to Ruskin to refer to the Guild of St. George.

13. Arnold also saw as part of his project in *Culture and Anarchy* the reorientation of workers who bought into the present system. The laborer who "looks forward to the happy day when [he] will sit on thrones with . . . middle-class potentates" participated in England's provincialism. So, too, did that part of the working class "which gives all its energies to organising itself" for political power, because "it is a machinery, an industrial machinery . . . and external goods, which fill its thoughts, and not an inward perfection." Matthew Arnold, *Culture and Anarchy,* ed. J. Dover Wilson (Cambridge: Cambridge University Press, 1932), 104–5.

14. What follows is not intended to be a full summary of Ruskin's educational ideas and proposals in *Fors*, but rather a suggestion of the way in which the text as a whole serves to educate its readers. For a brief survey of Ruskin's discussions of education in *Fors* and its relation to his other works, see the editors' introduction to volume 27 of the Library edition, and chapter 10 of J. A. Hobson, *John Ruskin, Social Reformer* (London: Nisbet, 1898). Two studies have tried to make a coherent educational theory of Ruskin's corpus: William Jolly, *Ruskin on Education: Some Needed But Neglected Elements* (London: Allen, 1894), who compares Ruskin to the leading educational theorists of his time, and Hilda Boettcher Hagstotz, *The Educational Theories of John Ruskin* (Lincoln: University of Nebraska Press, 1942), who summarizes Ruskin's ideas on the education of workingmen (113–17).

15. Edith Hope Scott, *Ruskin's Guild of St. George* (London: Metheun, 1931), 6.

16. John Stuart Mill, *Principles of Political Economy with Some of Their Applications to Social Philosophy*, 5th ed., 2 vols. (London: Parker, 1862), 2:334.

17. Arnold, *Culture and Anarchy*, 202.

18. In *Dreams of an English Eden,* Spear notices several connections between Ruskin's social and political ideas in *Fors* and the shape of *News from Nowhere* (230–33). He does not, however, note the many similarities between the life of Ruskin's Guild and the life of the Morris's community of the future.

19. Allan Bloom, *The Closing of the American Mind: How Higher Education Failed Democracy and Impoverished the Souls of Today's Students* (New York: Simon & Schuster, 1987), 29.

20. Ibid., 30.

21. The use of Rousseau's phrase from the *Social Contract* is deliberate. Ruskin invites a comparison between the political purpose of his later works with that of Rousseau, linking himself in *Praeterita* with the tradition of the *"contrat social"* (35:321). For a more detailed look at the Ruskin/Rousseau connection, and at Ruskin's development in *Fors Clavigera* of Rousseau's concept of a "general will," as well as his emphasis on national culture, see my forthcoming "Ruskin and the Cult of Community."

22. Anthony Burgess, *Urgent Copy* (New York: Norton, 1968), 48.

How Oliver Twist Learned to Read, and What He Read

Patrick Brantlinger

Indiana University

AFTER running away from Sowerberry the undertaker, Oliver rests by a milestone which tells him he has seventy miles to go to London. This isn't surprising, unless we ask how Oliver can read the milestone? It seems unlikely that a pauper orphan would know how to read—"picking oakum" is the chief education he gets from the workhouse—and all Sowerberry teaches him is how to look mournful at funerals.

Perhaps it's Oliver's good fortune that, discounting Fagin's anti-school for pickpockets, he never attends any school. Throughout Dickens's novels, schools are places of tyranny and miseducation. Noah Claypole has been to a charity school, which seems to have taught him nothing but cruelty and low cunning; though apparently better educated than Oliver, Noah, alias "Morris Bolter," joins the criminals. But maybe Dickens says nothing about Oliver's schooling because he takes it for granted. In fact there were schools for pauper children in the late 1830s. Even under the Old Poor Law a pauper schoolmaster might teach in a parish workhouse—a kindly old man fills that role in the first of the *Sketches by Boz*. But it was more often the case, as one historian of "schools for the people" wrote in 1871, that "the only sort of information which the [workhouse] young had to interest them, was a rehearsal of the exciting deeds of the poacher and the smuggler, or the . . . adventures of abandoned females."[1] On the other hand, the Benthamite drafters of the New Poor Law of 1834 stressed education as the key to eliminating pauperism.[2] Yet well into the 1840s little progress was made toward providing adequate workhouse schools. Qualified teachers were nonexistent, salaries rock-bottom, and classroom conditions wretched.

Nevertheless, a child in Oliver's circumstances *might* have learned how to read, though probably not very well. An 1838 survey of about five hundred workhouse children ages nine to sixteen showed that 87 percent could read at a minimal level or better, though only 53 percent knew how to write (West, 39). More surprisingly than Oliver's literacy is the fact that the thieves can read. Of course Fagin is literate: he regularly reads *The Hue and Cry,* an actual police gazette containing the latest crime reports. After the Dodger is arrested on only a minor charge, Charlie Bates laments that his friend may never be written up in *The Newgate Calendar*—literary fame of sorts.[3] Even Sikes can read. Although he worries about the Juvenile Delinquent Society's spoiling boys by teaching them to read and write, Sikes learns about Fagin's arrest from a newspaper (*OT,* 447). And when Nancy meets Mr. Brownlow and Rose Maylie at midnight on London Bridge, she tells them that she had almost turned back because of "horrible thoughts of death, and shrouds with blood upon them. . . . I was reading a book tonight . . . and the same things came into the print . . . I'll swear I saw 'coffin' written in every page . . . in large black letters" (*OT,* 490).

In a novel full of improbabilities, a few more may seem insignificant. But books and reading are a central feature of the story, as is more obviously the question of Oliver's education. Will his ultimate teachers be Brownlow and the Maylies, or Fagin and Sikes? It's while Brownlow examines a bookseller's wares that the Dodger and Charlie Bates pick his pocket (fig. 1). It's while returning books to that same bookseller that Oliver is recaptured by the thieves, who make great fun of his apparent bookishness. Between these episodes, Oliver is impressed by the "great number of books" in Brownlow's house—books written, as Dickens says, "to make the world wiser"—and Brownlow tells Oliver: "You shall read them, if you behave well" (*OT,* 145). He adds that Oliver may one day "grow up a clever man [and] write books," although Oliver replies that he would just as soon read them and, perhaps, be a bookseller himself.

The motif of books and reading does not entail a contrast between literacy and illiteracy, but between two dramatically different sorts of reading. The first is represented by Brownlow's library—books "written to make the world wiser." The second, which I shall call criminal reading, is represented by the text Fagin makes Oliver read just before Sikes takes him to burglarize

Figure 1. The Dodger and Charlie Bates picking Mr. Brownlow's pocket.

the Maylies. Fagin insists Oliver keep a candle burning so that he can read the book, and then locks him up with it. Oliver

> turned over the leaves. . . . It was a history of the lives and trials of great criminals; and the pages were soiled and thumbed with use. Here, he read of dreadful crimes that made the blood run cold; of secret murders that had been committed by the lonely wayside [and] of men . . . tempted . . . to such dreadful bloodshed as it made the flesh creep, and the limbs quail, to think of. The terrible descriptions were so real and vivid, that the sallow pages seemed to turn red with gore. [*OT*, 196]

Such criminal reading must be part of Fagin's plan to educate—or brainwash—Oliver by "slowly instilling" into the boy's "soul the poison which he hoped would blacken it, and change its hue forever" (*OT*, 185). Fagin's antibible for criminals is probably one of the many versions of the Newgate Calendar. Perhaps the first was the *Compleat History of the Lives and Robberies of the Most Notorious Highwaymen, Foot-Pads, Shop-Lifts, and Cheats,* published in 1719. The long list of such books includes *The Tyburn Chronicle* of 1768, *The Malefactor's Bloody Register* of 1796, and George Borrow's *Celebrated Trials* of 1825, down to twentieth-century versions and reprints. In such an anthology of crime, Dickens may have read about Ikey Solomons, the most likely real-life model for Fagin.[4]

The fact that the thieves can read raises the question, much debated in the 1830s and 1840s, about the correlation between crime and education. *What* the thieves read raises the further question about a criminal or underworld culture, the mirror opposite or double of legitimate, bourgeois culture. The idea of criminal versus lawful reading is related to the popular versus high culture dichotomy, and therefore to *Oliver Twist* as a "popular" crime novel—indeed, to Dickens's entire career as "popular" and "populist" writer. Does *Oliver Twist* belong in Brownlow's improving library, or is it also criminal reading? The debate in the early 1840s about the viciousness of "Newgate novels" made the answer less than clear to Dickens himself.

Dickens believed he was on the side of law and order, but he was unnerved by the public response to *Jack Sheppard*. William Harrison Ainsworth's Newgate novel began to appear in *Bentley's Miscellany* while *Oliver Twist* was still running its course in that journal. (Ainsworth succeeded his friend Dickens as its editor early in 1839.) So popular was *Jack Sheppard* that by the autumn of 1839 there were eight stage versions playing in London, including a musical that helped make "flash" songs like "Nix My Dolly, Pals, Fake Away" hits of the day. In both *Jack Sheppard* and his earlier crime novel *Rookwood*, featuring the exploits of the eighteenth-century highwayman Dick Turpin, Ainsworth seemed to champion "faking" or thieving, and so did much of the London reading and play-going public. Jack Sheppard souvenirs were sold at some theaters, including Sheppard bags containing burglars' picklocks, while the robber's putative grave at Willesden was visited by hundreds of sightseers.[5]

"Sheppard-mania," as Keith Hollingsworth calls it, might have passed harmlessly into oblivion, but on the fifth of May, 1840, Lord William Russell was murdered by his valet, who later confessed that reading *Jack Sheppard* had inspired him to slash his master's throat. According to one journal, the murderer's confession proved that "that detestable book, 'Jack Sheppard' . . . is a publication calculated to . . . serve as the cut-throat's manual, or the midnight assassin's *vade-mecum*. . . . If ever there was a publication that deserved to be burnt by the common hangman it is *Jack Sheppard*."[6] The Lord Chamberlain's Office performed its duty of policing theatrical discourse by banning all new plays about Jack Sheppard (though not the eight versions already in performance). Writing of any sort which seemed to sympathize with criminals was suddenly the target of social as well as literary critics. Along with other "Literary Gentlemen" like Bulwer-Lytton, Dickens was accused of penning "gallows" tales (fig. 2). In *Catherine*, his parody of Newgate fiction, Thackeray included Dickens among the writers of criminal literature:

> Breathless to watch all the crimes of Fagin, tenderly to deplore the errors of Nancy, to have for Bill Sikes a kind of pity and admiration, and an absolute love for the society of the Dodger [is the result of Dickens's great but misused power as a novelist]. All these heroes stepped from the novel on to the stage; and the whole London public, from peers to chimney-sweeps, were interested about a set of ruffians whose occupations are thievery, murder, and prostitution.[7]

And after the great popular success of *Oliver Twist*, "The public wanted . . . more sympathy for thieves, and so *Jack Sheppard* [made] his appearance [with] his two wives, his faithful Blueskin, and his gin-drinking mother, that sweet Magdalen!" Thackeray concludes: "in the name of common-sense, let us not expend our sympathies on cut-throats" (*C*, 186).

Dickens defended himself in the 1841 preface to *Oliver Twist*, arguing that he had not romanticized crime. But his contention

THE LITERARY GENTLEMAN.

Figure 2. Conjuring up Gallows Literature. From *Punch*, 12 February 1842.

that portraying thieves as they really are renders them unsympa-
thetic is feeble. No matter how realistic or even how moralizing,
any crime story can be construed, or misconstrued, as teaching
vice instead of virtue. Moreover, Dickens anticipated Thackeray's
guilty verdict by the very inclusion in *Oliver Twist* of the motif
of criminal reading. Dickens himself suggested the analogy between *Oliver Twist* and the Newgate Calendar; and Fagin's act
of giving Oliver criminal reading reflects Dickens's belief that
crime stories can make converts.

That Oliver is repelled instead of won over by Fagin's book
doesn't gainsay the possibility of such a conversion. The book's
"pages were soiled and thumbed with use"; perhaps it has been

the main antibible in Fagin's school for pickpockets. Furthermore, Oliver's improbable ability to read it has the paradoxical effect of putting him on the same level, at least educationally, with the criminals; insofar as knowledge is the antithesis of innocence, then Oliver shares their guiltiness as well as their literacy. It's at least clear that somewhere in Dickens's thinking lurks an equation between crime and literacy, instead of between—as might be expected—crime and illiteracy. On the mythic level, of course, knowledge and guilt have always been equated, as with Fagin's prototype Satan, while everyone knows that "ignorance is bliss." When Dickens represents illiteracy in later novels, he tends to equate it with innocence rather than crime. I'm thinking, for instance, of Joe's painful reading lessons in *Great Expectations,* and of Boffin's in *Our Mutual Friend.* In neither novel does Dickens treat learning as an unmitigated blessing. The schoolmaster Bradley Headstone turns homicidal. Joe's illiteracy corresponds to his good-natured innocence, Pip's literacy to his selfish ambition. The literary allusions in *Great Expectations,* moreover, are nearly all to crime stories–Wopsle, for instance, belabors Pip with lines from *The London Merchant* about an apprentice who murders his master—criminal literature reenforcing Pip's guilt. In these later novels also, then, illiteracy seems less troublesome than criminal literacy or the threat posed by certain types of reading, of which *Oliver Twist* as a "Newgate novel" is itself an example.

But most liberal Victorians including Dickens believed in a direct correlation between crime and ignorance, with education as the main cure: far better to pay for schools than for prisons (see West, 121–34). The epigraph to Thomas Beggs's 1849 *Inquiry into the Extent and Causes of Juvenile Depravity* defined crime as "ignorance in action." The Reverend Henry Worsley said exactly the same in his 1849 book also on "juvenile depravity": "The causes of ignorance are the causes of crime."[8] And Dickens chimed in with his 1848 *Examiner* article entitled "Ignorance and Crime," advocating state education: "Side by side with Crime, Disease, and Misery," Dickens wrote, "Ignorance is . . . certain to be found. The union of Night with Darkness is not more certain."[9] Yet in *Oliver Twist,* Dickens appears to reject the equation between ignorance and crime by making his criminals readers and by pointing to the existence of a criminal literary subculture.

Besides the mythic association of knowledge with guilt, several ideological factors help to explain the thieves' literacy. While Dickens and many of his contemporaries believed that ignorance caused crime, they were unable to believe that illiteracy caused crime. Mounting statistical evidence indicated a correlation between criminality and *some* rather than *no* schooling; it became common to admit that criminals were often at least semiliterate, while continuing to insist that they were woefully ignorant. Of course it's comforting to stress the ignorance of criminals—why else would they commit crimes? To acknowledge that criminals might know what they are doing—that they are somehow smarter than their victims—*that* is the dangerous proposition. Yet then as now there were educated criminals like Bradley Headstone, and literate, white-collar crimes such as forgery and embezzlement. And then as now criminals often outsmarted their victims, the police, and the courts. In *Oliver Twist,* the Bow Street runners Blathers and Duff are doubly outsmarted. First, they fail to capture Sikes, Toby Crackit, or even Oliver. Second, they are misled by Dr. Losberne, who wishes to protect Oliver, and who gets rid of them as quickly as possible. Thus *both* the criminals *and* the respectable bourgeoisie foil the police.

By the late 1830s, statistics had become a flourishing social science, with so-called "moral" or criminal statistics a leading branch. Further, according to Margaret May, the "key breakthrough" in the emergence of the modern concept of juvenile delinquency was a direct offshoot of this development and thus coincided with the publication of *Oliver Twist*. In 1839, the first secretary of the London Statistical Society, R. W. Rawson, demonstrated that "the correlation between age and type of crime was [a] fundamental 'law' of crime." He showed that "criminal activity began early in life and reached a peak between sixteen and twenty-five. . . . Joseph Fletcher, another prominent member [of the Society], concluded that since over half of those sentenced were under twenty-five 'there is a population constantly being brought up to crime.'"[10] Dickens hated statistical "laws" as much as he hated the New Poor Law, and in the 1830s he satirized societies like Rawson's in both the Pickwick Club and the Mudfog Association (fig. 3). But despite his antipathy to statistics and his obvious resistance to the idea that children could be criminalized, Dickens produced a novel in which juvenile delinquency is a major theme.

In 1833 the French statistician A. M. Guerry had contended that education did not lead to a reduction in the crime rate, but the reverse. According to Michael Cullen, British social investigators "became obsessed with Guerry's little book" on "moral

Figure 3. "Automaton Police Force and Real Offenders." From Dickens's "Mudfrog Association," *Bentley's Miscellany,* **1836.**

statistics." Thus in 1835 the economist W. R. Greg tried to refute Guerry, but "like Guerry's French data, at first sight [Greg's Dutch data] showed a direct, not inverse, relationship between the areas of high crime and high education. Greg was forced back on the observation that where there was the greatest quantity of education then crimes of violence were the least. The overall excess . . . was due to crimes against property."[11] Similarly, in *Progress of the Nation,* G. R. Porter argued that "although there was a greater proportion of offences in the more enlightened departments [of Guerry's France], the criminals were . . . among the uninstructed . . . where ignorance abounds, the standard of morals must be low."[12] But Porter himself offered figures showing that, while the population of Britain between 1805 and 1841 had increased 79 percent, and while schooling had also been on the rise, the crime rate had increased 482 percent (3:198). Porter tried to downplay these distressing figures by showing that crimes committed by illiterates and semiliterates had risen at a much faster rate than those committed by literate and well-educated criminals, but the evidence was far from convincing.

By shifting the definition of semiliteracy, it was possible to arrive at the opposite conclusion—namely, that education and not ignorance caused crime.

Disagreeing with liberal advocates of education as social cure-all, both radicals and conservatives interpreted the soaring crime rate as a function of education instead of the reverse. On the radical side, Engels insisted that the proletariat were better educated than ever before (though thanks to their own efforts, not to the bourgeoisie), but also that they were more criminal than ever before—"there is more crime in Britain than in any other country in the world." And "the criminal statistics prove that [the] social war is being waged more vigorously . . . and with greater bitterness every year." The bourgeoisie fail to see, said Engels, that "the individual crimes of which they read will one day culminate in universal revolution."[13]

Conservatives also believed that education fomented discontent which in turn fomented both crime and sedition. In 1807 Samuel Whitbread's bill, calling for a national system of schools at which all poor children would receive two years free education, was defeated largely because, as one opponent declared, educating "the poor . . . would be . . . prejudicial to their morals and happiness; it would teach them to despise their lot in life . . . it would enable them to read seditious pamphlets, vicious books, and publications against Christianity."[14] And at the time of the Reform Bill of 1832, Francis Place could still write: "Ministers and men in power, with nearly the whole body of those who are rich, dread the consequences of teaching the people more than they dread . . . their ignorance" (Hammond, 46). "How can we be cheerful," says Mr. Flosky in *Nightmare Abbey*, "when we are surrounded by a *reading public*, that is growing too wise for its betters?" And in *Crotchet Castle*, Dr. Folliott remarks that "robbery perhaps comes of poverty, but scientific principles of robbery come of education." In the latter novel, the economist Mr. Mac Quedy neatly sums up these views: "Discontent increases with the increase of information."[15]

Thus, despite the dominance among liberals of the wishful view that ignorance caused crime while education cured it, there were many reasons to believe the opposite.[16] As Engels understood, there was and continues to be a murky connection, or perhaps multiple connections, between individual or private crime and collective or public rebellion and revolution. Further, radical romanticism identified the highest forms of artistic vision with revolutionary, utopian political vision, as in Blake's *Milton* and Shelley's *Prometheus Unbound*. And the utopian rebel was also often likened to the anarchistic figure of the bandit or the criminal with noble principles, as in Byron. By a short declension from public to private, one could thus arrive at the astonishing view, ironically expressed by Thomas De Quincey, that murder was "one of the fine arts." Writing in *Household Words* in 1850, W. H. Wills expressed a similar view: "If thieving be an Art (and who denies that its more subtle and delicate branches deserve to be ranked as one of the Fine Arts?), thief-taking is a Science."[17] The metaphoric links between art and crime carried on a subterranean existence throughout the nineteenth century, down to and beyond Oscar Wilde's 1889 essay on Thomas Wainewright, painter, critic, and master poisoner, whom Dickens encountered during one of his tours of Newgate. Wilde's theme is also mine: "There is no essential incongruity between crime and culture."[18]

But quite apart from metaphoric links between crime, revolution, art, and therefore the highest forms of culture, those with most knowledge of the lives of criminals often expressed the view that education rather than ignorance caused crime. In her 1851 book *Reformatory Schools*, Mary Carpenter cited many reports showing, as one put it, that "the proportion of the wholly uneducated in gaol, is [actually] *less* than the proportion [in] the population at large."[19] The warden of Edinburgh Gaol testified that, for the year ending 30 September 1846, the number of prisoners in his charge who could neither read nor write was only "317 out of 4, 513 [or less than one-fourteenth]; 292 could read well; 85 could read and write well, and 3 had received a superior education" (Carpenter, *RS*, 27). The safest conclusion from such figures might have been that there was no correlation between crime and literacy, but the warden then offered the disturbing observation that "the number of re-commitments of those who can read well, [was] much greater than" among complete illiterates (Carpenter, *RS*, 27).

Narrowing the focus to the Artful Dodger's crowd, juvenile delinquents, produced similar results. According to the evidence gathered from "hundreds of . . . juvenile prisoners," Mr. Cotton, the Ordinary of Newgate, concluded that "juvenile delinquents, as a class, were not destitute of education . . . on the contrary, a very large portion of them had received a considerable degree of instruction" (Carpenter, *RS*, 19). At Wakefield Prison, declared an Inspector of Prisons in 1847, "every care is taken of the boys, and . . . the education given them is such as would qualify them for almost every situation attainable in their state of life, [yet] the frequency of recommitments has not diminished, but . . . increased."[20] Clever young jailbirds, moreover, often feigned illiteracy in order to be sent to the prison school rather than to the treadmill or oakum room. They thus swelled the figures for illiteracy; it was of course not possible for illiterates to pretend to read and write, and there were no incentives, at least in prison, for doing so (see Graff, 267).

Such revelations made it impossible to think of illiteracy as a cause of crime. But liberal faith in education as a panacea for all social problems ran strong, as it does today. The question was thus reformulated as one of religious or moral ignorance instead of illiteracy, and of improper or even criminal schooling instead of no schooling. For some social observers, no schools would have been better than those which existed. In his 1834 *Blackwood's Magazine* article on the "Progress of Social Disorganization," Archibald Alison contended that bad schools produced bad—that is, criminal—students. He pointed out that "crime has more than *tripled* in the last twenty years, during which time more has been done for the education of the poor, than in the whole previous periods of English history."[21] What was Malthus's nightmare of the world overrun with population, he wondered, to the far more nightmarish prospect of the world overrun with criminals? The clock could not be turned back, however—Alison didn't advocate the abolition of schools—but the criminalization of society would continue to outstrip the population explosion unless education could be placed on a sound religious basis. Otherwise "the greatest of all blessings," knowledge, would prove to be "the greatest of all curses . . . the Press will become an engine of vast power for the introduction of infidelity, discontent, profligacy, and corruption . . . all the safeguards of religion and virtue will speedily give way, and one unbridled torrent of licentiousness overwhelm the land" (Alison, 240).

One of the authorities cited by Alison was the ex-convict Charles Wall, who in his book *The Old Bailey Experience* (1833) condemned the schools founded by the National Society for Promoting the Education of the Poor for producing graduates "fully qualified to figure on the *pavé* as pickpockets."

> The very calling together so many low-born children daily, without some plan . . . for a moral guardianship over them, justifies the assertion, that they are taught *immorality*, and . . . *crime*. . . . There is nothing of a mental nature performed in [such schools]: a hundred boys at one time are taught to bawl out Lon–lon–don–don, London, with a few more words, which leads them . . . to learn just enough of

reading to enable them to peruse a twopenny life of [Dick] Turpin, or Jonathan Wild, proceeding to the lives of the bandits in regular course. [Alison, 232][22]

Wall's mention of "the lives of the bandits" is one of many occasions when such literature was cited as a direct cause of crime. R. H. Horne told the Children's Employment Commission of 1842 about working-class children in the Wolverhampton area who did not know the name of the queen and had never heard of "St. Paul, Moses [and] Solomon," yet who had "a general knowledge of the . . . life of Dick Turpin, the highwayman, and . . . Jack Sheppard, the robber and prison-breaker" (quoted in Engels, 127). The chaplain of the Preston House of Correction testified in 1847 that over one-third of the nearly fifteen hundred prisoners he had interviewed were "ignorant of the Saviour's name, and unable to repeat the Lord's Prayer." Yet about one-half had "read, or heard read, books about Dick Turpin and Jack Sheppard" (Carpenter, *RS*, 23). And in Henry Mayhew's *London Labour and the London Poor*, a professional thief declared that, in the cheap lodging houses where he slept, "on Sunday evenings the only books read were such as 'Jack Sheppard,' 'Dick Turpin,' and the 'Newgate Calendar'. . . . These were read with much interest."[23] John Binny, who interviewed this thief, believed that a "very fruitful source of early demoralization is . . . penny and halfpenny romances. . . . One of the worst of the most recent ones is denominated, 'Charley Wag, or the New Jack Sheppard, a history of the most successful thief in London.' To say that these are not incentives to lust, theft, and crime . . . is to cherish a fallacy." Binny advocated a strict censorship by the police to end "this shameful misuse of the art of the printing" (Mayhew 4:302).

Besides literature directly about crime, there were in the late 1830s many forms of reading which could be interpreted as criminal. In his concern for the "profligacy" of journalism, Alison was reacting, in part, to the so-called "War of the Unstamped Press"—that is, the battle against censorship and the "taxes on knowledge" waged from 1819 to 1836 by radical publishers such as Richard Carlile, Henry Hetherington, and William Hone. Dickens began his career as both a journalist and a novelist just as this war was winding down—the stamp duty on newspapers was reduced to a penny in 1836 and finally abolished in 1855. The fight against censorship must have given Dickens a vivid conception of the link between criminality and at least certain kinds of political discourse. Between 1830 and 1834, there were perhaps as many as 750 prosecutions for publishing and selling unstamped journals.[24] Leigh Hunt, on whom Dickens modeled Harold Skimpole in *Bleak House,* had been jailed for two years (1813–15) for comments on the Prince Regent he published in *The Examiner;* George Cruikshank could easily have followed him for illustrating such satires as Hone's bestselling *The Political House that Jack Built* (1819). The libel and stamp laws seemed as unjust to reform-minded writers as the poor laws—so unjust, in fact, that they threatened to make *all* reading and writing criminal.

This is, of course, a general threat implicit in any form of censorship: if one sort of discourse can be outlawed, then it's conceivable that all discourse can be outlawed. Such a paranoid prospect, moreover, seems only to increase the urgency would-be censors feel to fix absolute boundaries—between cops and robbers, but also between virtuous and vicious, clean and unclean, high and low forms of culture. The literacy of Dickens's thieves reveals just how arbitrary all such boundaries are. Policing discourse always involves criminalizing certain types of culture and, because they cannot be silenced, fencing them off from other types and then patrolling the fences more or less coercively. Literary criticism is a mild form of such policing; legal censorship is obviously more coercive—as Richard Ohmann says in *English in America,* "Better the MLA than the FBI."[25]

As the Gradgrindian prohibition against fairy tales in *Hard Times* indicates, Dickens understood that censorship could criminalize even the most innocent forms of discourse. The evangelicals were much more censorious than the utilitarians, as he also understood. The Society for the Suppression of Vice, founded by members of the Clapham Sect in 1802, was especially sharp after children's books which, it held, have been "a most successful channel for the conveyance of infidel and licentious tenets." It sought to eradicate "Infidelity and Insubordination, fostered by . . . the Press, [which has] raised into existence a pestilent swarm of blasphemous . . . and obscene books and prints" (Wickwar, 36). Some evangelicals included all novels in the category of "obscene" and therefore criminal reading.

Dickens detested evangelicalism even more than he detested utilitarianism. Yet in common with evangelical reformers like Lord Shaftesbury, he championed the Ragged Schools, the first of which were founded in 1843.[26] Dickens took a special interest in the one in Field Lane, Fagin's Saffron Hill neighborhood, and both he and their founders hoped such efforts would help solve the crime problem. This hope is evident in the vice/virtue contrast in John Leech's design for the *Ragged School Union Magazine* (fig. 4). But the struggle against moral darkness was far from easy. In his 1846 *Daily News* essay, "Crime and Education," Dickens described Ragged School children as "low-browed, vicious, cunning, wicked; abandoned of all help but this [the Ragged School]; speeding downward to destruction; and UNUTTERABLY IGNORANT."[27]

In the Ragged School movement generally, religious and moral instruction was felt to be more urgent than instruction in reading and writing, and teaching the students not to steal seems to have been the first order of business (fig. 5). At the Field Lane school, Dickens pointed out, the students could not even "be trusted with books," apparently because they would damage or pilfer them; "they could only be instructed orally; they were difficult of reduction to anything like attention, obedience, or decent behaviour" ("Crime and Education," 28). Through the 1840s and 1850s, reformers including Dickens shifted their hopes from voluntary, charity schools to the far stricter discipline of reformatory and industrial schools, as in Mary Carpenter's work with juvenile delinquents. She began her career by opening a Ragged School in Bristol in 1846, but was soon advocating much more thoroughgoing measures to deal with what she called "the perishing and dangerous classes."[28]

No more than intensifying police and prison discipline, however, did intensifying educational discipline solve the crime problem. And like the strictest schooling, even the purest reading could have effects opposite from those intended. One of the more disturbing accounts of literate juvenile delinquents cited by Carpenter came from a ragged school teacher:

> The most thoroughly unprincipled and unimpressible boy I ever taught . . . was one who had been long . . . in a Church of England Sunday School, and was thoroughly acquainted with all the facts of Scripture, together with various points of theology, which he would willingly have discussed, had I permitted him. He gloried in having been mentioned in the newspaper as the head of a gang of thieves, and is now in prison. [Carpenter, *RS*, 93]

If reading Scripture cannot cure crime, then no reading can. But what if reading Scripture can inspire crime, just as reading *Jack Sheppard* was held to do? This real-life Artful Dodger with theological savvy was only a step removed from the mass murderer whose case Michel Foucault unearthed and published in

Figure 4. Design by John Leech for the *Ragged Union School Magazine*.

Figure 5. The Lambeth Ragged School. From *The Illustrated London News*, 11 April 1846.

1973: "I, Pierre Rivière, having slaughtered my mother, my sister, and my brother. . . ."[29] Rivière was a twenty-year-old peasant who in June 1835, just as Dickens was beginning his career, committed the murders for which he was executed. Foucault found his case fascinating partly because, like Oliver and the thieves in Dickens's crime story, Rivière was surprisingly literate. Though supposedly barely able to read and write, in his teens "he eagerly took to the reading of . . . philosophical works. [And from] irreligion he turned to great piety" (Foucault, 10). Indeed, he claimed that his inspiration to kill his mother, sister, and brother came not from reading crime stories like *Jack Sheppard*, but from reading the Bible. When the judge insisted that "God never orders a crime," Rivière offered a reply worthy of James Hogg's "Justified Sinner": "God ordered Moses to slay the adorers of the golden calf, sparing neither friends nor father nor son. . . . I was specially inspired by God as the Levites were" (Foucault, 21).

Like the judge's, our first response is to think Rivière crazy, but this overlooks the paradox Foucault stresses. Rivière did not just confess orally to the police; he wrote a forty-page "memoir" explaining how he was the author—*auteur*—both of the murders and of the story of the murders. He even explained that he had planned to write the memoir at the same time that he planned the murders. Both by committing his crimes and by inscribing them in a legible text for a literate audience, Rivière staked his claim to authorship—that is, to the very cultural authority associated with literacy—with the Bible, of course, but also, in the shadowy way I have been tracing, with the writing and reading of crime stories. Rivière thus sought a double—albeit in our eyes, dubious—celebrity, at once criminal and literary, which Foucault has now helped him achieve, just as Norman Mailer's *Executioner's Song*, for better or worse, has immortalized Gary Gilmore. So far from eradicating crime, in this way too, through criminal writing, literacy can be seen to encourage it, to redouble it through representation, just as today the electronic mass media are said to encourage crime by continuously representing it. But this is the dilemma of cultural authority in general, which can and does empower robbers as well as cops—a dilemma manifest in the inextricable doubleness or moral ambiguity of all crime stories and perhaps of all novels, including *Oliver Twist*.

For Dickens and many other observers between the 1830s and 1860s, the idea of education split apart: there was genuine education, represented by the private lessons Oliver takes while with the Maylies; and then there was miseducation or even criminal education, represented by Fagin's antischool for pickpockets.[30] Culture as reading or literature also split apart. The naive assumption that all books made the world wiser gave way to a battle of the books, a warfare between two sorts of culture: virtuous and vicious, sacred and profane, elite and popular, bourgeois and proletarian (fig. 6). This warfare between two types of culture, one legitimate or hegemonic and the other rebelling against that hegemony, was of course not new, as the antiquity of laws against libel, heresy, and pornography shows.[31]

Indeed, executioner's songs and celebrations of outlaws like Robin Hood have always been a mainstay of the sort of popular culture Mikhail Bakhtin calls "carnivalesque." Echoing Bakhtin, Lennard Davis contends that the novel's origins were not just carnivalesque but criminal; he thus ironically appears to agree with those nineteenth-century evangelicals who wished to outlaw all secular fiction.[32] During the Renaissance there emerged a distinctive "news/novel discourse," Davis argues, a blend of fiction and quasi-journalism featuring roguery and crime, as in Robert Greene's "cony-catching" pamphlets, and from this already criminal discourse the modern novel took shape. Contrary to Davis,

Figure 6. Oliver and Bill Sikes in a tug-of-war over books.

in *The Novel and the Police* D. A. Miller contends that, in a sense, the novel *is* the police. So far from being criminal in nature, the novel is an ideological extension of the long arm of the law. Miller is not exactly arguing the case in defense of novels, however, because for him the police is the enemy.[33] Maybe we should split the difference between Davis and Miller. The novel is often rebellious, vulgar, criminal—perhaps never more so than when it is about criminals, as in *Jack Sheppard* and *Oliver Twist*. But the novel is just as often conservative and authoritarian—an ideological form of social control—perhaps never more so than when it is about the punishment of criminals, as again in *Jack Sheppard* and *Oliver Twist*. Clearly a single novel can lead a double life by playing both roles in a cultural game of cops and robbers, crime and punishment.

As an embryonic mystery novel, *Oliver Twist* shares in the Manichaean, structural doubleness of all mystery novels: secrecy and detection, guilt and innocence, crime and punishment. Its sharp divisions of setting, character, and plot, mirroring this doubleness, Dickens likened to the "streaky bacon" of stage melodrama. "It is the custom on the stage, in all good murderous melodramas, to present the tragic and the comic scenes, in as regular alternation, as the layers of red and white in a side of streaky bacon" (*OT*, 168). At the level of cultural history, the "streaky bacon" of *Oliver Twist* spans the contrast between high and popular culture, legitimate and criminal reading, and its melodramatic plot is structured to reveal what Peter Brooks calls "the moral occult."[34] At the level of biographical or psychoanalytic criticism, it expresses Dickens's notorious duplicity or ambivalence toward his deepest moral themes. As John Kucich declares, "Dickens has always appeared to his readers as a novelist of divided sensibilities. Irrepressibly drawn to rebellious . . . or even murderous displays of passion, Dickens also . . . circumscribe[s] human experience within inflexible moral boundaries." Kucich then cites Humphry House's well-known remark about the contrast between the murder of Nancy and "'the earnest moralities of the Preface! To understand the conjunction of such different moods and qualities in a single man is the beginning of serious criticism of Dickens.'"[35]

Thus do theories of the novel as uneasy, divided genre and of Dickens as uneasy, divided self echo the same anxious questions raised by the early Victorian debates about crime and education and about criminal reading. Does fiction about crime prevent or promote it? If certain types of reading promote crime, then how can it be maintained that literacy is beneficial to society or that culture can save us from anarchy? As I've tried to suggest, behind these questions lurks another one, concerning the processes that enforce the criminalization of certain types of literature—in other words, the processes of policing discourse. That these processes usually backfire isn't a pessimistic conclusion. If the ordinary police have not figured out how to stop crime, neither, thank goodness, have the cultural police figured out how to stop the carnivalesque. As Mr. Sleary puts it, "the people mutht be amuthed." Despite Gradgrindism, the circus goes on, and Dickens rightly takes his place in the show.

At the end of his career, Dickens turned criminal—or, at least, criminal reader. For his final tour he composed a reading of the murder in *Oliver Twist*. At first, he could not make up his mind to perform this reading. "I have no doubt that I could perfectly petrify an audience. . . . But whether the impression would not be so horrible as to keep them away another time, is what I cannot satisfy myself upon."[36] John Forster for one objected "because such a subject seemed to be altogether out of the province of reading."[37] Besides, Dickens's health was precarious. Edgar Johnson says that "in deciding to add the murder of Nancy to his repertory, he was sentencing himself to death"—a kind of self-murder by reading (Johnson 2:1104). But Dickens relished petrifying his audience. During one performance at Clifton in 1868, there was "a contagion of fainting. . . . I should think we had from a dozen to twenty ladies taken out stiff and rigid" (quoted in Forster 2:451). Dickens called the Clifton reading "by far the best Murder [he had] yet done." Indeed, he often spoke of his performances in the role of Sikes bludgeoning Nancy as "murders" he'd committed, and he joked about his "murderous instincts." "I have a vague sensation of being 'wanted' as I walk about the streets," he declared. "There was a fixed expression of horror of me, all over the theatre, which could not have been surpassed if I had been going to be hanged. . . . It is quite a new sensation to be execrated with [such] unanimity" (quoted in Johnson 2:1107). Of course this was mock execration, but it was also the dark, obverse side of the celebrity that had come to him as a novelist. For Pierre Rivière, execration and celebrity were identical. In both cases, murder and authorship were after all not so far apart. Though able to read, Bill Sikes didn't write his own crime story as Rivière had done—Dickens did that for him, and then resurrected Sikes as his favorite criminal alter ego, the murderer of Nancy over and over again, and the ghostly double of one of the great authors of his or any other age.

Notes

1. George C. T. Bartley, *The Schools for the People* (London: Bell & Daldy, 1871), 274.

2. E. G. West, *Education and the Industrial Revolution* (New York: Harper & Row, 1975), 143. Hereafter West, cited in the text.

3. Charles Dickens, *Oliver Twist* (Harmondsworth: Penguin Books, 1985), 390. Hereafter *OT*, cited in the text.

4. In *Prince of Fences: The Life and Times of Ikey Solomons* (London: Vallentine, Mitchell, 1974), J. J. Tobias contends that, mainly because Solomons's physical description doesn't match Fagin's, Dickens must not have had him in mind as a model. But Solomons was notorious; Dickens undoubtedly knew about him; and something of his career and character must have rubbed off on Fagin.

5. Keith Hollingsworth, *The Newgate Novel, 1830–1847* (Detroit: Wayne State University Press, 1963), 139–43. See also S. M. Ellis, *William Harrison Ainsworth and His Friends*, 2 vols. (London: Lane, 1911), 1:363–80.

6. Quoted in Hollingsworth, *The Newgate Novel*, 145–46. See also Philip Collins, *Dickens and Crime* (Bloomington: Indiana University Press, 1968), 257–59.

7. William Makepeace Thackeray, *Catherine*, ed. George Saintsbury, The Oxford Illustrated Thackeray (London: Oxford University Press, n.d.), 185. Hereafter *C*, cited in the text.

8. Henry Worsley, *Juvenile Depravity* (London: Gilpin, 1849), 23.

9. Charles Dickens, "Ignorance and Crime," *Miscellaneous Papers*, ed. P. J. M. Scott, 2 vols. (Millwood, N.Y.: Kraus Reprints, 1983), 1:109.

10. Margaret May, "Innocence and Experience: The Evolution of the Concept of Juvenile Delinquency in the Mid-Nineteenth Century," *Victorian Studies* 17, no. 1 (September 1973):17.

11. Michael J. Cullen, *The Statistical Movement in Early Victorian England: The Foundations of Empirical Social Research* (Hassocks: Harvester Press, 1975), 139–40.

12. G. R. Porter, *The Progress of the Nation*, 4 vols. (London: Knight, 1843), 3:211–12; further references cited in text.

13. Friedrich Engels, *The Condition of the Working Class in England*, trans. W. O. Henderson and W. H. Chaloner (Stanford, Calif.: Stanford University Press, 1968), 146; 146; 149. Hereafter Engels, cited in the text.

14. Quoted in J. L. and Barbara Hammond, *The Town Labourer: The New Civilization, 1760–1832* (Garden City, N.Y.: Anchor Books, 1968), 49. Hereafter Hammond, cited in the text.

15. Thomas Love Peacock, *Nightmare Abbey* and *Crotchet Castle* (New York: Capricorn Books, 1964), 71, 213, 219.

16. See Harvey J. Graff, *The Literacy Myth: Literacy and Social Structure in the Nineteenth-Century City* (New York: Academic Press, 1979), chap. 6. Hereafter Graff, cited in the text.

17. [W. H. Wills], "The Modern Science of Thief-Taking," *Household Words* 1 (1850):368. See also Thomas De Quincey, "Murder Considered as One of the Fine Arts" (1827, 1839), in *Thomas De Quincey*, ed. Bonamy Dobree (London: Batsford, 1965), 84–103.

18. Oscar Wilde, "Pen, Pencil, and Poison," in *The Soul of Man under Socialism and Other Essays*, ed. Philip Rieff (New York: Harper & Row, 1970), 98.

19. Quoted in Mary Carpenter, *Reformatory Schools for the Children of the Perishing and Dangerous Classes and for Juvenile Offenders* (1851; reprint, London: Woburn Press, 1968), 31. Hereafter Carpenter, *RS*, cited in the text.

20. Quoted in Mary Carpenter, *Juvenile Delinquents* (1853; reprint, Montclair, N.J.: Patterson Smith, 1970), 174.

21. Archibald Alison, "Progress of Social Disorganization," *Blackwood's Magazine* 35 (1834):235. Hereafter Alison, cited in the text.

22. *The Old Bailey Experience* consisted mainly of the series of five articles Wall published in *Fraser's Magazine* between June and November, 1832, under the general title, "The Schoolmaster's Experience in Newgate" (June, 521–33; July, 736–49; August, 12–23; October, 285–301; November, 460–98). Francis Place was the first to attribute these articles to Wall, and also to deduce that Wall was probably an ex-convict. See Walter E. Houghton, ed., *The Wellesley Index to Victorian Periodicals*, 4 vols. (Toronto: University of Toronto Press, 1972), 2:332.

23. Henry Mayhew, *London Labour and the London Poor*, 4 vols. (1861–62; reprint, New York: Dover Books, 1968), 4:302. Hereafter Mayhew, cited in the text.

24. See William H. Wickwar, *The Struggle for Freedom of the Press, 1819–1832* (London: Allen & Unwin, 1928), 30. Hereafter Wickwar, cited in the text.

25. Richard Ohmann, *English in America: A Radical View of the Profession* (New York: Oxford University Press, 1976), 252 n.11.

26. Philip Collins, "Dickens and the Ragged Schools," *Dickensian* 55 (1959):94–109; see also Collins, *Dickens and Education* (London: Macmillan, 1964), 86–93.

27. Charles Dickens, "Crime and Education," *Miscellaneous Papers*, 1:28.

28. For Mary Carpenter, see Jo Manton, *Mary Carpenter and the Children of the Streets* (London: Heinemann, 1976), and also J. Estlin Carpenter, *The Life and Work of Mary Carpenter* (London: Macmillan, 1881).

29. Michel Foucault, ed., *I, Pierre Rivière*, trans. Frank Jellinek (New York: Pantheon Books, 1973). Hereafter Foucault, cited in the text.

30. See Charles Wall, "The Schoolmaster's Experience," *Fraser's Magazine* (November 1832), 469: "All who discuss or write on this subject dwell on there being nurseries of petty crime, and schools of capital crime," and he proceeds to quote testimony to this effect. In "The Modern Science of Thief-Taking," Wills notes also that the London police use the term "school" to mean gang of thieves (369).

31. See Walter Kendrick, *The Secret Museum: Pornography in Modern Culture* (New York: Penguin Books, 1987), 95–97.

32. Lennard J. Davis, *Factual Fictions: The Origins of the English Novel* (New York: Columbia University Press, 1983); see also Davis, *Resisting Novels: Ideology and Fiction* (New York: Methuen, 1987).

33. D. A. Miller, *The Novel and the Police* (Berkeley: University of California Press, 1987).

34. Peter Brooks, *The Melodramatic Imagination: Balzac, Henry James, Melodrama, and the Mode of Excess* (New York: Columbia University Press, 1985), 5.

35. John Kucich, *Repression in Victorian Fiction: Charlotte Brontë, George Eliot, and Charles Dickens* (Berkeley: University of California Press, 1987), 201.

36. Quoted in Edgar Johnson, *Charles Dickens: His Tragedy and Triumph*, 2 vols. (New York: Simon & Schuster, 1952), 2:1102. Hereafter Johnson, cited in the text. For the text of "Sikes and Nancy," see Philip Collins, ed., *Charles Dickens: The Public Readings* (Oxford: Clarendon Press, 1975).

37. John Forster, *The Life of Charles Dickens*, 2 vols. (Boston: Osgood, 1875), 2:448. Hereafter Forster, cited in the text.

The Jew as Victorian
Cultural Signifier:
Illustrated by Edward Lear

Ina Rae Hark

University of South Carolina

O NE of the ways cultures "educate" their members is to in-
scribe them within a discourse of ideological similitude
that itself requires the generation of discourses of exclusion, defining those apart from the culture as Other. The "conditioned
imagination" of such discourses in turn produces what Michael
J. C. Echeruo identifies as the "exo-cultural stereotype" in which
the individual member of the exo-culture "functions within a
frame of attitudes created by a tradition outside his person";
furthermore "it becomes impossible to assimilate him completely
into the artist's culture or to write about him other than what
he is to the artist's culture—a type."[1] While cultural pressures
in the past few decades have greatly inhibited the giving of free
expression to such stereotypes in Anglo-American public discourse, the Victorians exercised no such self-censorship. The ex-
panding empire was bringing a wide range of peoples, different
in race, ethnicity, cultural practices, and religion into the English
consciousness, producing new exo-cultural types and reenforcing
or modifying older ones. Victorian comic writing, relying as it
did on graphic caricature and exaggerated, one-dimensional
characterization, sanctioned the portrayal of the non-English
Other through, to our eyes, distastefully racist images. To con-
textualize these images, however, results in a more complex impression of the process of Other-making. In this paper I shall
consider a frequently caricatured Victorian group, the Jews, as
presented in the writings and drawings of Edward Lear, to dem-

onstrate the multivalence of exo-cultural stereotypes and the dangers of generalizing from any single example.

Consider the illustrated nonsense poem by Lear, one of the "Teapots and Quails" sequence in which each verse has the structure "AA & B / CC & B / set him a B-ing / and see how he B-s."[2] Here the *word* "Jews" functions in the first instance as a purely material paradigmatic signifier whose signified is completely irrelevant. It appears in the poem's syntactic chain because it meets the preliminary formal requirements of having one syllable, being a noun, and rhyming with "pews" and "mews." "Crews," "screws," or "hues" would serve here just as nicely. The illustration, however, completes the sign by making the signified of "Jews" two men with beards, large noses, and the multiple hats of the old clo' dealer. For the signifier "Jew" to call forth such a signified (itself a pictorial signifier for actual Jewish people) is hardly surprising in the context of Victorian comic discourse. Caricatures similar to Lear's can be seen, for instance, in the following *Punch* cartoon, the illustrations to Aytoun's "The Lay of the Levite," and Gilbert's "The Bishop and the Busman."[3]

Since the legal resettlement of Jews in England under Cromwell, the marks of Jewish identity had gradually shifted from

Edward Lear, "Tea Urns & Pews," from *Teapots and Quails and Other New Nonsense*.

MOSAIC ORNAMENTS.

Cartoon from *Punch*, as reprinted in *Victorian Jews through British Eyes.*

Aytoun's "The Lay of the Levite," from *The Book of Ballads.*

Gilbert's "The Bishop and the Busman," from *The Bab Ballads*.

being predominantly signifiers of villainy, of the Satan-Judas Christkiller, bloodsucking usurer, ritual murderer and mutilator, to being signifiers of buffoonery. The old clo' man, without a medieval villain-prototype, arrived opportunely for assimilation into this comic model:

> During this period [1656–1800] of one and a half centuries, some indigent, immigrant Jews settled in the provinces. Most Jews began work at the lowest mercantile stage—peddling. Many progressed from street traders to shopkeepers to merchants, concurrently providing tangible material from which the stage Jew as a comic, old clothes peddler was molded.[4]

There is further evidence that this particular representation of the Jew as old clo' man had a dominant place in Lear's use of the Jewish exo-cultural stereotype. In his nonsense song "Mr. and Mrs. Spikky Sparrow," the family expands its wardrobe with a trip to "Moses' wholesale shop"; again, in a letter to Chichester Fortescue, when summoning up signifieds for the "Turk, Hebrew, or Heathen," he produces, as a companion to "A Turk with 5 wives," the exo-cultural stereotype "a Jew working hard for little old clo' babies."[5] Do we therefore conclude that this was the first image of the Jew to pop into a Victorian's mind, that Lear was a typical Victorian, and so, when he was faced with the free-floating signifier "Jew," it naturally popped into his? The codes cultural ideologies generate rarely function so monolithically. Most exo-cultural stereotypes vary, not just across cultures, but across cultural discourses produced by the same individuals.

We do not have to leave Lear in order to make this case. His industrious life and travels spawned a wide range of cultural discourses embodied in a number of distinct verbal and visual forms: paintings and drawings, nonsense poetry and prose, travel books, massive correspondence, thirty volumes of surviving diaries. And in them the signifier "Jew" calls up a wide variety of signifieds in addition to the conventional comic caricature: (1) amusing peasants given to non-English, and therefore improper, antics; (2) "picturesque" exotics suitable for commodifying for sale to orientalist Britons; (3) the people of Old Testament history; (4) a cohesive religious group whose unity was a refreshing contrast to the endlessly squabbling, straining-at-gnats factions within Christianity; (5) aristocratic patrons and personal friends; (6) a noble and gifted people often unjustly maligned by the ignorant and persecuted by the zealot. The occasions and audiences of the various discourses, and the cultural construction of those discourses, to a large part determine how the sign will operate.

Before examining the Jew as constructed in these disparate Learian discourses, some general remarks about Lear's relation to the dominant Victorian cultural ideology are in order. He certainly subscribed to it, but he had not been educated into it through the usual channels of school and class. The youngest son of a middle-class stockbroker who lost most of his money when Edward was three, Lear probably obtained less than a year of formal schooling, receiving the bulk of his education from his older sisters at home. At fifteen he began supporting himself through his art work. Yet once he came under the patronage of the Earl of Derby, when he lived at Derby's Lancashire estate, Knowsley, in order to sketch the specimens in the menagerie, Lear frequently found himself befriended by aristocrats and high-ranking civil servants. Lear felt his position in these circles as marginal; he was both a part of and apart from the imperial power relations in which so many of his friends and patrons engaged. "Read D Telegraphs," he would record in his diary of 5 October 1880, "certainly it is bad to have a fanatic as prime Minister, but 'dirty landscape painters' have no vote in that matter."[6]

So at times Lear even constructed his countrymen as Other, with scattered barbs on the habits of "Anglo-Saxons" and the unbearable "thikphogged" English climate, and the fabrication of a Danish grandfather named Lor. In fact the Leares—a Dorset name from which the second *e* was eventually dropped—had been London merchants since the seventeenth century. And as soon as he found himself among foreigners, Lear clearly placed himself as an Englishman for whom all non-English were Other. To him, as to so many Victorians of the middle and upper classes, not knowing a person's national or ethnic background, his "race" as they would call it, would prevent his completely knowing the person. Thus Lear's diaries and travel journals rarely fail to enumerate the racial composition of those with whom he traveled:

3 P.M.—Came on board the *Ferdinando,* an Austrian steamer running between Constantinople and Salonica; and a pretty place does it seem to pass two or three days in! Every point of the lower deck—all of it–is crammed with Turks, Jews, Greeks, Bulgarians, wedged together with a density compared to which a crowded Gravesend steamer is emptiness.[7]

But the ship is not large, & the sailors appear Turks & infidels: &

the passengers, always numerous, are apparently weary mixed—Jews, Germans, &&& . . . meanwhile heaps of Turks, Armeni, Arabs & other birds came in with their carpets. [Diary 24 March 1858]

[C]alled on the Rosens. R a pleasant friendly German, Mrs. R. I should say a Jewess,—& sharp. [Diary 28 March 1858]

Judging all by British example, he finds many deficiencies, as he complains of Italians "20 mad bulls would not stir an Italian out of a slow walk!" (SL, 34) and "Poor dear owls of Romans!— why they cannot yet black shoes or cook a potato" (SL, 61). Peace of mind returns only when among one's own. "It is delightful," Lear explains of his stay with the Sidney Smith Saunders family at Preveza, "after roaming over the most uncivilised places, to find a nook stamped with the most thoroughy English character in one of the spots where you would least expect it" (EL Greece, 174).

The farther he traveled from Northern Europeans,[8] the more Lear expected to find incompetence, sloth, vermin, dirt, threats on his person and property, and, the frequent repository for his fears of the strange and hostile, vicious barking dogs. Usually his fears were self-fulfilling, and when they were not, he registered his surprise: "Constantinople is much more oriental in character than Pera the Frank quarter, & the costumes are more picturesque. The streets are narrow—but far cleaner than I had expected" (SL, 86).

Therefore, the most unflattering remarks about Jews contained in Lear's writings refer to orientalized Sephardic Jews encountered in the Near East. His 11 September 1848 anecdote about the Jews of Salonica bears quoting at length:

Salonica is inhabited by a very great proportion of Jews; nearly all the porters in the city are of that nation, and now that the cholera had rendered employment scarce there were literally crowds of black-turbaned Hebrews at the water's edge, speculating on the possible share of each in the conveyance of luggage from the steamer. The enthusiastic Israelites rushed into the water and, seizing my arms and legs, tore me out of the boat and up a narrow board with the most unsatisfactory zeal . . . From yells and pullings to and fro, the scene changed in a few minutes to a real fight, and the whole community fell to the most furious hair-pulling, turban-clenching, and robe-tearing, till the luggage was forgotten and all the party was involved in one terrific combat. [EL Greece, 20]

Eventually police came and beat the rioters, after which "some six or eight were selected to carry the packages of the Ingliz, which I followed into the city, not unvexed at being the indirect cause of so much strife" (*EL Greece*, 20). The rowdy conduct of the Jews at Salonica made such an impression on Lear that almost twenty years later he would refer to them in his diary as a standard of ludicrous behavior: "I have never known G[iorgio] laugh so much, since the days of the moneythrowing Jew at Salonica" (Diary 2 February 1867).

The non-English oriental Jew served Lear as raw material that was subsumed in the wider discourse of the exotic that he packaged in prose and pictures in order to earn a living. Chloe Chard, reviewing a recent centenary exhibit of Lear's paintings, notes "the intensity of their fascination with the foreign and exotic."[9] His descriptions of foreign Jews and their habitations frequently reveal this fascination:

A few Jews in dark dresses and turbans; Jewesses, their hair tied up in long, caterpillar-like green silk bags, three feet in length. . . . [*EEL Greece*, 23]

[At Monastir] the stream, deep and narrow throughout the quarter of private houses and palaces, is spanned by two good stone bridges and confined by strong walls; but in the lower or Jews' quarter, where the torrent is much wider and shallower, the houses cluster down to the water's edge with surprising picturesqueness. [*EL Greece*, 36]

How picturesque are those parts of the crowded city in the Jews' quarter, where the elaborately detailed wooden houses overhang the torrent, shaded by grand plane, cypress, and poplar! [*EL Greece*, 39]

The repeated references to the picturesque here and throughout the travel books are not simply the overuse of a tourist cliché. Lear valued such scenes because they literally possessed suitability for being made into pictures. Lear apparently found Jewish subjects particularly picturesque. On his very first painting excursion outside of England in 1838 he visited Frankfurt and painted *Frankfurt, The Jews' Quarter*.[10] In 1870 he made an effort to "inspect the new Synagogue" at Turin, although it proved not picturesque but "most hideous!" (Diary 18 July 1870).

The saleability of art with Jewish subjects seems to have derived from the general Victorian fascination with things oriental. V. D. Lipman observes that "the Jew of Asia or Africa, in so far as the British public was conscious of him, was an exotic figure, perhaps pitiable if oppressed, perhaps picturesque if viewed as a variation on the Arab."[11] Lear frequently inscribed lower-class

Jews met abroad into this orientalist discourse, a discourse that Edward Said has described as "a dynamic exchange between individual authors and the large political concerns shaped by the three great empires—British, French, American—in whose intellectual and imaginative territory the writing was produced."[12] Indeed, a man Said cites (see pp. 35ff.) as a particularly salient purveyor of this discourse, the English envoy to Egypt from 1882 till 1907, was Evelyn Baring, Lord Cromer, who in his younger days had been a fast friend of Lear's (as was his cousin Thomas, Lord Northbrook.)

Lear further had good reason to assume that Anglicized, native-born British Jews of wealth and position might wish to recuperate their oriental past: "Sir J. Reid says I must do a large Jerusalem and get Sir Moses M. or Rothschild to buy it" (LEL, 88). While representations of present-day Eastern Jews, merely picturesque to the European gentile, might make their sophisticated Anglo-Jewish brethren uneasy, the landscapes once inhabited by their ancestors, the biblical Hebrews, presented prospects for historical grandeur and reminders of a heroic past. When Lear made his trips to Egypt and Palestine in 1858 and 1867, he deliberately scouted out locations for paintings suitable for sale to wealthy English Jews or acquired advance commissions for such paintings. His negotiations with Lady Waldegrave, wife to his friend Fortescue and daughter of the famous Jewish tenor, John Braham, are typical:

My stay in Jerusalem—or rather opposite the city—for I pitched my tents on the Mt. of Olives when I had ascertained the point I thought you would like best for your picture,—was the most complete portion of my tour: i.e. I was able to attend thoroughly & to the best ability to what I was doing, in peace & quiet. [SL, 149]

The uppermostest subject in my feeble mind just now is my Palestine visit. I read immensely on the matter, and am beginning to believe myself a Jew, so exactly do I know the place from Robinson, De Stanley, Lynch, Beaumont, Bartlett, & the old writers from the Bordeaux Pilgrim to Maundsell, not to speak of Stanley, & Josephus, whose works I can now, thank goodness, read in their natural garb. Now my particular idea at the present hour is to paint Lady Waldegraves 2nd picture from *Masada* whither I intend to go on purpose to make correct drawings . . . My reason for this choice is, that not only I know the fortress of Masada to be a wonder of picturesqueness, but that I consider it as embodying one of the extremest developments of the Hebrew character, i.e. constancy of purpose, & immense patriotism. [*LEL*, 69–70]

To be sure, the assumption that wealthy Jews would always want a rendering of Palestine from him sometimes led to disappointment:

> Baroness Rothschild was to come at 3.30— . . . Mrs. R.—and her sister, than whom 2 more ugly women I never saw. Mrs. R. looked at the 25 drawings in mano—& all talked & frittered & bored me to death—& holily glad was I when they went. My anger & distress is great, & although I had divided sheets of paper for Palestine drawings, I now do not know what to do. [Diary 18 January 1865]

These business considerations further mingled with a sincere interest in biblical lore to lead Lear to try to trace events from Hebrew history as he journeyed through the present-day Middle East: "Some parts of Jewish *History* (I don't mean traditions, speaking eagles & Lions dens,) are most touching & grand" (*SL*, 307). Lear could be sensitive to the similar interests of his Jewish patrons because he did not make invidious comparisons between the biblical Hebrews and present-day Jewry, a common practice in nineteenth-century cultural discourse. A passage from Coleridge's *Table-Talk* for 14 August 1833 provides an often-repeated example of the more prevalent attitude:

> The two images farthest removed from each other which can be comprehended under one term, are, I think, Isaiah—"Hear, O heavens, and give ear, O earth!"—and Levi of Holywell Street—"Old Clothes!"—both of them Jews, you'll observe.[13]

The one term "Jews" comprehended both Isaiah and Levi for Lear as well, but disjunctive signifieds for a single signifier never caused him undue amazement, as the deadpan tone of his limericks would demonstrate.

Lear's discomfiture with Jews, when there was some, related primarily to ethnicity, culture, and class. Their otherness as non-Christians did not enter into any negative feelings he might have, for Lear, while a proponent of a generalized Christian good will toward men and a regular churchgoer, nevertheless detested the institutional discourse of Victorian Christianity. The exclusion clause of the Athanasian Creed never failed to infuriate him. He regularly recorded adverse reactions to the narrow-mindedness, dullness, or downright blasphemous lies he perceived in Sunday sermons. The crabbed asceticism of the monks at Mount Athos evoked a barrage of invective and the conclusion that if what I saw be Xtianity, then the sooner it be rooted out, the better for humanity. A Turk with 5 wives, a Jew working hard for little old clo' babies—these I believe to be far nearer what Jesus Christ intended man to become than those foolish & miserable monks. [SL, 139]

A hater of all strife and discord who was saddened by accounts of the Franco-Prussian War and of skirmishes on various battle-fields of empire, Lear found quarrels among various Christian sects and factions almost unbearable: "The War *is* a horror.—I am going to turn Moslem as fast as I can, being sick of sham Xtianity, the only religion now rampant" (SL, 228). In his religious discourse, therefore, the Jew becomes a model of unity of religious purpose to be evoked as a set-off to the fractious and disgraceful Christian:

And this forsooth at a place of example for Turks & Jews!—this at the very place where he whom they believe the founder of their faith, died!—By Heaven!—if I wished to prevent a Turk, Hebrew, or Heathen from turning Christian, I would send him straight to Jerusalem! I vow I could have turned Jew myself, as one American has actually lately done.—At least the Jews do not lie:—they act according to their belief: & among themselves they are less full of hatred & malice (perhaps—for bye the bye they excommunicated Sir M. Montefiore in 3 synagogues because they said he tried to introduce Xtian modes of life–) than the Xtian community. [SL, 155]

As the cautionary note about Montefiore indicates, in writing the Jews as a harmonious spiritual community untouched by theological discord or hypocrisy, Lear is no more engaging in balanced representation than in writing them as voluble exotics scrambling for shekels on the docks of Salonica. Various discourses simply produced various Jews.

The discourse of superior class and rank, of course, produced the best Jews. Lear had always preferred the Jewish aristocrat manqué Disraeli to the evangelical Gladstone: "now who can hold the balance against fierce Radicals & Demagogues?" he wrote of Disraeli's death in his diary of 20 April 1881. If many wealthy Jews were Lear's patrons, some, like many equally well-placed Christians, were genuine friends as well. Underemphasized by his biographers is a particularly strong relationship with the family of Sir Francis Goldsmid, who, unlike Lady Waldegrave and Disraeli, remained observant as well as ethnic Jews, "of Jewish race and religion," as the *Dictionary of National Biography* phrased it.[14] Moreover, Sir Francis and his father, Sir Isaac Lyon Goldsmid, had long been what we would today term "Jewish activists." Both lobbied for and wrote pamphlets concerning the removal of Jewish disabilities. Sir Isaac's efforts in behalf of the Jewish Disabilities Bill caused Sir Robert Inglis to quip: "The title of the bill ought to be 'a bill to enable an hon. gentleman to come from the lobby into the body of the house.'"[15] Sir Isaac would later become the first English Jew to be created a baronet. Francis would in his turn become the first Jewish Queen's Counselor, would establish one of the first Jews' Infant Schools, and would go into Parliament for Reading in 1860.

A year after Sir Francis had been elected to Parliament (two years after he had succeeded to the baronetcy), he met Lear through Henry Bruce, Lord Aberdare, and, in March 1861, purchased a large painting of Civitella from him. From 30 September through 4 October of that year Lear was the Goldsmids' guest at St. John's Lodge. In his diaries he remarks upon the particular charms of the Jewish women and reflects "I did not think such pleasant times were ever again to be." Dinners, correspondence, and sales of pictures to the family would continue until Lear's death; the name of Goldsmid's nephew Julian Goldsmid, who assumed the baronetcy upon Sir Francis's death, appears in the list of correspondents at the front of the last of Lear's diary volumes, that for 1887. Throughout the diaries and letters many expressions of deep affection for Lord and Lady Goldsmid and their relations appear:

> Miss G. has all the talent of her race, & is very amiable. [*LEL*, 227]

> Miss Goldsmid, a sister of Sir F. G. is here, & is a pleasant contrast to the ordinary run of society. [*SL*, 175]

> Also Fr. Goldsmid wrote: they, alack! go on Monday. [Diary 4 April 1862]

> [The picture] was bought by one of the very kindest men I have known, Sir F. H. Goldsmid. [Diary 1 January 1870]

He grieved over deaths in their family, especially that of Sir Francis in a freak accident—"a fall from a Railway Carriage while in motion—at Waterloo Station":

> dear good Lady Goldsmid got to the Hospital only to find he had just died!—How constantly kind these 2 good people have been to me. [Diary 5 May 1878]

> *Julia Goldsmid died on* the morning of last Monday, the 7th . . . This event distresses me greatly. [Diary 12 March 1870]

Nor did the grief fade quickly. Three months after the death of Goldsmid's daughter Julia, Lear welcomed the arrival of a mutual acquaintance because "it was a pleasure to have someone to talk to about Julia Goldsmid" (Diary 26 August 1870). A visit to St. John's Lodge on 1 June 1880 reawakened "memories of Sir Francis!" (Diary 1 June 1880).

Any feelings against Jews that Lear harbored never transferred to the Goldsmids,[16] although he was well aware that their Jewishness would color the attitudes of his compatriots. Awaiting a visit by Julia to Corfu in 1862 he muses: "Next week Miss Goldsmid comes—what the fine & pious world will say to a live Jewess remains to be seen; what does it matter that she is good, sensible, accomplished, & handsome? If she don't believe in the supernatural attributes—birth, &c., &c.,—of course she must go to 'L.—'" (*LEL*, 221–22). A further comment about this visit in the same letter to Fortescue, however, reveals the class component of most of Lear's close friendships with Jews: "Miss G. had determined I find, not to go to the Synagogue here,—& had she not done so, I should have deterred her if possible from going there. For as the Jews here are all of the lowest orders, the advent of a Lady might have brought 'Confusion on the little Isle'" (*LEL*, 225).

Nevertheless, Lear did speak out against overt anti-Semitism regularly, as in the following excerpts from letters to Fortescue:

> Concerning the buzzim of intelligence, I am displeased, (since I wrote,) with some of Miss Emily Beaufort's writing. She wonders forsooth, that there is a traditional terror of the Cross or "anything shaped like a cross" among the poor "ignorant Jews" at Jerusalem!— Has Emily then never heard of the Crusades, of the Spanish persecutions & Inquisition, of St. Bartholomew, of all the Popes, not to speak of Lord Chelmsford & Mr. Spooner? If she has not, the Jews have, she may take her davy. [*LEL*, 193]

> One word about the Jews:—the idea of converting them to Xtianity AT Jerusalem is to the sober observer fully as absurd as that you should institute a society to convert all the cabbages & strawberries in Covent Garden into pigeon pies and Turkey carpets. I mean that the whole thing is a frantic delusion. Are the Jews fools that they should take up with a religion professing to be one of love & yet bringing forth bitter hatred & persecution?—Have the Jews shown any particular signs of forgetting their country & their ancestral us-

ages, that you should fancy it easier for them to give up those usages in the very centre of that country they have been long attached to, & for the memory of which they have borne such & so much misery? Once again the theory of Jew-conversion is utter boshblobberbosh— nothing more nor less. [*SL*, 156]

If we might suspect that Lady Waldegrave's own Jewish heritage influenced these protestations, similar disdain for anti-Semites occurs in the diaries as well:

Came away meeting Richd Brocklebank who tho apparently an amia- ble fellow is fanatically religious & . . . don't believe but that a Jew must go to Hell,—He is also absurd about Janet K. S. [Diary 9 January 1880]

A—— Graham, with 2 white dogs. Wonderful asinine Tory!—spoke of the downfall of Austria—of their reward and consolation being the fact of never having admitted Jews into their society. [Diary 25 November 1861]

To read personal, all-inclusive anti-Semitism from the caricatured Jews in the "Tea Urns and Pews" verse would therefore be as much of a miscalculation as to discount the repeated occurrence of such images in a cultural discourse of exclusion or to deny that Lear frequently employed such an exclusionary discourse. Once he had decided upon "Jew" as one of the lexical signifiers in this sequence, he needed the most economical pictorial signi- fieds to accompany it, and any frequent Victorian consumer of comic/pictorial representation would have recognized the beard- ed, old clo' caricature. Given that the resulting sign almost had to be derogatory, the question shifts to why Lear chose the signi- fier "Jew" from all the other available rhyming words. For his nonsense, full as it is, in the limericks, of persons from all over the globe, refuses many opportunities for the kind of dismissive exo-cultural stereotyping found in his journals and letters and in the general run of Victorian comic representation. Jews do not appear pictorially in them or any other nonsense pictures save for the one in "Tea Urns and Pews." The dress of the limerick characters who belong to other non-English groups may be na- tionally "appropriate" according to the prevailing stereotype, but there are no gross caricatures of ethnically typical physical fea- tures in the illustrations. And the only verse to convey any kind of ethnic slur occurs in the limerick in which the Quaker woman whom the Old Man of Jamaica has married exclaims "O lack!

I have married a black!"[17] Lear did in fact admit to an almost aesthetic revulsion against black skin, writing to Ann in 1849 of some "blacky moors" he encountered in Egypt: "but you know I never liked blackies, though you *did* make me walk round that chimneysweeper 33 years ago" (*SL,* 102). Nevertheless the conclusion of the limerick merely reports that his wife's remarks "distressed that Old Man of Jamaica," hardly an authorial endorsement of her prejudice.

In the "Teapots and Quails" sequence no ethnic/national group other than Jews appears both pictorially and lexically. Words that define social roles—"wives," "kings," "sailors," and "sweeps"—are accompanied by pictures of suitably garbed people. Additional drawings of humans pictorially represent "mumps," "whiskers," "swings," and "guns." The latter case involves the only other exocultural stereotype in the sequence's drawings, as the guns are wielded by two caricatured Chinese.[18] All the pictured, individual *he*'s whom the verses set a'going resemble the generic, ethnically nonspecific nonsense humans in the limerick illustrations. So the Jews are here, in unflattering caricature, perhaps only because the conjunction between the Jews-mews rhyme and an opportunity to draw them as terrorized by the mewing cat in the illustration appealed to Lear's sense of fun. Since the instance is a unique one, we can only speculate.

Finding in the "Teapots and Quails" sequence perhaps the most anti-Semitic representation of Jews in all Learian discourse has particular irony, for nonsense theorists have long asserted that nonsense breaks down the arbitrary signifying chains through which cultures naturalize their ideologies. Ann Colley cites another of the "Teapots and Quails" verses, "Thistles and Moles," as making "even more explicit" the "principle of serialization" in the nonsense "which separates objects and words and forces the reader to take experience as a shopping list of places, events, and items."[19] Nonsense, in other words, calls into question the ontology of Other-making, of the production of exo-cultural stereotypes. In Lear's limericks, the conflict between the protagonists and "they," the voice of the dominant cultural ideology, shows that he was quite conscious of this function of nonsensical discourse. That the caricatured Jews of "Tea Urns and Pews" intrude into this least exclusionary of all Learian discourses of the Other demonstrates that mere consciousness of the workings of cultural ideology cannot categorically make the individual immune to having it spoken through him.

Notes

The research for this article was partially funded by a Research and Productive Scholarship grant from the University of South Carolina Sponsored Programs and Research division.

1. Michael J. C. Echeruo, *The Conditioned Imagination from Shakespeare to Conrad* (London: Macmillan, 1978), 13.

2. Edward Lear, *Teapots and Quails and Other New Nonsense,* ed. Angus Davidson and Philip Hofer (London: Murray, 1953), 28. (A collection of poems left in manuscript, unpublished, at the time of Lear's death.) In printing the verse, the editors alter the punctuation in the ms. In this essay I will retain the original punctuation.

3. The *Punch* cartoon is reprinted in *Victorian Jews through British Eyes,* ed. Anne and Roger Cowen (Oxford: Oxford University Press, 1986), 17. The Aytoun and Gilbert illustrations are taken from the following editions: *The Book of Ballads, edited by Bon Gaultier* (Edinburgh: Blackwood, 1877), 68 and *The Bab Ballads,* ed. James Ellis (Cambridge: Belknap Press of Harvard University, 1970), 105.

4. Linda Zatlin, *The Nineteenth-Century Anglo-Jewish Novel* (Boston: Twayne, 1981), 17. For other considerations of the portrayal of Jews in the literature and art of England, I am indebted to Harold Fisch, *The Dual Image* (New York: Ktav, 1971); Montagu Frank Modder, *The Jew in the Literature of England* (Philadelphia: Jewish Publication Society, 1939); and Edgar Rosenberg, *From Shylock to Svengali* (Stanford, Calif.: Stanford University Press, 1960).

5. *Edward Lear: Selected Letters,* ed. Vivien Noakes (Oxford: Clarendon Press, 1988), 139, hereafter indicated in the text as *SL.* References to Lear's other private discourse—additional letters and diaries—are to the following sources: *Letters of Edward Lear,* ed. Constance Strachey (London: Unwin, 1907), hereafter *LEL; Later Letters of Edward Lear,* ed. Constance Strachey (New York: Duffield, 1911), hereafter *LLEL;* and the thirty unpublished, bound holograph diary volumes for 1858 through 1887; hereafter Diary and the date; in the collection of the Houghton Library, Harvard University, used by permission of the Houghton Library.

6. Lear had overheard a fellow guest at an inn dismiss him as a "dirty landscape painter," and Lear adopted the epithet as an ironic defiance of his acknowledged cultural marginality.

7. Edward Lear, *Edward Lear in Greece* (London: Kimber, 1965), 17; reprint of *Journals of a Landscape Painter in Greece and Albania* (1851). Hereafter, *EL Greece,* cited in the text.

8. To be fair, Lear did save his strongest bigotry for an Anglo-Teutonic people, the Germans, whom he irrationally detested.

9. Chloe Chard, "Pursuit of the Alluring Alien," *Times Literary Supplement* (4 June 1988), 16.

10. See Vivien Noakes, *Edward Lear 1812–1888* (New York: Abrams, 1986), 96, the catalogue of the Royal Academy exhibition of Lear's paintings, for a reproduction and history of this drawing.

11. V. D. Lipman, "The Victorian Jewish Background," in Cowen, *Victorian Jews,* xix.

12. Edward Said, *Orientalism* (New York: Pantheon Books, 1978), 15.

13. Quoted in Fisch, *Dual Image,* 5.

14. *Dictionary of National Biography* (London: Oxford University Press, 1917), 18:81.

15. *Hansard Parliamentary Debates* (July 1833), 1079; quoted in *DNB* 18:84.

16. Aytoun, whose comic portrayals of Jews were far more vicious than Lear's, was also friendly with the Goldsmids. Lear noted their mutual acquaintance when reporting a conversation with Aytoun in his diary of 19 October 1862.

17. *The Complete Nonsense of Edward Lear,* ed. Holbrook Jackson (1947; reprint, New York: Dover, 1951), 41.

18. Caricaturing the Chinese had appealed to Lear very early. A letter to Eliza Drewitt in 1831 contains an "Ode to the little China-Man," accompanied by a sketch that emphasizes the Chinaman's long eyebrows, high cheekbones, and "screwed up mouth" (*SL,* 11–12).

19. Ann Colley, "Edward Lear's Limericks and the Reversals of Nonsense," *Victorian Poetry* 26 (Autumn 1988): 292.

Learning to Punish: Victorian Children's Literature

John R. Reed

Wayne State University

I F culture is the text each member of a community must learn to interpret, punishment is one of its most obvious grammars for neophytes. Education is a premiere form of social management, and modern societies are generally aware of the degree to which their populations are aculturated through organized public education. Introducing young people to an institutional culture involves the delineation of values, which in turn requires an explanation of approval and blame. Consequently, one important purpose of education is to teach the consequences of wrongdoing. For example, children must be made to appreciate the significance of intentionally inflicted pain. Different cultures have different methods of punishment, and their educational schemes differ in applying those schemes to their citizens. Most modern educational systems forego physical punishment; they employ systems that withhold privilege or encourage obedience and approved performance through a hierarchy of rewards. In the United States these rewards are generally material; in Japan, they are psychological.

England at the beginning of the nineteenth century offers an interesting cultural moment when ideas about punishment were changing, thereby calling for a revision of values. The bloody code of capital punishment—so notorious in the eighteenth century—was being replaced with more "humane" forms of punishment, and the concept of rehabilitation was emerging as a new objective. During these years many reform movements gained force, notably reform of prisons and of the penal code.

But other reforms were instrumental in adjusting changed attitudes toward wrongdoing to the culture at large. One of these was the reform in education.

During the early nineteenth century, several different educational reforms occurred. The universities were reformed, the public schools offered a new model, and opportunities were extended to the laboring and poorer classes. Evangelicalism affirmed the value of literacy, and the Sunday School movement it promoted encouraged the teaching of secular and religious subjects in a moral context. Philanthropic organizations encouraged the creation of ragged schools and the improvement of the "national" schools. One consequence of this emphasis upon education was a larger reading public, especially among the young. In what follows, I shall examine some ways in which the growing body of literature written specifically for young people, or utilized in their education, treated the subject of punishment. All the works I discuss were very popular in their own day and remained so for many years after. These works represent actual practices and serve as handbooks for the instruction of parents and children, in the process institutionalizing changing values and methods of dealing with misconduct.

Gillian Avery asserts that there is a clear increase in the savagery of child punishment as one moves backward from Victorian to Georgian times, and this pattern parallels actual legal practice.[1] Physical means of correction like flogging are mentioned regularly, but so are other forms of threat and humiliation. A notorious and often-cited example occurs in Mrs. Sherwood's famous children's tale *The History of the Fairchild Family* (1818). When the Fairchild children get into a quarrel, their father immediately disciplines them by whipping their hands and making them stand in a corner unfed through the morning. But this is not all. To emphasize the enormity of sibling conflict, the father later takes them to gaze upon the remains of a hanged man:

> Just between [the house] and the wood stood a gibbet, on which the body of a man hung in chains: it had not yet fallen to pieces, although it had hung there some years. The body had on a blue coat, a silk handkerchief round the neck, with shoes and stockings, and every other part of the dress still entire: but the face of the corpse was so shocking, that the children could not look at it.[2]

This, Mr. Fairchild says, is the final outcome of one brother's hatred for another. He explains that, left to its own selfish and resentful nature, the human heart inclines to such barbarities.

Only dependence upon God and the example of Christ can spare man from such consequences of his depravity.

Much of the evangelically inspired literature for children emphasized human depravity and the need to trust in divine providence and its scheme of retribution and redemption. But another body of early juvenile literature was less concerned with intimidating children into accepting their culture's moral code than with providing pragmatic formulas for successful adaptation to that culture. One of the most enduring children's stories of this kind was Thomas Day's *Sandford and Merton* (1783–89). Day, though a religious man, took a materialist approach to punishment. On the whole, his story is more about avoiding the consequences of unwise behavior than about the need to punish. He argues for a *reasonable* life. Nonetheless, punishment must be addressed in a world arranged according to moral values. The first specific reference to punishment in Day's story describes how an ill-tempered tailor in India is immediately punished by the elephant he injures.[3] The stories of "The Good-Natured Little Boy" and "The Ill-Natured Little Boy," provide a version of the industrious and idle apprentice syndrome. One boy performs a series of spontaneous good deeds and is rewarded for them the same day. The other commits a series of offences which result in retributively similar injuries. Punishment is quick, certain, and appropriate to the wrong committed. This is an organic pattern of justice, based as much upon good sense as upon moral law. Mr. Barlow, the mentor for Sandford and Merton, explains that a sensible man will behave well to all around him, since he never knows when he may need help himself (101). The last extended treatment of punishment as such occurs when little Tommy Merton (the pampered, upper-class child) wants to punish a cat that has killed his pet robin. Mr. Barlow says: You can't punish him if you haven't disciplined him. The disciplining, however, takes the form of some painful behavior modification for the cat, but this pain is viewed as education, not punishment. Tommy also wants to punish the rabbits that have killed his newly planted trees, but Mr. Barlow suggests that the wise move is not to avenge oneself upon the rabbits for what is natural in them (seeking nourishment), but to protect the trees instead. Here practical sense is offered as a countermeasure to sheer retributive impulse.

Day's story emphasizes a due subordination to the social order and patience in the face of human hardships, but also suggests that reasonable people can achieve a great measure of contentment through virtuous and frugal behavior. Maria Edgeworth, influenced by Day's work, also emphasized acceptance of social roles and the use of reason over outright punishment as the chief means of dealing with wrongdoing among children, as did other writers like Hannah More and Mrs. Trimmer.

If evangelical writings emphasized physical and emotional chastisement to correct childish misbehavior and rationalists preferred reason to both of these, another school of thought considered direct pain a useful and commonsensical device for simple training. As with Day's "educated" cat, Captain Frederick Marryat's characters must learn correct behavior through physical suffering. Corporal punishment is both discipline and punishment. The education of young Johnny Easy in *Mr. Midshipman Easy* (1836) is a clear example. Like Day's Tommy Merton, young Jack Easy has been spoiled by his family and become so dangerously ungovernable that finally the family agrees to send him to school, but to one where flogging is not permitted. Dr. Middleton, the family medical advisor who takes Johnny to the school, asks how Mr. Bonnycastle, the master of the school, can manage without flogging. The educator replies, "I can produce more effect by one caning than twenty floggings."[4] He has not abandoned corporal punishment, but refined it. He explains to Dr. Middleton:

> "Look at that cub, doctor, sitting there more like a brute than a reasonable being; do you imagine that I could ever lick it into shape without strong measures? At the same time, allow me to say that I consider my system by far the best. At the public schools, punishment is no check; it is so trifling that it is derided: with me punishment is punishment in the true sense of the word, and the consequence is that it is much more seldom resorted to." [20]

He explains further that fear and love are the two strongest impulses in human nature and that appeal to the former never fails. He puts his method to use immediately with little Johnny, striking him with his cane each time the boy refuses to do as he's told. When he has thus wrenched compliance from the child, he sends him supperless to bed to "facilitate" his studies the next day. Marryat intrudes at this point to approve Mr. Bonnycastle's method. "Pain and hunger alone," he observes, "will tame brutes, and the same remedy must be applied to conquer those passions in man which assimilate him with brutes" (24). He adds that while Johnny's family sleeps confident that he isn't being birched, Johnny himself is already "so far advanced in knowledge as to have a tolerable comprehension of the *mystery of the cane*" (25).

Marryat approves physical punishment, but advises that it be used sparingly. Later in the novel, Jack himself fights a shipboard bully to protect a young midshipman and resists the institutionalized brutality of the navy.

Corporal punishment remained an important ingredient in the Victorian attitude toward children, and became a notorious shared experience of boys who attended the English public schools. But if an emphasis upon physical pain as a consequence of wrongdoing remained a significant element in introducing children to their culture, new and subtler features were equally significant. Early moralistic children's fiction sought to make inherently wicked children obey the strictures of religion and thus become good citizens. More secular writers wanted to employ logic in achieving similar results. But a characteristic tendency in the Victorian years was to teach children to punish themselves. This approach was assisted by the growing belief that children came into this world fallen but not evil. In fact, a familar figure in the literature of the middle years of the century is the pure child who succeeds in converting wayward adults, a reversal of the Georgian pattern of benevolent adult disciplining child. There are numerous examples of the good effects of self-incrimination in Victorian literature. A whole genre developed in the public school novel from Thomas Hughes's *Tom Brown's Schooldays* (1857) and Frederick W. Farrar's *Eric, or Little by Little* (1858) clear to the end of the century. But I would like to glance at a special category of tales that utilize the natural world as their instructive library.

Mary Howitt's *Sketches of Natural History* (1834) was inspired by a sympathy for animals and a positive view of children, but was, in the early nineteenth-century manner, more informational than moralistic. Mrs. Gatty, one of the most popular moral educators of the Victorian period, reversed the equation, offering a skeleton of natural history to carry the weight of a substantial moral lesson. Mrs. Gatty's *Parables from Nature* first appeared in 1855 and continued through five series until 1871. Each parable was designed to help the juvenile audience learn how to become a part of society. "The Law of Authority and Obedience" uses a community of bees to demonstrate that social order requires hierarchical structures where some guide and some labor. A group of bees, discontented because they do not see the justice of one bee being queen when they were created equal, sets out to found a republic where all are working bees. But they cannot agree on rudiments of social life and finally must return to the

order of the hive. "Training and Restraining" criticizes the desire
for individual freedom. The wind convinces flowers in a garden
that the poles and strings that support them and the careful
pruning with which they have been tended are the offensive tyr-
annies of gardeners. The flowers liberate themselves and are
promptly devastated by wind and rain so that most must be
scrapped by the gardener. The lesson is clear to the young mistress of the house:

> "now, at last, I quite understand what you have so often said about
> the necessity of training, and restraint, and culture, for us as well
> as for flowers, in a fallen world. The wind has torn away these poor
> things from their fastenings, and they are growing wild whichever
> way they please. I know I should once have argued, that if it were
> their *natural* mode of growing it must therefore be the best. But
> I cannot say so, now that I see the result. They are doing whatever
> they like, unrestrained; and the end is, that my beautiful GARDEN
> is turned into a WILDERNESS."⁵

One recognizes here kinship with Matthew Arnold's more complex indictment of doing as one likes.

"The Law of the Wood" inculcates the necessity of mutual accommodation by showing that the spruce trees who wish to prolif-
erate without consideration for their neighbors are the first to
be singled out by the woodsman's axe. "Kicking" is the story
of a lively colt that doesn't wish to be ridden and thinks that
it is serving itself by kicking and therefore discouraging riders
until one day he throws a young girl who is injured; he is severely
disciplined by his master, a discipline that is a kindness too, for
Firefly the colt comes to feel guilt for injuring his young mistress
and learns that submission is not bad. "Animals under man—
servants under masters—children under parents—wives under
husbands—men under authorities—nations under rulers—all
under God,—it is the same with all:—in obedience of will is the
only true peace" (268).

Mrs. Gatty's nature parables were popular, but the most striking work of this kind was Charles Kingsley's *Water-babies* (1863).
This children's story traces the growth of young Tom the chimney
sweep's soul after his "husk" has been purged in a stream (i.e.,
he drowns). Living in a pond and protected by water fairies,
Tom learns about the ways of nature, which are remarkably an-
thropomorphic. The important turn of events for our present
purpose is Tom's encounter with Mrs. Bedonebyasyoudid, who

explains why Tom is punished in kind for tormenting water crea-
tures even though he doesn't realize he has been doing wrong:

> "And so, if you do not know that things are wrong, that is no
> reason why you should not be punished for them; though not as
> much, not as much, my little man" (and the lady looked very kindly,
> after all), "as if you did know."
> "Well, you are a little hard on a poor lad," said Tom.
> "Not at all; I am the best friend you ever had in all your life.
> But I will tell you; I cannot help punishing people when they do
> wrong. I like it no more than they do; I am often very, very sorry
> for them, poor things: but I cannot help it. If I tried not to do
> it, I should do it all the same. For I work by machinery, just like
> an engine; and am full of wheels and springs inside; and am wound
> up very carefully, so that I cannot help going."[6]

Those who don't listen to Mrs. Doasyouwouldbedoneby, she says,
must inevitably answer to her.

This is a modernized version of the law of cause and effect;
it assumes as Thomas Carlyle and George Eliot did in their different ways that we sow the seeds of our own destinies. For the
one, whatever punishment we receive is what we deserve; for
the other, it is the result of invariant consequence. But the significant distinction in Kingsley's scheme, at least insofar as it applies
to children, is that this process is natural and does not require
external authority to make it happen. Kingsley openly rejects
corporal punishment. When Mrs. Bedonebyasyoudid does not
flog or browbeat Tom after an offence, Kingsley remarks, "But
perhaps the way of beating, and hurrying, and frightening, and
questioning, was not the way that the child should go; for it
is not even the way in which a colt should go if you want to
break it in and make it a quiet serviceable horse (215–16). Mrs.
Gatty's Firefly might disagree. But what is clear here is that Kingsley does not merely use episodes from nature to illustrate a moral,
he *trusts* nature as a foundation of morality because it literally
embodies the divine purpose. Poetic justice governs this world.
The crows who kill one of their kind for refusing to steal grouses'
eggs die when they consume a dog's carcass laced with strychnine.
Grimes, the master who had abused Tom when he was a chimney
sweep, suffers the Dantean punishment in his afterlife of being
immovably fixed in a chimney. Kingsley, avid fisherman that he
was, could not resist interjecting that the best way to cure a salmon
poacher is to put him under water for twenty-four hours.
Kingsley said that the doctrine of his book was "your soul makes

your body, just as a snail makes his shell" (86). What we become, in his scheme, is the consequence of our own actions. But the significantly Victorian version of this model is that we develop over time and learn from our past acts in what amounts to an evolutionary pattern, and Kingsley makes overt references both to evolution and devolution in his tale. The burden now is on the individual, even the individual child, to learn from natural events and internalize those values. No religious faith is necessary in *Water-babies;* the morality is pragmatically designed for social coexistence. Of course Kingsley stresses the existence of a higher power, but he insists that we learn God's purpose by looking at the world around us and in our own heart.

Two widely separated articles from the *Quarterly Review* indicate the direction and dimension of the change represented by *Water-babies.* In an article on children's fiction in 1842, Elizabeth Eastlake complained about the increasing appeal in juvenile literature "solely to *reason*" in the infant.[7] She associated this trend with American juvenile literature that, she said, revealed the calculating character of Americans.[8] A quarter of a century later, a similar review article by Bennett G. Johns deplored the heavily religious approach of Mrs. Sherwood's *The Fairchild Family* whose purpose, he said, was to impress on the minds of children "their own utter, entire, unmitigated, constant wickedness in thought, word, and action; their love for wickedness, and their fitness for hell to which they are all most surely and infallibly doomed, and to which they must go unless God specially saves them."[9] The author championed a more enlightened position assuming that "the conscience of a child, taught fairly to love what is pure, brave and true, is tenderly alive to a sense of every injustice as a departure from his own high standard."[10]

Of course that high standard was instilled by adult authorities, but, projected on the juvenile population, it revealed a new perspective on society as a world in which children (and adults) are not "corrected" by physical punishment, but encouraged to "good" behavior by imitating a "natural" code in which wickedness, being unnatural, injures itself, and in which education can transform misguided souls into worthy citizens who have learned to edit their own worst inclinations. As adult society more and more endorsed the model of an integral, self-directed individuality, it displayed for its children a paradigm in which childhood itself became the model of redemptive self-correction in a developmental scheme. The soul of the state makes the body of the state, just as a snail makes his shell. Matthew Arnold in his post-

Hegelian manner believed that the state could be the population's own best self; similarly, the child, in learning to aspire to its own best self through introspection could contribute to that evolving progressing and developing political entity.

The nineteenth century experienced a radical transformation in its way of perceiving blame and punishment. One major feature of that transformation involved the realization that human nature, like external nature and its various species, is not fixed but mutable. That being so, it seemed reasonable to assume that it was mutable toward good and that, when institutions were not employing educative and other rehabilitative schemes to effect that change, individuals could be doing it for themselves. At one simple level this is the positive doctrine of self-help, but at a far more rudimentary and intimate level this training for participation in a progressive world alterable for the better started in the nursery when young children began to learn the new plot by which they were to shape their lives.

Notes

1. Gillian Avery, *Nineteenth-Century Children: Heroes and Heroines in English Children's Storeis, 1780–1900* (London: Hodder & Stoughton, 1965), 204ff.

2. Mary Sherwood, *The History of the Fairchild Family*, pref. Barry Westburg (New York: Garland, 1977), 57.

3. Thomas Day, *The History of Sandford and Merton* (London: Darton & Hodge, n.d.), 3; further page references in the text.

4. Frederick Marryat, *Mr. Midshipman Easy*, introd. David Hannay (London: Macmillan, 1932), 19; further page references in the text.

5. Mrs. [Margaret Scott] Gatty, *Parables from Nature* (London: Dent, n.d.), 38–39; further page references in the text.

6. Charles Kingsley, *The Water-babies* (Ann Arbor: University Microfilms, 1966), 196–97; further page references in the text.

7. Elizabeth Eastlake, "Children's Fiction," *Quarterly Review* 71 (December 1842): 62–63.

8. Ibid., 82.

9. Bennett G. Johns, "Children's Fiction," *Quarterly Review* 122 (January 1867):73.

10. Ibid., 62.

Cracking the Code of the School Story: Telling Tales about Telling Tales

Beverly Lyon Clark

Wheaton College

*T*OM *Brown's Schooldays* (1857) was not the first school story. Nor is the school story always about a boy who wins acceptance at school when he fights the school bully, scores winning runs, and refuses to tell tales though wrongly accused of cheating or stealing. This standard characterization, focusing as it does on stories about the British public school, ignores the many stories about smaller private schools, which tended to foster different relations among schoolchildren and between children and authorities. It ignores the many school stories written before *Tom Brown's Schooldays* and also many later ones, including British girls' stories and American stories for both boys and girls. The neglect of these other school stories is unfortunate for their own sakes. But also these stories outside the canonical mainstream, often by women, can provide greater insight into the assumptions and contradictions of the mainstream—into such assumptions as the prohibition against telling tales.

Probably the best capsule statement of the contradictory assumptions underlying British schooling comes from George Orwell, writing in the midtwentieth century of his early-twentieth-century experiences: he tells how the "religious, moral, social and intellectual" codes at school "contradicted one another if you worked out their implications." In particular, "the tradition of nineteenth-century asceticism" was at odds with "the actually existing luxury and snobbery of the pre-1914 age," respect for hard work clashing with respect for inherited position: "Broadly, you were bidden at once to be a Christian and a social success, which is impossible."[1] In school stories as in real schools, a public school boy was supposed to be a meek Christian but also popular with his peers. Yet authors often suppressed one of the terms. The stories in the Tom Brown tradition may have paid lip service to Christian piety, but they really celebrated boys as boys, their loyalty to one another rather than to adult authorities or to the higher truths of religion.

More than earlier writers for children, Thomas Hughes revealed the opposition between student and teacher.[2] He was, it seems, the first writer of school stories to endorse the child's perspective in opposition to the moral righteousness of parents and teachers. True, he doesn't stress this opposition in *Tom Brown's Schooldays:* instead, he warps some of Dr. Arnold's ideas, aligning them with young Tom's ideas of what a Rugby education is for, especially the boy's preference for sports.[3] True, too, Hughes's narrator preaches at the reader from time to time, trying to enforce his adult moral authority on the child reader. But Tom's boyish perspective is central to the novel, with its focus on sports over academic work[4] and on loyalty to other boys over loyalty to adults.

One marker of Hughes's shift is his attitude toward telling tales. While a code against tattling must have existed at least since 1546, when the *OED* first notes the appearance of "tell tales out of school," the code had not been particularly encouraged in children's literature—at least not in the form that prohibits telling on peers. Many early writers assumed that telling tales was acceptable, even desirable; they valued moral goodness over peer loyalty, fidelity to God over fidelity to friends. In one story in the anonymous *Tales of the Academy* (ca. 1820), for instance, the virtuous Osric thinks nothing of telling his master of the romantic Paul's fancies about becoming a hermit to reenact *Robinson Crusoe*—and there is no hint that Osric is anything but right to tell on Paul. Or when early writers do acknowledge the schoolchild ethic of not telling tales, they generally beat a hasty retreat. Yet a few early writers like Dorothy Kilner and Susannah Strickland—and especially Emily May—explore the issue enough to elicit some of its contradictions.[5] They may then leave their fictional incidents unresolved and the implications unexplored, but they still raise key questions: Under what circumstances should a child tattle on others? Should her fundamental allegiance be to peers or to authorities? Will tattling cause her to forfeit any chance of influencing her schoolmates? For whose good does she tattle—and how does the valence shift if she will benefit materially from the tattling? Margaret Atwood, adopting the persona of a nineteenth-century writer of one of these probing, problematic school stories, might almost be addressing such fictional incidents when she writes, "There was something they almost taught me / I came away not having learned."[6]

In *Tom Brown's Schooldays* Hughes displaces the literary tradition of the past onto Tom's past: a weakness of the preparatory school that Tom attended before Rugby is the extent to which the ushers encouraged "tale-bearing, which had become a frightfully common vice in the school in consequence, and had sapped all the foundations of school morality."[7] At Rugby, on the other hand, an admirable sixth-form leader won't pry even when he knows there's bullying going on: "that only makes it more underhand, and encourages the small boys to come to us with their fingers in their eyes telling tales, and so we should be worse off than ever" (*TBS*, 110–11). Later the sixth form proclaims that reporting incidents to masters is "against public morality and School tradition," and "any boy in whatever form who should thenceforth appeal to a master without having first gone to some praepostor and laid the case before him, should be thrashed publicly and sent to Coventry" (*TBS*, 155). The need for such a proclamation may suggest that the code is not yet second nature. At least not for the older boys, though, curiously, it seems to be for younger ones. For Tom and his friends believe in the code implicitly, even doubting the propriety of telling older boys of Flashman's bullying. Instead they resolve as a group to defy the bully—acting on the advice of an older boy who has conveniently overheard their discussion.

Thereafter the boys in British school stories need no such proclamations. Imagine Kipling's Beetle tattling on Stalky, or Wodehouse's Psmith on Mike. Yet not all school stories written after *Tom Brown's Schooldays* assume, unproblematically, the codes that Hughes endorses. Late nineteenth-century British girls' stories, for instance, are often silent on the issue of talebearing. Perhaps going to school was itself an act of subversion—and why subvert that, why liberate oneself from something that is itself liberating?[8] When girls' stories do acknowledge the code, they generally accept its force, even if they express some ambivalence about adhering to it. In Annie Buckland's *Lily and Nannie at School* (1868), for instance, Lily is prevailed upon to read a forbidden novel and not to tell on herself or other girls, yet the narrator and also Lily's mother make it clear that her actions are wrong. Not until the twentieth century, in stories by Angela Brazil and the like, does the British girls' school story appropriate the codes and tone of the canonical boys' stories.

American school stories, too, even those for boys, followed a rather different path from that of the recognized British tradition. In the nineteenth century they stayed closer to the older, pre-Hughesian norms, even when acknowledging Hughes's influence. They tended to convey mixed or contradictory messages about talebearing, or even to endorse it. Oliver Optic's hero in *In School and Out* (1864) feels no compunction about informing his principal of the plotting of a secret schoolboy society. Edward Eggleston's Jack, in *The Hoosier School-Boy* (1883), does indeed submit to a whipping by a tyrannical master rather than tell who put gunpowder in the school stove, but the narrator lets us know that "in the present instance, Jack ought, perhaps, to have told."[9] Even Louisa May Alcott, in *Little Men* (1871), seems evasive on the issue of talebearing—or rather she reworks the theme through displacement: a new boy bears the blame for having stolen some money but not because he is protecting someone else, as we might expect in a canonical story; he is subsequently protected by an even more recent newcomer, who wrongly claims to be guilty and thus tells a different kind of tale, redefining the telling of a tale as the telling of a lie. Only in the twentieth century do American boys' tales like Claude Moore Fuess's *Andover Way* (1926) enact and enforce the ethic.[10]

As these examples may suggest, to find the issue of talebearing treated with complexity, to tease out the tensions and contradictions, we do well to seek outside the accepted canon of the school story. One book in particular gives free play to the contradictions associated with talebearing, even if not so much intentionally as unintentionally—not so much through the turmoil of a character's reflections as through what seems to be confusion in the narrative. E. J. May's *Louis' School Days* would not perhaps be called better than *Tom Brown's Schooldays*. But it is more revealing: it shows the schoolboy code under pressure, leading to uncertain, even contradictory, results. Published in 1850, May's book was in its fourth edition by 1855.[11] Its popularity shows its resonance for readers in this decade of transition from adult to schoolboy codes in children's literature, from loyalty to truth to loyalty to peers. May is pathbreaking in the way she problematizes talebearing—the way she bridges, even if in juryrigged fashion, the moral righteousness and reverence for authority upheld by the earlier school stories and the subversion of traditional authority to be ushered in seven years later by *Tom Brown's Schooldays*.

Central to May's book are contradictions regarding talebearing. On the one hand, deciding whether to report other boys' misdeeds to adult authorities is a litmus test of peer solidarity: boys expect other boys not to tell tales. Yet closing one's eyes to another's misdeeds is not right in the eyes of God. And in other respects, *Louis' School Days* is a profoundly religious book, like other school stories before Hughes: it's clear that school authorities are to be obeyed; only bad boys disobey.[12] Certainly Louis, despite a checkered first year at Ashfield Academy, is committed to obedience. His popularity soars and plummets, though, as he is accused of using an illicit translation to help him with exercises, then names names, then unflinchingly takes the blame due another boy and forgives the boy for not speaking up, then preens himself on his virtue, then is revealed to have divulged confidential information to an adult, then fears to confess to a practical joke and thus implicate another, then is accused of stealing apples but refuses to tell tales to clear himself, and then finally is restored to good favor. May seems a little uncertain at times in charting Louis's popularity—it's hard to see how, at his most priggish, he can be as popular as she claims he is. And her treatment of talebearing reflects her uncertainty: sometimes Louis seems aware of the code against talebearing, sometimes not; sometimes boys punish those who violate the code, sometimes not.

When Louis is accused early in his first term of using the illicit translation, for instance, he thinks nothing of implicating others. He feels no compunction about saying who had put the book in question near his books; he denies having taken it out of a classroom and attempts to incriminate a boy named Ferrers. But others believe that Louis, the newer boy, is guilty—and he is "looked upon as an unworthy member of the little society to which he belonged" (*LSD*, 70), not just by Dr. Wilkinson but by his schoolmates in the upper classes. Still, there is no hint that Louis's unpopularity is due to tattling. Instead, it seems due to being presumed guilty of cheating, to having been caught perhaps (or rather apparently caught), to denying the charge instead of confessing—and hence presumably, given all the evidence, lying.

Yet soon afterwards we are assured that there is indeed a schoolboy prohibition against telling tales. A younger boy, un-

aware of the source of Louis's disgrace, admits to having seen
Ferrers fetch the illicit book. The boy prefaces his admission
by saying, "It won't be telling tales out of school to tell you,
Louis" (95–96). Young Alfred has a sufficiently keen sense of
schoolboy honor to know that he shouldn't tell a master what
he saw, though it may be acceptable to tell another boy, especially
a friend. And Louis knows enough at this point to admonish
Alfred not to tell others about Ferrers's action—not to tell tales
to clear Louis of suspicion. Yet the endorsement of the code
here underscores how, earlier, Louis was violating schoolboy
norms. Furthermore, it's curious that, as in *Tom Brown's Schooldays,*
younger boys seem to have a surer grasp of the code than some
of their elders do. Are older boys, as they approach adulthood,
increasingly co-opted by adult authority? But then why would
an older boy like Louis, in the course of the book, increasingly
adhere to the schoolboy code? Or is May influenced by a Romantic view of childhood, of the child as more in touch with clouds
of glory, with truth? But then why are May's religious precepts
at odds with the code against talebearing that the child endorses?

Later, after Ferrers has confessed to his dire deed and Louis
has been basking in moral approbation, the latter is charmed
by an imprudent and flattering family friend, a Mrs. Paget, into
prattling on about school life, particularly about Ferrers's mis-
deed. The prattle then becomes known at the school, thanks to
a boy who has overheard Louis's conversation and subsequently
enrolled. Thus the virtuous Louis, who had prevented Alfred
from tattling even to save Louis's reputation, has in effect been
tattling to an outsider: one boy angrily calls him a telltale and
hypocrite.

His consciousness heightened with respect to telling tales, Louis
then encounters several boys and a servant with what he realizes
must be illicit apples. Louis doesn't want to bear tales, as he
tells his virtuous friend Charles, but he feels uneasy about not
doing so. He states that the servant Sally "is always doing forbidden things for the boys." Charles urges him to tell Dr. Wilkinson,
but Louis doesn't want to "get the boys into such a scrape," nor
does he want to be called a sneak. And despite Charles's admonitions that "if they are bad boys they deserve it," and that "if
we conceal evil, when we may remove it by mentioning it, we
make ourselves partners in it," Louis doesn't tell (262). He doesn't
question whether indeed the boys have committed evil, as a
twentieth-century reader might (when a child raids the cookie
jar do we consider her evil or simply naughty?). Instead he tries

to dodge the incompatibility between the schoolboy and Christian codes through uneasy evasions about fearing to be called a sneak and also through class and gender prejudice, through latching onto the servant as the most guilty party.

Later still, Louis is reluctant to admit to a practical joke, to having taken what turns out to be the only copy of an essay that his estranged friend and mentor Hamilton wants to submit for a prize. Louis is even more reluctant, once found out, to divulge who had put the idea into his head: "I do not mean to say who was with me. He was not to blame for what I did" (295). Through the adroit questioning of Hamilton, who has strong suspicions about which boy it was anyway, Louis nonetheless lets the name slip. In the give-and-take that follows, another boy remembers Louis's indiscretion with Mrs. Paget and accuses him of being "a tell-tale—a traitor—in the camp." Yet Louis is astute enough to counter the charge: "If there hadn't been another as great . . . you would never have known of me; but you bear with him because you can't turn him out" (296). That is, the indiscretions with Mrs. Paget would never have been discovered if a new boy had not told on Louis. And Louis's phrasing here suggests May's characteristic uncertainty: Louis doesn't stop at the semicolon but goes on to vitiate his argument—why shouldn't the boys have to bear with Louis too because he can't be turned out? Furthermore, the new boy is not the one who is distrusted here, as when Louis accused Ferrers of using an illicit translation. And while it's true that this dialogue may catch some of the slips and uncertainties of actual conversation, May doesn't elsewhere seem to be aiming at this kind of verisimilitude: she might almost be trying to make Louis self-deconstruct.

In any case, well-schooled by now in the niceties of schoolboy honor, Louis subsequently refuses to tell Hamilton whom he suspects of a later theft of apples. He himself is wrongly accused but refuses to state his suspicions; Hamilton expostulates against Louis's "mistaken notion of honor," which leads to "doing an injury to others as well as yourself. You must remember, that these evil-disposed boys are still mixing with others, to whom their example and principles may do much harm, independently of the evil done to themselves by being allowed to sin with impunity" (308). Louis responds:

> I am called a tell-tale, and I know I deserve it; but the worst is, they call me a hypocrite, and say that religious people are no better than others. I could bear it if it were only myself, but it is more,

and I have given reasons for them to say all kinds of things. . . .
But do not make me tell any more tales. I have promised,
Hamilton—I dare not—I *will* not break my promise! [309]

The overabundance of his excuses shows how strongly Louis is
drawn to the schoolboy code, despite its conflict with his understanding of Christian principle. He admits that he doesn't like
being called a telltale. We may or may not fully believe him when
he claims that it's worse still to be called a hypocrite and therefore
bring oppobrium on religious people. And in case all that isn't
enough—and presumably it isn't, for what follows is in fact the
most telling reason with Hamilton—Louis has promised not to
tell.

And Louis doesn't tell. But he is cleared—the wrongly accused
schoolchild inevitably is in school stories, as if the author too
doesn't dare trust only in heavenly rewards, as if he or she finds
the secular seductive. The virtuous Charles steps forward to make
an accusation to Dr. Wilkinson—thus becoming a telltale, though
he is not so called. As Hamilton tells Louis (thereby becoming,
in a regress that could soon become dizzying, a kind of telltale
himself), Charles told Dr. Wilkinson that the culprit was surely
not Louis but probably one of the boys to whom Charles had
earlier seen Sally give apples. Sure enough, when accused, Sally
confesses—or rather blames one of these other boys—thereby
becoming a telltale and deflecting some of the opprobrium we
might otherwise be tempted to assign to Charles. In any case,
Hamilton goes on to admire what he calls Charles's "truthful
independence" (318).

But what are we to make of Charles's talebearing? Why, with
all his "truthful independence," didn't he tattle about the earlier
apple incident when it happened, especially given his willingness
at the time to berate Louis for not tattling? Will Charles tattle
only to save a friend? But surely that's not sufficiently principled.
Will he tattle only when he is certain of his accusations? But
he wasn't certain here. And what should we make of his relative
unpopularity and, further, the fact that "never once, from the
first day he came to school, had he on any occasion incurred
the displeasure of his masters; and yet no one cared for him,
for he had lived only for himself" (265).[13] Much as some oppobrium is deflected from Charles to the dubious Sally, some that
might earlier have adhered to Louis is now deflected to the para-
gon Charles.

Nevertheless, Louis likes Charles, and Hamilton admires him.

Further endorsement is that Charles wins the medal for good conduct at the end of the term. Of the various end-of-term prizes, this one is, Dr. Wilkinson has told us, "the greatest of all" (129). There had, in fact, been considerable fanfare when Louis won it the previous term, after having meekly borne scorn and blame when wrongly accused of using the illegal translation: Louis had not only been chosen by Dr. Wilkinson—in effect being rewarded by an adult authority for adhering to the schoolboy code—but he had received the acclaim of his schoolmates. So Charles is merely following in the footsteps of Louis, the character with whom the reader presumably sympathizes. Yet the luster of Charles's meritorious conduct is slightly dimmed when we learn that Hamilton, the most likely other candidate, had "privately signified to the doctor his wish to withdraw all claim to the medal" (322). Why he should withdraw is never made clear—as if the purpose of telling us is only to tarnish Charles's achievement. Further, May buries the announcement of the medal in a paragraph detailing many prizes, unlike the many paragraphs that had heralded the award to Louis.

Still, Charles wins the medal. And, overall, his virtue is endorsed. Even his talebearing is not for the sake of personal aggrandizement but to clear wrongful accusations against another (though we may wonder if the prospect of winning the medal was entirely absent from his mind). Yet despite this endorsement of the talebearing Charles, May lacks the courage of her convictions: the progress of her story shows Louis more or less increasingly accepting the schoolboy prohibition against bearing tales—and accepting it despite its conflict with the dictates of religion, with the necessity of removing bad examples, of expunging evil. We are led to believe that Louis is nonetheless religious—that he will eventually enter the ministry. Still, toward the end of her story only Charles, a relatively peripheral character, and with all the ambiguity accorded by lack of popularity, violates the schoolboy code in the name of religion.

Now maybe we shouldn't make too much of May's inconsistencies. It's important to keep in mind, as Gill Frith has noted with respect to girls' stories, that such a schoolchild code is often a narrative device, "subject to adaptation according to the demands of the narrative. . . . What matters, in fact, is not *what is done*, but *who does it*. Whether the character concerned has the reader's sympathy, or the reverse."[14] And that's true in part. But the inconsistencies also illuminate the fault lines of conflicting loyalties, even conflicting ideologies. Other writers are rarely guilty of lapses as puzzling and resonant as May's—either their technique is equal to their story or, more often, they choose a plot that evades the contradictions associated with talebearing.

Such evasion appears in May's sequel: *Mortimer's College Life* (1856) evades the contradictions, giving little play to the issue of talebearing. In only two incidents is anything like talebearing broached. The first is only a brief mention. Still at Ashfield Academy, Louis learns of the straitened circumstances of his former schoolmate Ferrers, who has been obliged, upon the death of his father, to become apprenticed to a stationer. We might not make much of the fact that the boy who tells Louis of Ferrers's plight is referred to as an informer—"'It is a just punishment for him,' said the informer"[15]—even though Ferrers had been involved in one of the talebearing incidents of the first volume. Yet later when Louis does visit Ferrers—and visits him out of interest and concern, unlike others who simply come to gape— Ferrers says, "I don't believe you come to carry the tale of what the apprentice is doing, and how he looks. I know *you* are above that" (62). Thus May displaces the code against talebearing to a realm more acceptable to adult moral authorities: in part Louis is remaining loyal to a (former) schoolmate, but the code against talebearing is also redefined as a matter of Christian kindness, of not rubbing in a change in fortune, not allowing oneself to be governed by the superficial niceties of social standing.

In the other incident, at Oxford, something like talebearing does occur, though it is carefully hedged and qualified, as if May now has control of this trope (or Louis now so fully subscribes to religious authority that talebearing is less fraught with anxiety). Through the machinations of his cousin Frank—whom May allows to regress to some of the careless practical joking that had characterized him in the first part of *Louis' School Days*—Louis has agreed to host a musical gathering in his rooms, subject to certain conditions, including an early hour of adjournment. Yet Frank and his friends get out of hand, boisterous and rowdy; they deceive Louis as to the time and lock the door so that he can't get out. When a don or two come to object, Frank even goes so far as to fire a pistol he has found lying around (he says he thought it wasn't loaded)—though fortunately no one is hurt. When faithful old Hamilton stops by the next day, Louis tells the whole story, for Louis is still bound to him by ties of friendship. Yet Hamilton has now received his degree and is serving as Louis's private tutor—and thus has ties and loyalties to the college authorities as well. Hamilton gets the revelers to sign a statement exculpating Louis and presents it to the head of the college. The onus of talebearing is thereby displaced onto Hamilton, a peer who is no longer a peer, and dissipated even further by his ability to persuade the guilty parties to incriminate themselves: Louis seems little to blame, for either the rowdiness or the talebearing. Nor does May get at all exercised about the issue—she's not at pains here to explore it. In part she seems more in control: she knows better how to present the contradictions associated with talebearing so that they seem more resolved, to tidy the traces of disruption.[16]

Yet in *Louis' School Days* the trope does cause disruption. Poised on the cusp of change, May documents the fissures between (and within) a religious view of authority and a newer child-centered one. She records—even if unwittingly—the tensions between new expectations and old conventions, or between the conventions of school and the outmoded conventions of the pre-Hughesian school story, or between the precanonical and the canonical school story, or perhaps between instructing and delighting the reader, or between didactic and normative indoctrination.[17] She marks the stresses that arose in the transition from a relatively sex-integrated literature to a sex-segregated one, one that could allow middle- and upper-class boys increasing authority:[18] the transition, in the history of school stories, from views espoused primarily by women writers to those espoused primarily by men.

For the gaps in the book, the inconsistencies, could be explained in part by May's crossdressing. She is a woman who gives only the initial of her first name on the title page, hiding the "Emily" behind the "E."[19] She has not herself attended the kind of boys' school of which she writes: at one point she admits, "I do not mean to particularize the subjects for examination given by Dr. Wilkinson to the two upper classes, for this simple reason, that my classical and mathematical ignorance might cause mistakes more amusing to the erudite reader than pleasant to the author."[20] Yet the admission is unnecessary: rare was the school story, before or after Hughes, that particularized such subjects. May tentatively takes on the trappings of male authority, yet she is apologetic; she is anxious about her authority, unconsciously feeling the need for cultural myths that give authority to women who mother "sons."[21] It may be that in *Louis' School Days* she is writing about her experience in a girls' school, dressing it in trousers, in effect anticipating the stresses of the transition from private to more public girls' schools, from an emphasis on dependency to one on peer loyalty, a transition that started in the

midst of the century whose midpoint she straddles.[22] Or she may
be bringing her experience of girls' schools to bear on what she
has heard of boys' schools. Or even if she is simply rehearsing
what she has read in earlier school stories, she doesn't acknowledge that, as an outsider, as a woman writing of a boys' school,
she can bring insights and interrogations that most men seemed
unable to; it's as if, less committed to the system—to the system
of the genre, to the educational system, to the imperialism that
the educational system buttressed—a woman like May felt less
need to justify it, less need to present a perfect front.

   May's uneasiness can be seen in the roles she allots the two
most prominent women in the book, marginal though they remain: neither the servant Sally nor the family friend Mrs. Paget
is altogether trustworthy, one abetting a kind of stealing, the other
a kind of talebearing. Women are thus associated both with those
who might oppose talebearing, not wanting their evil deeds to
come to light, and those who elicit it, however imprudently. It's
significant that the males who try to elicit talebearing, Charles
and Hamilton, are not seen as imprudent. May displaces onto
Mrs. Paget, the imprudent elicitor of tales, some of the negative
associations readers might have with talebearing (though maybe
also, ambiguously, showing the undesirability of talebearing by
associating it with a woman, and thereby undermining some of
May's religious import). Similarly with Sally: her association with
some naughty boys (or are they evil?) serves as a lightning rod
for their evil (she led them astray) and as a marker of their evil
(their actions must be dubious if their confederate is both a
woman and a servant). That is, at the same time that she is a
sign of their evil, she may also, if she led them astray, if she
is somehow responsible, imply that they are merely naughty. The
presence of Sally intensifies the hesitation between—and consequent foregrounding of—the evil and the naughty. In like manner, the presence of the two women foregrounds and intensifies
the contradictory attitudes toward talebearing.

   And much as these women are ambiguously associated with
both opposing and eliciting talebearing—and with negative sanc-
tions either way—so perhaps is May: she has trouble locating
herself, locating a narrative stance. As if mirroring the narrator's
attitude toward Mrs. Paget, May seems to doubt her own trust-
worthiness, perhaps also her prudence. Yet despite—or perhaps
because of—her uncertainties May broaches fundamental issues:
she hints at the fundamental deviousness of all authors who tell
tales about telling tales. Is telling tales in the sense of telling

on someone ever far from telling tales in the sense of lying? Can we ever trust what we are told? Is there inevitably something dubious about the teller? Do we inevitably doubt the status and abilities of authors who tell such tales? May foregrounds and problematizes the question of peer authority to such a degree that she sabotages her own adult authority.

And by raising questions—by calling into question the cosmetic unities of subsequent male authors, who gloss over the ways in which peer authority undermines adult authority, including au- thorial authority—May sheds light on the fissures between (and contradictions within) the predominantly female tradition of the school story before (and after) Hughes and the male tradition, the public tradition, afterwards. For Thomas Hughes channeled the school story into the mode in which it received public acclaim—establishing the canon of the school story as it flourished for almost a century afterwards. After Hughes, there were Talbot Baines Reed, Rudyard Kipling, P. G. Wodehouse, Hugh Walpole, among many others. But no woman contributed to this canon, as it is now constructed. Not that women weren't writing school stories, and sometimes brilliant ones like Evelyn Sharp's *Making of a Schoolgirl* (1897). But that's a subject for another essay.

Notes

I am grateful to the National Endowment for the Humanities for providing time with which to research school stories, and to Roger Clark and Toni Oliviero for incisive comments on an early draft of this essay.

1. George Orwell, "'Such, Such Were the Joys . . . ,'" *Partisan Review* (1952); reprinted in *Such, Such Were the Joys* (New York: Harcourt, 1953), 45.

2. I speak advisedly here of earlier writers for children—and when I speak of school stories I will mean school stories presumably intended for children. There was, however, another tradition that influenced Hughes, one less explicitly addressed to children: what Margaret M. Maison, in "Tom Brown and Company: Scholastic Novels of the 1850s," *English* 12 (1958):100–03, calls the scholastic novel. This tradition endorses some of the rough-and-tumble manliness and willingness to defy authority that appear in Hughes's work. For a discussion of Hughes's use of such sources, see Patrick Scott, "The School and the Novel: *Tom Brown's Schooldays*," in *The Victorian Public School: Studies in the Develop- ment of an Educational Institution*, ed. Brian Simon and Ian Bradley (Dublin: Gill, 1975), 44–46.

3. But see Scott, "*Tom Brown*," 52–55, for a discussion of how Tom does increasingly adopt Arnold's values. Arnold's goals were, in order: religious principles, gentlemanly conduct, intellectual pursuits—with enough exercise to stay healthy; Hughes elevated sports and devalued academic work. And if Hughes debased Arnold, his followers often debased Hughes—shifting, for instance, his emphasis on self-reliance to an emphasis

on competition. See Isabel Quigly, *The Heirs of Tom Brown: The English School Story* (London: Chatto, 1982), 50.

4. J. A. Mangan argues that it was not the boys but the masters and headmasters who initiated the emphasis on games in the 1850s—to discipline the boys' unruliness. Yet the growth—the metastasis—of athleticism in the late nineteenth century was certainly fueled by the boys' own enthusiasm. Still, it's worth teasing out some of the contradictions in official attitudes of the time. The emphasis on games like cricket and football was both a pandering to boys' interests and a way of controlling their exuberance—a mode of control that acknowledged complete submissiveness was not possible. The consequent eclipse and even belittling of academic achievement was both a denial of what schools and masters pretended to stand for—in favor of boys' interests—and also an instrument for controlling the boys, creating, states Mangan, "compliant, uncomplicated, not-too-well-read boys who would challenge neither the intellectual nor the moral authority of older men—at least not openly." See *Athleticism in the Victorian and Edwardian Public School: The Emergence and Consolidation of an Educational Ideology* (Cambridge: Cambridge University Press, 1981), 106.

5. Frederic Farrar's *Eric; or Little by Little* (1858), though it follows *Tom Brown's Schooldays* by a year, is still in the tradition that gives religion precedence over peer loyalty. As P. G. Scott notes, it is a story about a private school rather than a public school. "The School Novels of Dean Farrar," *British Journal of Educational Studies* 19 (1971):163. Scott's comments about *Eric* could also apply to the earlier school story: "one of the culture-shifts since the high-Victorian period may have been a shift away from a morality of small-group life, with a corresponding diminishment of individual responsibility, and therefore of the tendency to melodrama in moral analysis" (177). In any case, as he wends his downward way, Eric is too attached to peer loyalty: it may seem admirable that he refuses to tell which boys have been using a crib even though that means he himself seems guilty. But his loyalty derives from too intense a hunger for popularity—too great an eagerness to win the "favour of man," resulting in "forgetfulness of God." Frederic W. Farrar, *Eric; or Little by Little: A Tale of Roslyn School*, in *The Victorian Age (1837–1900)*, ed. Robert Lee Wolff, vol. 5, no. 2 of Masterworks of Children's Literature (1858; reprint, New York: Stonehill & Chelsea House, 1985), 103. We are in fact told with approval of two boys who tell or threaten to tell tales. Yet while the incidents stress the boys' courage in braving their peers' contempt, the narrator also undermines their example. In one case, he explicitly disavows it: "I do not recommend any boy to imitate Owen in this matter" (23). He also distances us from the incident by making it occur before Eric arrives at school and by never allowing Eric to become very close to Owen, for all that Owen is always on the side of truth and justice, the side that Eric's better nature keeps urging upon him. In the other case, the narrator simply shows a boy threatening to tell a master about widespread cribbing, a boy concerned that a friend is being deprived of his rightful standing in the form—but we then get caught up in Eric's drunken debauchery and never learn the aftermath. Further, though the boy had been encouraged to take a stand against cribbing by an admirable older boy, the narrator refers to the advice as "well-meant, though rather mistaken" (142).

6. Margaret Atwood, *The Journals of Susanna Moodie: Poems* (Toronto: Oxford University Press, 1970), 27. In Susannah Strickland's *Hugh Latimer* (1828) the peer code against talebearing is most fully endorsed by a boy who is unduly influenced by peer pressure to snub a former friend whose mother runs a shop. Atwood is writing as the later Strickland, after the latter has married and emigrated to Canada. The "they" who "almost taught me," in "Departure from the Bush," are animals, representatives of the wilderness.

122 CULTURE AND EDUCATION IN VICTORIAN ENGLAND

The poem would thus seem to be addressing the opposite of what *Hugh Latimer* addresses, if the civilizing effects of school are opposed to the effects of the Canadian bush, though maybe what is almost learned is not so very different.

7. Thomas Hughes, *Tom Brown's Schooldays*, illus. S. Van Abbe (1857; reprint, London: Dent, 1951), 56. Hereafter *TBS*, cited in the text.

8. Not only are girls' stories relatively silent on the issue of talebearing, but there were far fewer girls' school stories, at least during the second half of the nineteenth century (and especially in the U.S.)—as if the school story itself was potentially dangerous for girls. Because of this relative dearth, and because of the incompatibility between what stories there were and the canonical stories, girls' school stories are virtually invisible in histories of children's literature. In her book on the school story Isabel Quigly devotes only one brief chapter to girls' stories. In his discussion of the history of the school story, "Two Little Worlds of School: An Outline of a Dual Tradition in Schoolboy Fiction," *Durham University Journal* 75, no. 1 (1982):59–71, Terence Wright mentions none about girls—not recognizing that one of the two traditions he traces, that following Farrar, derives from an earlier tradition of stories predominantly by women. Samuel Pickering, Jr., in "Allegory and the First School Stories," *Opening Texts: Psychoanalysis and the Culture of the Child*, ed. Joseph H. Smith and William Kerrigan (Baltimore: Johns Hopkins University Press, 1985), 42–68, is one of the few critics who acknowledge the existence of school stories before Hughes, though he is not concerned to compare them to the later stories.

9. Edward Eggleston, *The Hoosier School-Boy* (New York: Judd, 1883), 68–69.

10. In the British boys' tradition, on the other hand, it's generally not till the twentieth century that we encounter more complexity in treating the ethic. In the 1890s we may occasionally come across fairly rich treatments, as in George Manville Fenn's *Burr Junior* (1891): when Burr is wrongly accused of a theft, and he suspects that a friend is guilty, we watch his internal vacillations, his determination not to tell, his assuring himself that his mother at least will believe him, his dismay when it occurs to him that his uncle will learn of the allegation. But only in the twentieth century do we find, in the canonical mainstream, statements comparable to that in *The Hoosier School-Boy*, in which an adult criticizes the code. In Hugh Walpole's *Jeremy at Crale* (1927), a respected housemaster recognizes and to some degree accepts the schoolboy prohibition against talebearing but still makes clear his disagreement with that "ridiculous code of honour." *Jeremy at Crale: His Friends, His Ambitions and His One Great Enemy* (New York: Doran, 1927), 201.

11. Though of course it didn't compare in popularity to *Tom Brown's Schooldays*, which went into a fifth edition within seven months; see Scott, "*Tom Brown*," 35.

12. With the possible exception of Louis's cousin Frank, who is a carefree practical joker during the first half of the book but then settles down and even wins prizes at the end of the second term (though May allows him to revert to his earlier ways in the sequel, *Mortimer's College Life*, to provide some vivid incidents at Oxford that would not otherwise have ensnared the sedate Louis). Through Frank, May can make the point that hard work counts more than natural ability, for Dr. Wilkinson decides not to give Frank a prize at the end of the first term, despite Frank's strong examination results: "the doctor added that Frank Digby's indifference and idleness during the term had made him so unwilling that he should, by mere force of natural ability, deprive his more industrious class-fellows of a hard-earned honor, that he had not felt himself justified in listening to the [outside examiner's] recommendation, but hoped that his talents would, the following term, be exerted from the beginning, in which case, he should have pleasure in awarding to him the meed of successful application." E. J. May, *Louis' School Days: A Story for Boys* (1850; reprint, New York: Appleton, 1851), 128–29. Hereafter *LSD*, cited in the text. Then, as if feeling a little guilty about depriving Frank of his award,

May makes him work hard the second term and win several prizes. Still, rather like the private girls' schools that Joyce Senders Pederson describes, in "The Reform of Women's Secondary and Higher Education: Institutional Change and Social Values in Mid and Late Victorian England," *History of Education Quarterly* 19 (1979):69, this private boys' school tends to reward boys more for their behavior, for working hard, than for achieving academic excellence—or rather, May and Dr. Wilkinson are drawn both ways, acknowledge both kinds of merit, even if they try to reward one more than the other.

13. Charles even seems to be relatively unpopular with the author. For in the sequel Charles may be mentioned in a laudatory way several times, but we never see Louis interact with him—yet Louis does interact with at least half a dozen of the schoolboys we have met in *Louis' School Days*.

14. Gill Frith, "'The time of your life': The Meaning of the School Story," in *Language, Gender and Childhood*, ed. Carolyn Steedman et al. (London: Routledge, 1985), 118–19.

15. E. J. May, *Mortimer's College Life* (New York: Appleton, 1856), 50.

16. Not so for other contradictions. One such is the question of whether it is appropriate to strive for earthly glory at college. Hamilton discourses at great length to the effect that it's okay as long as one isn't seeking it merely out of personal ambition—but rather "your father expects you to make the most of your time," and "if you do not use the powers God has given you, in the situation in which he has placed you, you are not doing your duty: you are not doing MIGHTILY whatsoever your hands find to do" (*Mortimer*, 203). Further, "the more learning you have, the more you will be fitted for any sphere; and in your calling, you will in time have to answer all kinds of objections, and refute all denominations of arguments, not only among the illiterate, but among those who will respect your opinion little if you cannot boast the same amount of refinement in education as themselves; and the higher you are above such in attainments, the more will your opinion have weight" (203). So it's acceptable for Louis to compete for and win the Newdigate Prize—even to write a poem "allowed by all competent judges to be of no mediocre order, and far surpassing any which for years had gained the prize" (243). Yet, as if May isn't fully convinced on the issue, she crowns Louis's university career by having him win only third-class honors—as opposed to Ferrers's double first and Frank's first in mathematics and second in classics. Yet this "disappointment" is described without opprobrium (even if with a little too much eagerness to explain). The narrator has earlier described Louis as a creditable though not remarkable scholar. And here she notes,

> whether owing to accident, or nervousness, or to the desultory nature of his own arrangement of his studies, or to want of sufficient ability, or all together, we do not pretend so [*sic*] say. Some said he had not application enough, and that if Hamilton had not made him work, he would not have done even as much as was accomplished. Certain it was he was not idle, and earnestly strove to do his duty; but perhaps his efforts flagged just where they would have been of such signal service to him in his examination; and though possessing a considerable amount of scholarship, he was too deficient in critical accuracy and the hundred minutiae so essential to a first-class man, and which were attained by many his inferiors in mind, though not in perseverance. [262]

17. For an illuminating discussion of the nineteenth-century shift in children's literature from the didactic to the normative, a shift that displaced the transmission of values rather than eliminating it, see Patrick Scott, "The Schooling of John Bull: Form and Moral in Talbot Baines Reed's Boys' Stories and in Kipling's *Stalky & Co.*," *Victorian Newsletter* 60 (1981):4–5.

18. According to Elizabeth Swegel, this transition to a sex-segregated literature, fueled by increases in the market for children's books, the rise of the middle class, and the increasingly "sharp differentiation of male and female roles," was "well underway by the mid-nineteenth century." "'As the Twig is Bent . . .': Gender and Childhood Heading," in *Gender and Reading: Essays on Readers, Texts, and Contexts,* ed. Elizabeth A. Flynn and Patrocinio Schweikart (Baltimore: Johns Hopkins University Press, 1986), 170. But see also Samuel Pickering, Jr., "Allegory and School Stories," who points out that early school stories were differentiated by sex, in part "simply mirror[ing] contemporary education" (52) for the middle and upper classes, but also in order to inculcate somewhat different values. Boys could fight, for instance, to overpower evil. Girls, however, needed "to conquer the urge to fight," to internalize struggle, with the result that any fights that did occur "represented the general breakdown of social order" (56). Still, toward the middle of the nineteenth century sex segregation increased, as did class segregation. See Gillian Avery, *Childhood's Pattern: A Study of the Heroes and Heroines of Children's Fiction, 1770–1950* (London: Hodder, 1975), 71.

19. Her name is so well hidden that at least one early reviewer, quoted in the advertising supplement in *Mortimer's College Life,* assumes she is a male—"someone who can recall his own youth." And although her gender is correct in S. Austin Allibone's *Critical Dictionary of English Literature and British and American Authors Living and Deceased from the Earliest Accounts to the Latter Half of the Nineteenth Century* (1870), her first name is given as Edith (she is described as being "favourably known as the author of a number of juvenile works which have obtained considerable celebrity both in England and in the United States"); it's not until the dictionary's supplement that her name appears as Emily, though even then the compiler lists only a late work of hers, apparently not connecting her with the Edith in the earlier volume.

20. May, *LSD,* 114. May includes no comparable disclaimer in the sequel—and she even sprinkles her dialogue there with a few Latin and even Greek phrases, a *multum in parvo* here, an *argumentum ad hominem* there.

21. See Jane Miller, *Women Writing about Men* (New York: Pantheon Books, 1986), 114.

22. See Pederson, "Reform of Women's Education," 68–71, 83.

From Schoolroom to Stage: Reading Aloud and the Domestication of Victorian Theater

Alison Byerly

Middlebury College

C HARLOTTE Brontë's Lucy Snowe has a divided response to her first theatrical performance: it is "a marvellous sight: a mighty revelation . . . a spectacle low, horrible, immoral."[1] Her reaction encapsulates a puzzling contradiction in Victorian society. The nineteenth century saw a strong revival of interest in theatrical productions, but also, Jonas Barish points out, the development of a "puritanical distrust of qualities like mimicry, ostentation, and spectacle."[2] The Victorian taste for "spectacle" has been much discussed by recent critics.[3] But the Victorians' fascination with the theater was matched by a profound uneasiness about an art form whose purpose was, in a sense, deception, and whose medium was the human body. Theatricality is associated with duplicity in many Victorian novels. Becky Sharp, that "splendid actress" and "perfect performer," employs her considerable histrionic skills to deceive her friends as well as to garner applause in amateur theatricals,[4] while George Eliot's works are full of women like Gwendolen Harleth and Rosamond Vincy whose skill at social acting denotes their lack of a moral center.

Yet one type of performance was acceptable in any Victorian home and eventually became a lucrative form of public entertainment: reading aloud. Victorian antitheatricalism found a perfect outlet in reading performances, which represented a domestication of theater, a compromise for people who wished to be enter-

125

tained but were suspicious of overt theatricality. The importance of reading aloud to the careers of those authors who practiced it professionally has been amply demonstrated by Philip Collins.[5] Reading aloud can also be situated in the larger context of the Victorian educational reform movement. The appropriation of this domestic pastime by educational societies and, ultimately, professional entertainers, reflects a blurring of the boundary between education and entertainment that was typical of Victorian culture.

Reading aloud was one of the few shared recreations available in the Victorian household. In general, Jenni Calder suggests, entertainment occurred at "dubious localities" like the theater, music hall, and pleasure gardens, while the home was reserved for more edifying activities, like gathering "in the parlour to read *The Old Curiosity Shop* or bowdlerized Shakespeare together."[6] Eventually, however, the theater of this characteristically Victorian pastime shifted from home to stage, as professional performers began to make careers out of publicly reciting poetry, fiction, and drama. Once an activity practiced only by the upper classes, reading aloud became a form of popular entertainment which was enjoyed by working people as well. Solo performers like Charles Mathews, Albert Smith, and Fanny Kemble paved the way for authors themselves to perform in public. Wilkie Collins, A. Conan Doyle, and Charles Dickens were among the many British writers who read their own work aloud to paying audiences. Though they became increasingly dramatic, even sensational, recitation performances were able to escape the taint of theatricality for three reasons: because of their origin as a form of private recreation, because of their association with the educational reform movement, and because of their reliance upon the power of the individual voice to confer authenticity where a cast of characters would suggest artifice. The most popular Victorian readers, as we will see, presented themselves as lecturers (rather than actors) in order to emphasize the domestic and educational connotations of reading aloud. It was the activity's dual status as a form of education and a form of entertainment which made reading aloud seem the perfect expression of the novelist's project, as suggested by the fascination it held for two very different Victorian novelists, Charles Dickens and George Eliot.

Jane Austen's proto-Victorian novel *Mansfield Park* exemplifies the ambivalent feelings about theatricality which would later become general in Victorian England. The amateur theatricals

which the Bertrams and the Crawfords enthusiastically promote
are condemned by Fanny and Sir Thomas, whose objections are
never fully explained or justified. The subsequent elopements
of Maria and Julia are implicitly blamed on the dangerous inti-
macy established during the rehearsals; nevertheless, the theatricals are charged with a "mysterious iniquity," in Barish's words,[7]
which has been a source of puzzlement to critics. The novel's
well-known reading scene clearly locates the source of this iniquity in the nature of acting itself. When Henry Crawford begins
to court Fanny, his greatest obstacle is the bad impression created
by his skillful acting. But Crawford manages to entrance Fanny
with his reading of Shakespeare, which embodies "a variety of
excellence beyond what she had ever met with." While Fanny
recognizes that his reading is "truly dramatic," it does not offend
her as his acting had done.[8]

Why would dramatic reading be acceptable when acting is not?
One difference is that when the reader assumes a variety of
roles—"The King, Queen, Buckingham, Wolsey, Cromwell, all
were given in turn" (255)—there is no danger of his losing himself
in any of them. Lionel Trilling has pointed out that the antitheatricalism of Rousseau and his followers was based on a fear
of "the attenuation of selfhood that results from impersonation."
The actor diminishes his own integrity by deliberately cultivating
the art of "counterfeiting himself, of putting on another character
than his own." The spectator, too, is in danger of contracting
this "characteristic disease of the actor."[9]

In *Mansfield Park*'s private theatricals episode, the perils of impersonation are painfully clear: the actors and actresses hide
behind their fictive roles, evading responsibility for actions
performed in the guise of their assigned characters. Though
engaged to Mr. Rushworth, Maria Bertram flirts with Henry
Crawford, her lover in "Lover's Vows," and Edmund shows
an indiscreet enthusiasm for rehearsing love scenes with Mary
Crawford. Desires which would otherwise remain hidden are expressed through the players' various personas. But, as Fanny recognizes, this sort of identification with a character does not occur
when a single speaker is reading all the parts, and the written
text is present as a reminder that the spoken words are not the
speaker's own.

Henry and Edmund discuss the subject of reading aloud, com-
plaining of the "common neglect of the qualification" in young
boys' education (675), but clearly the Bertram boys were trained
readers; earlier, Tom had asked, "How many a time have we

mourned over the dead body of Julius Caesar, and to be'd and not to be'd, in this very room, for [Sir Thomas's] amusement? And I am sure, *my name was Norval,* every evening of my life through one Christmas holidays" (257).[10]

In fact, at this time well-educated young boys were commonly given elocution lessons. In the course of the eighteenth century, "elocution" became a powerful offshoot of the larger field of rhetoric, eventually replacing attention to style, content, and logic with an emphasis on declamation. In the period between 1800 and 1850, Wilbur S. Howells notes, "elocutionary rhetorics . . . flourished in such abundance on all levels of education as to make the term rhetoric almost everywhere synonymous with the art of delivering speeches with the correct accent, the appropriate emphasis, the proper pause, and the fitting gesture."[11] The prominent American grammarian Lindley Murray published three "readers": the first, *The English Reader, or Pieces in prose and poetry . . . Designed to assist young persons to read with propriety and effect* (1808), was such a success that it was followed by two sequels, in 1815 and 1816, which were as popular in England as in America. Murray's books were essentially anthologies of literary excerpts, with a minimum of instructive comment. Later manuals dealt with more advanced matters of technique. J. W. Keene's *Selections for Reading and Elocution: A Handbook for Teachers and Students* (1876), for example, contains detailed discussions of orthophony and the elements of expression as well as a variety of readings including "Hamlet's Advice to the Players," Hazlitt's "The Character of Hamlet," and De Quincey's "The Knocking at the Gate in *Macbeth.*"[12] The inclusion of such pieces implies that the student is expected to be attentive to dramatic considerations.

This emphasis on theatricality is not surprising, since, as Frederick W. Haberman points out, the "general interest in delivery so noticeable after 1750 is traceable in part to the renewed popularity of the theatre," and to "the personal influence of the great actor David Garrick, [and] to the pedagogy of the two actors, [Thomas] Sheridan and [John] Walker, who adapted stage delivery to certain forms of social discourse."[13] The actor George Vandenhoff, who was noted for his fine enunciation of Shakespeare, explained his own technique in *Plain System of Elocution* (1845).[14] Another handbook, B. H. Smart's *The Practice of Elocution: A Series of Exercises and an Outline Course of English Poetry* (1820) actually provides stage directions for the reader; each phrase is followed by a number, and footnotes in the text denote the emotions he should strive for at each point: (1) fear (2) disgust (3) regret (4) contempt (5) spiteful anger, and so on.[15]

The proliferation of elocution textbooks suggests that the ability to read aloud—and, especially in the later examples, to read dramatically—was an important accomplishment which the average middle- to uper-class person might be called upon to display. For those who, like Edmund, had to exercise this talent regularly as part of their clerical duties, it was more than an accomplishment: it was a professional qualification. Edmund laments to Henry Crawford: "How little the art of reading has been studied! How little a clear manner, and a good delivery, have been attended to!" (675). This problem eventually led to books like *Garrick's Mode of Reading the Liturgy of the Church of England* (1840), by Richard Cull, and *Use of the Voice in Reading and Speaking, a Manual for Clergymen and Candidates for Holy Orders* (1894), by T. J. Russell.[16] Crawford claims that he himself could not preach without a "London audience," their appetites whetted by expecting him "for half-a-dozen Sundays together" (257), suggesting that he sees preaching as a performance rather than a heartfelt sharing of God's word. Reading aloud, as we will see, is situated somewhere between acting and preaching, combining the drama of performance with the appearance of sincerity.

Reading aloud was originally an "accomplishment," an exercise for schoolchildren, but gradually it came to acquire the status of entertainment. One practical reason for reading a new novel, poem, or periodical aloud was to enable everyone in the family to enjoy it immediately. Philip Collins describes the anguish of a young child whose father would "retreat into his study with the new Dickens installment, shut the door, and begin his private perusal and rehearsal for the evening's family reading: the children could hear his chuckles and guffaws, but had to wait for hours before they could share the joke."[17] Henry James recalls in his *Autobiography* an occasion on which he hid behind a tablecloth, after having been sent to bed, in order to listen surreptitiously to an older cousin's reading of *David Copperfield*—until the Murdstones' ill-treatment of David made him break into "sobs of sympathy" that disclosed his presence.[18] But reading aloud was not exclusively the province of literary families; it was common in middle- and upper-class households, as many fictional instances of reading aloud suggest. Elizabeth Gaskell's Molly Gibson behaves like a daughter to the daughterless Mrs. Hamley by reading poetry and "mild literature" with her.[19] In Charlotte Brontë's *Shirley,* Caroline Helstone teaches Robert Moore a lesson about pride by having him read *Coriolanus* to her—although she finds that he does not excel at comic scenes, and has to read those parts herself.[20] Reading aloud was a suitable pastime for ladies, but it was the gentleman's prerogative to take center stage when the whole family was listening. As Mademoiselle Hortense tells Caroline, "when the gentleman of a family reads, the ladies should always sew" (115).

Once an exclusively middle- and upper-class entertainment, by the mid-nineteenth-century reading aloud was enjoyed by the working classes as well. The increase in popular literacy from the eighteenth century onward led to—and was aided by—the creation of the first Mechanics' Institutes in 1823, followed by Atheneums, Polytechnics, People's Instruction Societies, and similar institutions.[21] Many of these societies were sponsored by utilitarian reformers who feared that members of the working class did not know how to employ their own time wisely. Peter Bailey links the proliferation of "dramatic readings" at working men's clubs in Leeds and other industrial cities with a national trend toward "rational recreation" which originated in a middle-class effort to educate the working classes in "the social values of middle-class orthodoxy."[22]

But while they may have originated in a paternalistic social agenda imposed by the middle class, these societies were sustained and imitated by the working classes themselves. Working men started their own clubs, in which they sold beer to cover costs and took turns reading aloud.[23] Because triple-decker novels, and even periodicals, were beyond the means of most working-class families, many regular pubs and coffeehouses bought books and newspapers to be shared by their customers; in 1849, five hundred coffeehouses in London had libraries attached. Reading aloud was a convenient way to share these materials, and some establishments even hired readers.[24] According to the anonymous *Memoirs of a Working Man* (1845), workers occasionally read to each other on the job.[25]

By the late 1850s many churches and working men's organizations were sponsoring regular "Penny Readings." These events were not lectures, but meetings at which the members themselves took turns reading. The movement spawned its own journal, *Penny Readings,* which came out in monthly numbers with a selection of prose and verse suitable for recitation. Martha Vicinus calls penny readings "one of the most successful forms of working-class entertainment in the nineteenth century." Culture was made available "at a price and in a form that appealed to respectable families, courting couples, and ambitious young men. With the theatre and the music-hall considered off-limits to the respectable, readings and soirees, as they were called, became a popular substitute."[26] The name "soirees" suggests that imitation of the upper classes was one appeal of the entertainments.

Readings may have become popular because they were more respectable than theater, but as time went on "readings" began to resemble theatrical performances more and more. The elocution manuals mentioned earlier were intended as textbooks for students, but another class of books catered to a different audience: the professional elocutionist. Daniel Staniford's *The Art of Reading: containing a number of useful rules, exemplified by a variety of selected and original pieces, together with dialogues, speeches, orations, addresses, and harangues* (1807) and, later, Jacob W. Shoemaker's collection *Best Things from Best Authors: Humor, pathos, and eloquence . . . comprising numbers one, two, and three of the Elocutionist's Annual* (1875) are typical.[27] The fact that there was a market for books which were intended to form a repertoire for professional speakers suggests that such speakers enjoyed considerable success. Professional elocutionists and their more theatrical cousins, "virtuoso" or solo performers, were important precursors of literary readers like Charles Dickens.

Charles Mathews was one of the first successful solo performers and exerted considerable influence on Dickens, who saw him perform many times. Mathews was an actor who achieved notable success in a wide variety of character roles and gradually developed a one-man program which showcased his versatility. His first shows were lectures of a sort, narratives in which he would recount a journey and act out the parts of the various people he met along the way. "The Mail Coach Adventure," in 1817, was followed by "A Trip to America" in 1824, and finally these shows were replaced by his famous "At Homes." These were advertised simply as "At Home with Mr. Charles Mathews," and consisted of a mix of monologues, dialogues, and farces. He developed what he called the "monopolylogue," a drama in which he acted all the parts; at first he presented dramatic excerpts like "Hamlet's Advice to the Players," but later he wrote his own scripts, which often satirized his contemporaries.[28] He was clearly a model for Dickens both in the convivial, almost domestic, atmosphere he established in his "At Home" performances, and in his legendary talent for playing many diverse roles.

The lectures of the famous solo performer Albert Smith also helped pave the way for Dickens's readings. Smith, like Mathews, gave lectures on his various travels, but he also illustrated these talks with increasingly elaborate visual aids, culminating in his hugely successful "Ascent of Mont Blanc" show. Smith, the thirtieth man to make this reputedly difficult ascent, gave a stirring account of the difficulties of the journey, using as a backdrop for his talks a series of stunning panoramas painted by William Beverley. His success was repeated year after year; Beverley made new views and Smith added new characters, but the show ran for several years with the same basic format.[29] Smith differed from other solo performers by presenting himself as an author, not an actor, and though some derided him as a "vulgar showman," he was able to attract family audiences to his highly respectable entertainments. Dickens hired Albert Smith's brother Arthur as manager for his own reading tours.

Fanny Kemble was another actor who made a successful transition from the stage to the lecture hall. Kemble was of course not the first member of the great theatrical family to give public readings. Her grandfather, John Philip Kemble, read occasionally, perhaps in imitation of the actor-rhetorician Thomas Sheridan, whose 1763 "Attic Mornings" is sometimes credited with originating the literary recitation as a form of entertainment; Kemble attended at least one of Sheridan's readings.[30] Her aunt, Sarah Siddons, was asked by the royal family to read at Windsor. Mrs. Siddons enjoyed reading so much that she frequently read Shakespeare to her friends, and, after her retirement, gave two seasons of public readings at the Argyll Rooms.[31] Charles Kemble, Fanny's father, was also invited to read privately for the royal family, and he read Shakespeare publicly for several years after his retirement.[32] But Fanny was the first Kemble to prefer reading to acting. Her brilliant acting career lasted only from 1829 to 1834, when she married Pierce Butler and retired from the stage. After the collapse of her marriage, she returned briefly to acting in 1847–48, but when Charles discontinued his readings and gave Fanny the immense volume of Shakespeare in which he had written his own performance notes, she thankfully abandoned acting forever and began the public readings of Shakespeare which would be her main source of income for more than twenty years.

Fanny Kemble had in fact always hated acting; at the height of her fame, she wrote in her journal, "How I do loathe the stage! these wretched, tawdry, glittering rags, flung over the breathing forms of ideal loveliness . . . horror! horror! how I do loathe my most impotent and unpoetical craft!"[33] Charles Lamb's influential essay "On the Tragedies of Shakespeare" had popularized the idea that Shakespeare was better appreciated on paper than on the stage, and Kemble felt that readings were a way of rescuing Shakespeare from the "mockery," the "disgusting travesty" of incompetent productions.[34] She said of her readings that the loss of "dramatic effect" would be compensated for by the "possibility of retaining the whole beauty of the plays as poetical compositions."[35] But she seems to have felt that not only incompetent productions, but all theatrical productions, were fundamentally spurious. In an essay, "On the Stage," which she wrote for *Cornhill Magazine* in 1863, Kemble distinguishes between "drama" and "theater," insisting that the "dramatic in human nature . . . has no relation . . . to that which imitates it, and is its theatrical reproduction; the dramatic is the *real*, of which the theatrical is the *false*."[36]

Fanny Kemble's decision to make a career out of reading Shakespeare's plays was prompted partly by financial need—one practical reason for the popularity of readings was of course that they reaped greater profits than full-scale theatrical productions—but also by a genuine desire to educate the public. Though her tour managers begged her to stick to the most popular Shakespearean selections, Kemble insisted on reading a wide variety of plays in order to popularize the lesser-known works. She also demanded that admission prices be kept low enough to make her readings accessible to all classes. Kemble was determined to present the great poet's works as pure drama, stripped of their theatrical trappings.

Michael Booth points out that "Shakespearean performances in the Victorian period became a battleground between supporters and opponents of the spectacular style."[37] To choose to read—or hear—a text that was intended to be acted suggests a deep repugnance for theatricality of any kind. Shakespearean readings by actors and actresses were so well-attended that one contemporary reviewer satirized the hypocrisy of the person "who shrinks from a theatre, but goes with a smug countenance to hear a Shakespearian reading . . . who will hear actors read and will not see them act."[38] Such audiences were able to tell themselves that they were being educated rather than entertained.

Charles Dickens's career as a reader seems in many ways a complete reversal of Fanny Kemble's. His love for the theater which she rejected is well known. She read literature aloud in order to preserve it from theatricality; he read literature aloud in order to infuse it with theatricality. But the opposite directions from which they approached the problem of theatricality con-

verged in the same perfect compromise. The unpretentious stag-
ing of Dickens's readings closely resembled Fanny Kemble's. Both
performed behind a reading desk. Their only "props" were desks,
lamps, and the texts themselves, all of which validated the fact
that they were playing the role of "reader," a role familiar to
most of the audience. While theatrical convention dictated that
spectators suspend their disbelief and pretend that actors *were*
the characters they portrayed, the conventions of the reading
performance worked to distance the reader from the various
roles he or she would perform.

The fact that Dickens's novels were customarily read aloud
in many homes probably contributed to his immediate success
as a reader. His public readings were "safe," respectable, because
they were simply an extension of a familiar domestic activity.
Dickens did his best to foster a familial atmosphere in his readings; he commonly prefaced his reading of *A Christmas Carol* by
asking his audience to "consider themselves a Christmas party
listening to a Christmas story."[39] But he also reworked his texts
into startlingly theatrical performances.

Dickens began by reading only Christmas books, then gradually
added excerpts from his novels to the repertoire. Dickens re-
hearsed the readings thoroughly, making additional cuts and
writing in stage directions for himself. He worked out several
different combinations of texts which would provide an even mix
of humor and pathos, and the final repertoire was clearly chosen
with a view toward exhibiting his skill as a character actor. Like
Charles Mathews, Dickens was noted for his ability to play a wide
variety of roles. Charles Kent described Dickens's remarkable
ability to present these characters with "a rapidity of sequence
or alternation, so astonishing in its mingled facility and precision,
that the characters themselves . . . were there simultaneously."[40]
Dickens's reading texts were essentially scripts which represented
his own dramatizations of his novels. A brief look at Dickens's
prompt-copy for "Sikes and Nancy," one of his most important
readings, shows how thoroughly theatrical those "readings" were.

Dickens wanted to include something unusual and memorable
in his farewell tour, and decided on the murder from *Oliver Twist*.
He may well have expected the sensationalism of the story to
be a strong selling point, since such readings were becoming increasingly popular; Thomas Hood's "Eugene Aram, the Murderer" was recited by Henry Irving and others with great success.
Many of Dickens's friends expressed reservations about "Sikes
and Nancy," fearing that the constant repetition of such a taxing

performance would affect Dickens's health (as it ultimately did). They may also have been afraid that the tale's violence would destroy the intimate atmosphere which Dickens cultivated in his readings. Dickens, however, knew what his audience wanted.

Dickens sensationalized the story of "Sikes and Nancy" through small changes in the diction of the reading version which heighten the tale's melodramatic qualities. Dickens's eventual choice of the title "Sikes and Nancy," rather than "The Murder from *Oliver Twist*," as in his premiere of the reading, suggests that he intended to draw attention to the shocking relationship between the two characters. In the reading version, the violence underlying Sikes and Nancy's sexual relationship is rendered more horrifying by Dickens's emphasis on Nancy's inability to leave Sikes even though she is fully aware of what he may do to her. In *Oliver Twist*, the reason Nancy gives Mr. Brownlow for her refusal to turn in her criminal friends is simply the loyalty she feels toward her compatriots. But in "Sikes and Nancy," Dickens adds a dramatic speech which stresses Nancy's simultaneous attraction and fear: "how can I say it with the young lady here!—among them, there is one—this Bill—this Sikes—the most desperate of all—that I can't leave. Whether it is God's wrath for the wrong I have done, I don't know, but I am drawn back to him through everything, and I should be, I believe, if I knew I was to die by his hand!"[41] Dickens reenforces the idea of a perverse attachment born of the prostitute's fallen condition by contrasting her diseased love— her "rotten" heart, she says in the reading version, cannot be "cured" (23)—with the normal, healthy love of a woman like Rose.

Most of the changes Dickens made in his reading text are for the purpose of "dramatizing" it, of making it more theatrical. But Dickens's keen sense of dramatic timing prevented him from reducing the story to simple dialogue: the narrator's role is just as important as the character parts in "Sikes and Nancy." Many of Dickens's notations to himself pertain to narrative passages. Three pages before the murder, when Sikes returns stealthily to his house, Dickens wrote in *"XX Murder coming XX"* as a reminder to read even this simple description with a sense of impending doom (35).

By emphasizing the narrator's role, rather than just reading the dialogue of the stories, Dickens ensured that his stories, dramatic as they were, would not be perceived as inappropriately theatrical. Dickens's "Protean voice," to use Charles Kent's term, was able to suggest many characters, but in a sense he was playing only one role: narrator of his own stories, a role in which his sincerity could not be questioned, since Dickens's narrators were popularly identified with Dickens himself. Taking on this part could involve none of the dangerous misrepresentation and disintegration of self that, as we saw earlier, were associated with acting.

In fact, the ability of a performer to assimilate a number of different voices argued against the possibility of the actor's own personality being subsumed in his or her role. A listener at one of Fanny Kemble's readings marveled that "a single voice by reading of a play could produce the effect which followed her simple introduction";[42] the contrast between her own simple speech and the crowd of voices she was able to evoke highlighted the fact that it was she herself, one person, who portrayed all of the characters. A reviewer for the *Illustrated London News* praised her ability to perform many roles, bringing both sexes and "different ranks of person and education" into "alternate prominence."[43] The same thing was said of Dickens's reading: "He gives a distinct voice to each character, and to an extraordinary extent assumes the personality of each . . . But then the man himself is also there."[44] In spite of its obvious disadvantages for dramatic representation, the solo voice was preferable to an entire cast because it seemed to signify the presence of a stable, sincere self behind the theatrical roles.

Dickens himself recognized, of course, that the apparent authenticity of the reading voice was an illusion. In *Our Mutual Friend,* which was written after Dickens had been reading regularly for several years, reading aloud is implicated in the masquerades which disguise so many of the characters from each other, and functions as a parody of efforts at self-improvement. Silas Wegg, who is taken for a "literary chap" by the uneducated Mr. Boffin because he knows the words to so many street-ballads, uses his position as hired reader to exploit Mr. Boffin's generosity. All of Wegg's readings start with a hearty meal and end with an exorbitant fee. But Wegg's reading sessions involve pretense on Boffin's part as well; in order to reenforce the miserly role which he has assumed for Bella's benefit, Boffin orders Wegg to read the lives of famous misers to him. The reading scenes are thus the locus of a double deception: Wegg enacts the role of literary chap and invaluable advisor while Boffin enacts the role of a man obsessed with wealth.

Our Mutual Friend's other reader, the boy Sloppy, applies his dramatic skill directly to the text. Betty Higden says to the Boffins: "You mightn't think it, but Sloppy is a beautiful reader of a newspaper. He do the Police in different voices."[45] Sloppy's skill at dividing his own personality into multiple roles is perhaps the result of his orphaned status. He has no stable identity of his own to preserve; he has "no right name . . . he took his name from being found on a Sloppy night" (201). Sloppy's evocation of the many voices of authority which have failed him suggests displacement and alienation, as T. S. Eliot recognized when he originally chose "He Do the Police in Different Voices" as his title for the polyphonic poem which became *The Waste Land.*

Although she never read publicly, as Dickens did, George Eliot was also a lifelong devotee of reading aloud. Nina Auerbach has suggested that George Eliot was innately theatrical in a way which has not been fully recognized. She led, Auerbach claims, a "divided life, whose painful care for its own privacy and artistic attentiveness to the private consciousness of others fought a hunger for self-dramatization and an irrepressible instinct for self-display."[46] Reading aloud may have represented a perfect compromise between those competing impulses. It was an acceptable forum for Eliot's desire to perform, and, at the same time, an essential part of her education as a writer.

The instructive function of Eliot's and Lewes's reading is clear if we compare what they were reading with what Eliot was writing at any given time. When Eliot first began writing fiction, she and Lewes started reading novels almost exclusively. Novels might seem an obvious choice for reading entertainment, but Eliot and Lewes, themselves experienced essayists and connoisseurs of good expository prose, at other times read such works as Layard's *Ninevah and Its Remains,* Ernest Renan's *Essais de morale et de littérature,* and Mendelssohn's *Letters* aloud.[47] Early in 1857, however, they were reading Elizabeth Gaskell's *Cranford,* Charlotte Brontë's *The Professor,* and *The Scarlet Letter.* They also enjoyed Gaskell's *Life of Charlotte Brontë;* rereading in that biography Lewes's famous correspondence with Brontë on the subject of Jane Austen may have reminded them of Austen's importance to any serious writer of fiction, because between February and June of 1857 Eliot's *Journal* records reading aloud every Austen novel except *Pride and Prejudice.*[48] Eliot was writing the second of her *Scenes of Clerical Life,* "Mr. Gilfil's Love-Story," at this time, and if one compares the opening of this story with the opening of her first story, "The Sad Fortunes of the Reverend Amos Barton," one can almost hear Austen's influence. "Amos Barton" begins with a friendly, intimate description of the narrator's memories of Shepperton Church:

> Shepperton Church was a very different-looking building five-and-twenty years ago. To be sure, its substantial stone tower looks at you through its intelligent eye, the clock, with the friendly expression of former days; but in everything else, what changes! . . . Pass through the baize doors and you will see the nave filled with well-shaped benches, understood to be free seats.[49]

"Mr. Gilfil," however, begins with a paragraph as detached and ironic as any of Austen's openings:

> When old Mr. Gilfil died, thirty years ago, there was general sorrow in Shepperton; and if black cloth had not been hung round the pulpit and the reading-desk, by order of his nephew and principal legatee, the parishioners would certainly have subscribed the necessary sum out of their own pockets, rather than allow such a tribute to be wanting. . . . An unreadiness to put on black on all available occasions, or too great an alacrity in putting it off, argued . . . a dangerous levity of character, and an unnatural insensibility to the fitness of things. [75]

The narrator seems to have absorbed Austen's satiric tone.

Tennyson was a favorite when Eliot and Lewes stayed in Dresden in 1867; they read "Enoch Arden," "Sea Dreams," "The Northern Farmer," and "Tithonus."[50] This sudden immersion in Tennyson is probably connected to Eliot's work on a verse drama, *The Spanish Gypsy*, at this time. Parts of that poem echo Tennyson's mellifluous sonority, and one of Pablo's songs is patterned after "In Memoriam"'s distinctive rhyme scheme. (Tennyson himself enjoyed reading his poems, and often brought a copy of his works when he visited Eliot and Lewes at the priory, just in case a reading was requested.)[51]

Eliot made a habit of reading her day's work aloud to Lewes in the evenings; dramatizing her writing in this way perhaps enabled her to imagine how her prose would sound when performed in other homes. Eliot's work was often read aloud, as letters from her friends and admirers attest: Alexander Main, compiler of *Wise, Witty, and Tender Sayings in Prose and Verse, by George Eliot* (1871), claimed to have spent several days reading Eliot aloud by the seashore, while Frederic Harrison reported after the publication of *Felix Holt* that he knew "whole families where the three volumes have been read chapter by chapter and line by line and reread and recited as are the stanzas of 'In Memoriam.'"[52]

Both Dickens and Eliot absorbed theatricality into their narrative art through the indirect route of reading aloud. Enacting the role of narrator helped each to develop a narrative mode which gave the impression of an authentic person behind the words. In a sense, reading their novels aloud permitted Dickens and Eliot to bring their distinctive narrative voices to life. Mikhail Bakhtin has pointed out that while poetic genres usually rely on a unified language system, the novel makes "social hetero-glossia" and "the variety of individual voices" the substance of its prose.[53] The solo reader's performance is thus a perfect analogue for the task of the novelist: to represent a crowd of voices through the range of one's unique voice; to render heteroglossia in such a way that it does not drown out the individual identity which gives a narrative coherence and meaning.

With its dual function of instructing and diverting, reading aloud represents the essence of what Victorian culture required from its pastimes, and of what Victorian fiction attempted to provide. As we have seen, reading aloud owed much of its popularity to its origins in the schoolroom and the home. Although readings became increasingly theatrical in the course of the nineteenth century, the Victorians continued to consider them—or conveniently pretended to consider them—educational as well as entertaining. Victorian antitheatricalism actually reenforced the enthusiasm for "dramatic readings." The scholastic and domestic connotations generated by the very idea of reading aloud rendered acceptable the titillation of the entertainment.

Notes

I would like to thank Nina Auerbach for her thoughtful comments on earlier drafts of this essay.

1. Charlotte Brontë, *Villette,* ed. Mark Lilly (Harmondsworth: Penguin Books, 1979), 339.

2. Jonas Barish, *The Antitheatrical Prejudice* (Berkeley: University of California Press, 1981), 299.

3. Michael R. Booth convincingly suggests that many aspects of Victorian culture—art, architecture, decoration—conspired to heighten visual perception and that this resulted in an unprecedented interest in the theater. See *Victorian Spectacular Theatre, 1850–1910* (Boston: Routledge & Kegan Paul, 1981); Martin Meisel has shown how nineteenth-century theater both absorbed and influenced major trends in art and literature. See *Realizations: Narrative, Pictorial, and Theatrical Arts in Nineteenth-Century England* (Princeton: Princeton University Press, 1983).

4. William Makepeace Thackeray, *Vanity Fair: A Novel without a Hero,* ed. John Sutherland (New York: Oxford University Press, 1983), 663, 76.

5. See especially Philip Collins, *Reading Aloud: A Victorian Métier* (Lincoln: Tennyson Society, 1972); Collins, "'Agglomerating Dollars with Prodigious Rapidity': British Pio-

neers on the American Lecture Circuit," in *Victorian Literature and Society: Essays Presented to Richard D. Altick* (Columbus: Ohio State University Press, 1984), 3–29; and Collins, ed., *Charles Dickens: The Public Readings* (Oxford: Clarendon Press, 1975).

6. Jenni Calder, *The Victorian Home* (London: Batesford, 1977), 134, 25.

7. Barish, *Antitheatrical Prejudice*, 304.

8. Jane Austen, *Mansfield Park*, ed. Reuben Brower (New York: Houghton Mifflin, 1965), 255; further page references cited in the text.

9. Lionel Trilling, *Sincerity and Authenticity* (Cambridge: Harvard University Press, 1971), 64.

10. The speech, from John Home's *Douglas* (1756), act 3, scene 1 ("My name is Norval; on the Grampian hills / My father feeds his flocks . . .") was a standard children's party-piece.

11. Wilbur Samuel Howells, *Eighteenth-Century British Logic and Rhetoric* (Princeton: Princeton University Press, 1971), 712–13.

12. J. W. Keene, *Selections for Reading and Elocution: A Handbook for Teachers and Students* (Boston: Small [ca. 1876]).

13. Frederick W. Haberman, "English Sources of American Elocution," in *History of Speech Education in America: Background Studies* (New York: Appleton-Century-Crofts, 1954), 108.

14. Critics praised his "enunciation and gesticulation," and his "really beautiful level speaking." See Donald Mullin, ed., *Victorian Actors and Actresses in Review: A Dictionary of Contemporary Views of Representative British and American Actors and Actresses, 1837–1901* (Westport, Conn.: Greenwood Press, 1983), 467–69; George Vandenhoff, *Plain System of Elocution*, 2d ed. (New York: Shepard, 1845).

15. Benjamin Humphrey Smart, *The Practice of Elocution: A Series of Exercises, and an Outline Course of English Poetry* (1820; reprint, London: Longman, Brown, Green, & Longman, 1855). This exercise book was a companion to Smart's popular *Theory of Elocution* (London, 1819), which Frederick W. Haberman calls "one of the best correlated and most philosophical of the textbooks" (122).

16. Richard Cull, *Garrick's Mode of Reading the Liturgy of the Church of England*, A new edition (London, 1840), cited in Howells, 713 n.51; T. J. Russell, *The Use of the Voice in Reading and Speaking, a Manual for Clergymen and Candidates for Holy Orders*, 2d ed. (New York: Pott, 1894).

17. Collins, *Reading Aloud*, 7.

18. Henry James, *Autobiography*, ed. Frederick W. Dupee (New York: Criterion Press, 1956), 69.

19. Elizabeth Gaskell, *Wives and Daughters*, ed. Frank Glover Smith (Harmondsworth: Penguin Books, 1969), 114.

20. Charlotte Brontë, *Shirley*, ed. Andrew and Judith Hook (Harmondsworth: Penguin Books, 1974), 116–17; further page references cited in the text.

21. Louis James, *Fiction for the Working Man, 1830–1850* (London: Oxford University Press, 1963), 4.

22. Peter Bailey, *Leisure and Class in Victorian England: Rational Recreation and the Contest for Control, 1830–1885* (London: Routledge & Kegan Paul, 1978), 86, 35.

23. Ibid., 95.

24. James, *Fiction for the Working Man*, 7.

25. Ibid., 8.

26. Martha Vicinus, *The Industrial Muse: A Study of Nineteenth-Century British Working-Class Literature* (New York: Barnes & Noble, 1974), 193.

27. Daniel Staniford, *The Art of Reading* (Boston: West [ca. 1803]); Jacob W. Shoemaker, ed., *Best Things from Best Authors* (Philadelphia: Shoemaker, 1875).

28. Richard L. Klepac, *Mr. Mathews at Home* (London: Society for Theatre Research, 1979), 1–23.

29. Raymond Fitzsimons, *The Baron of Piccadilly: The Travels and Entertainments of Albert Smith, 1816–1860* (London: Bles, 1967), 94–103.

30. See W. Benzie, *The Dublin Orator: Thomas Sheridan's Influence on Eighteenth-Century Rhetoric and Belles Lettres* (Leeds: University of Leeds School of English, 1972), 56, 63.

31. Roger Manwell, *Sarah Siddons: Portrait of an Actress* (New York: Putnam, 1970), 298, 304, 340 n.14.

32. J. C. Furnas, *Fanny Kemble: Leading Lady of the Nineteenth-Century Stage* (New York: Dial Books, 1982), 323.

33. Fanny Kemble, *Journal of Frances Anne Butler* (Philadelphia: Carey, Lea & Blanchard, 1835), 2:16–17.

34. Ibid., 17.

35. Eleanor Ransome, ed., *The Terrific Kemble: A Victorian Self-Portrait from the Writings of Fanny Kemble* (London: Hamilton, 1978), 215.

36. Fanny Kemble, "On the Stage," *Cornhill Magazine*, December 1863, 733.

37. Booth, *Victorian Spectacular Theatre*, 30.

38. "Readings," *The Saturday Review*, 4 October 1862, 411.

39. Philip Collins, "Some Uncollected Speeches by Dickens," *The Dickensian*, no. 382 (May 1977), 95.

40. Charles Kent, *Charles Dickens as a Reader* (1872; reprint, New York: Haskell, 1973), 256.

41. Philip Collins, ed., *"Sikes and Nancy" by Charles Dickens: A Facsimile of a Privately Printed Annotated Copy* (London: Dickens House, 1982), 19; further page references cited in the text.

42. Quoted in Leota S. Driver, *Fanny Kemble* (1933; reprint, New York: Negro Universities Press, 1969), 156.

43. "Mrs. Fanny Kemble," *Illustrated London News*, 10 August 1850, 124.

44. Collins, *Public Readings*, 4.

45. Charles Dickens, *Our Mutual Friend*, The Oxford Illustrated Dickens (Oxford: Oxford University Press, 1978), 198; further page references cited in the text.

46. Nina Auerbach, "Secret Performances: George Eliot and the Art of Acting," in *Romantic Imprisonment: Women and Other Glorified Outcasts* (New York: Columbia University Press, 1986), 253.

47. *The George Eliot Letters*, ed. Gordon S. Haight (New Haven: Yale University Press, 1954–79), 3:148–49; Haight, *George Eliot: A Biography* (New York: Oxford University Press, 1968), 428.

48. Haight, *Biography*, 225.

49. George Eliot, *Scenes of Clerical Life*, ed. Thomas A. Noble (Oxford: Clarendon Press, 1985), 7; further page references cited in the text.

50. Haight, *Biography*, 403.

51. Ibid., 438–39, 501.

52. *George Eliot Letters*, 4:440, 285.

53. Mikhail Bakhtin, *The Dialogic Imagination*, ed. Michael Holquist, trans. Caryl Emerson and Michael Holquist (Austin: University of Texas Press, 1981), 264.

Visualizing Victorian Schooling: Art as Document and Propaganda

Leslie Williams

University of Cincinnati

T HE problem of education in terms of cultural transmissions in nineteenth-century Britain involved three major demands. The first was simply a large scale quantitative demand for increased educational facilities made necessary by population pressure. In the nineteenth century 35–39 percent of the population was under fourteen years of age.[1] The second demand was a matter of rising expectations for literacy in that population. Further, there was a strong demand for a national culture and a corresponding awareness, almost ethnographic, of regional differences. Paintings and graphic works document some of the modes of cultural transmission, particularly those which the aristocrats and wealthy merchants who constituted the Edinburgh and London art markets found attractive or which the popular press found newsworthy. These images record a wide variety of schools and other methods for inculcating the young with knowledge.

Scottish painters were deeply aware of an alternate, nonliterate Gaelic culture in the North. It had been the source of inspiration for Robert Burns, Sir Walter Scott, James McPherson, and James Childe among the collectors of folklore. In art, it was seen almost in anthropological terms as in William McTaggart's *Going to Sea* (1858, fig. 1) in which the old salt's tale is so enthralling and so terrifying that the young lad about to become a cabin boy

Figure 1. William McTaggart, *Going to Sea*, 1858. Courtesy of Kirkcaldy Museum and Art Gallery, Scotland.

is having some qualms. While the painting is comic, it is also a comment on powerful storytelling. Similarly, about 1864 George Paul Chalmers began but never finished *The Legend* (National Gallery of Scotland), in which a traditional storyteller, an old shanachie in her dimly lit cottage, passes on a fascinating, slightly fearsome tale to a dozen spellbound young girls. The continuing importance of oral rather than written messages in Scottish households is seen as well in Hugh Cameron's *Responsibility* (1869, fig. 2). While the subject is ostensibly about the trivial matter of a child remembering a shopping list, it is a cultural expectation that the child will remember what she is told. Quite likely her mother could write the message down. Scotswomen were, in fact, more literate throughout the nineteenth century than their English sisters. It is, however, the oral tradition which is being commented upon here.

In England, the whole idea of schools or learning was contrary to the Wordsworthian or Blakeian ideal of childhood as innocence and unfettered freedom. William Collins, R.A., knew both Wordsworth and Blake and on one occasion stayed at Wordsworth's home. Their romantic idea of childhood is seen in his *The Nutting Party* (1831), which shows children at leisure finding food in nature with a broken fence in the background to imply a happy freedom from parental or societal control. *Returning to the Haunt of the Seafowl* (1833, fig. 3) by Collins is even more romantic, with children climbing about gathering birds' eggs on precipitous cliffs. They roam in perfect freedom, if at some risk. It is against this ideal of the innocent liberty of childhood that school was seen as a kind of wrongful imprisonment. Reluctance at submitting to authority, especially for the task of schooling, is usually treated as a humorous theme. In *The Sailing Match* (1831) by William Mulready, while local lower-class children—the children of nature—are fanning their toy boats across the stream, a middle-class mother hurries her young scholar past the idlers. He would prefer to play with the others, but education of a more formal nature is required for his anticipated position in society.

The Tory view of education for rural children is seen in Thomas Webster's painting *School: Morning* (1836, fig. 4), one of a pair which shows a group of boys reluctantly toiling up a hill to the start of school and then dashing out to freedom at the end of the day. Webster's patrons, among them King George IV, were far more interested in the comic aspects of schooling than the intellectual ones. *School: Morning* puts

Figure 2. Hugh Cameron, *Responsibility*, 1869. Courtesy of Aberdeen Art Gallery, Scotland.

Figure 3. William Collins, *Return to the Haunt of the Seafowl*, 1833. Courtesy of National Museums and Galleries on Merseyside (Walker Art Gallery).

suspicions of upward mobility to rest with an echo of the reassuring pastoral tradition. These rural children are depicted as reluctant to learn, or even such bumpkins as to be unable to learn (the one in a farmer's smock is shown scratching his head forlornly), and fearful of the punishment implied in not knowing one's lesson. The condescension of the upper classes toward such a figure is reiterated in the *Art Journal* in 1862 when an engraving of this work was published:

> The young clodpole in a round frock is trying to bring back some half forgotten word or sentence; he will never repeat his lesson "trippingly on the tongue."[2]

The contrast between the word "clodpole" and the concluding quote from Shakespeare shows in the language of the sentence the distancing between the educated, superior critic and the humorous, inferior rustic. It appeared to the nineteenth century an unbridgeable gap.

Webster showed school anticipated as a trial and a burden.

Figure 4. Thomas Webster, *School: Morning*, 1836, engraving.

In the morning the students drag themselves toward the school door, worrying over lessons, vaguely truculent. The care with which Webster indicated the sharp clear light of morning and the long soft light of a late afternoon was a very deliberate narrative effect. In *Evening*, an explosion of energy erupts from the doorway: hats flung off, legs flying, the students gleefully regain their freedom. This humorous antiintellectual bias was to some extent reassuring to Webster's aristocratic patrons. In their view, the stereotypic farmer's boy, Hodge's son, had no desire and, from Webster's representations, little ability to learn more than was good for him. Fear of a literate rabble was lulled by Webster's images, which enforced the upper- and middle-class belief that

> Nothing could be more dangerous to society than for the middle class to find their position perilled and their social relations dislocated by the upheaving of educated pauperism from beneath. To confer on the lower classes that knowledge which Lord Bacon widely identifies with power . . . is to prepare an assured way for a revolutionary pressure of class upon class. . . . The proper business of education is to fit a man to do his duty in that state of life to which it has pleased God to call him. It is very possible, with the best intentions, so to educate a man as to disqualify him for his position in life.[3]

And for some in the lower classes there was a fear of getting "above one's station." In *Larkrise to Candleford* when Edmund Thompson expresses a wish to go to Oxford when he grows up, his mother replies that "she hoped Edmund would not turn out to be clever. Brains were not good to a working man; they only made him discontent and saucy and lose his jobs. She'd seen it happen again and again."[4] The desire, apparently at all levels, that poor children conform to class norms in performance and expectations provided Victorian society with a remarkable mechanism for the suppression of mobility. This seemingly universal agreement that schooling was useless, if not dangerous, for the poor was certainly the social source for Webster's image of the dull ploughboy.

As to the quality of education, for most of the nineteenth century English liberty included absolute freedom from regulation for entrepreneurial schools. As Edward Baines, editor of the Leeds *Mercury* put it:

> We have as much right to wretched schools as to have wretched newspapers, wretched preachers, wretched books, wretched institutions, wretched political economists, wretched Members of Parliament and

wretched Ministers. You cannot proscribe all these things without proscribing Liberty.[5]

The idea of inspecting schools was spoken against in Parliament as an incursion on individual freedom. John Howard Hinton pleaded in 1843 that any inspection of schools would be "tyrannical and oppressive." For him, "what the country roused itself to resist was a scheme of national education. . . . Liberty of education is clearly necessary to liberty of conscience."[6] Such liberty allowed for some very picturesque forms of schooling, Dotheboys Hall among them. Dame schools, Madras schools, adventure schools, and public schools flourished and proliferated to fill the need for cultural transmission of which literacy was really only a part. William Shenstone's poem on the village dame school characterizes schooling as a taming process:

> In every village marked with little spire
> Embowered with trees, and hardly known to fame,
> There dwells in lowly shed and mean attire,
> A matron old, whom schoolmistress we name,
> Who boasts unruly brats with birch to tame;
> They grieven sore, in piteous durance pent,
> Awed by the power of this relentless dame,
> And ofttimes, on vagaries idly bent,
> For unkempt hair or tasked unconned, are sorely shent.[7]

Webster's dame school mistresses seem to have ruled with cane and frown and to have kept order as the first priority with teaching as a secondary possibility. The *Art Union* reviewer finds Webster's *A Dame's School* (1845, fig. 5) "up to the quaint verse of the poet." There is nothing in this picture to encourage a fear of educating the lower class:

The dame is seated by the window; spectacles on nose, intently following, or perhaps driving, the dunce of the school through his drawling lesson. He points with his finger to the dog's-eared and well-thumbed spelling book, and we hear him hesitate at every word of two syllables.

Very young children attended dame schools, not only to learn reading but, for the girls, to learn some little skill in sewing. This dual purpose can be seen in William Bromley's ironically titled *The Schoolroom* (1853, fig. 6), which is in fact simply a remarkably cozy, well-lit kitchen. The children are crowded onto benches. The little girls, occupied with their needles, exemplify

Figure 5. Thomas Webster, *A Dame's School*, 1845. Courtesy of Tate Gallery, London.

the physician William Buchan's complaint that "Miss is set down to her [embroidery] frame before she can put her clothes on."[8] The boys hold books or engage in more interesting activities such as the careful examination of a marble. There are fourteen children in the little room. The good dame points to the letters in her book with a pin for the edification of a young reader. The whole effect is warm and charming. One of Her Majesty's Inspectors "considered one of the reasons for the survival of the dame schools was that parents believed them 'warmer than the school.'" So the crowding of the children toward the fire may document one of the main benefits of the dame schools. Their value as educational institutions was very questionable. An 1858 report by the Reverend W. Warburton, Her Majesty's Inspector for the Berkshire, Hampshire, Wiltshire, and Isle of Wright area, considered them valueless except that they accustomed children "to some little restraint for certain hours every day."

> The greater part of the private dames' schools are held in dwelling rooms . . . It is one of the many ways of making their bread adopted by people scrambling for a livelihood in no certain or definite calling. The children in such schools frequently spend a great part of the school hours sitting on forms round the kitchen, with dog-eared

Figure 6. William Bromley, *The Schoolroom*, 1853. Courtesy of Sotheby's, Belgravia.

pages of spelling books in their hands, from which they are supposed to be learning, while the "schoolmistress" is engaged in sewing, washing or cooking.[9]

A more immediate reaction to the dame school is found in Mary Hughes's autobiography when she encounters one on her annual trip to her mother's family farm in Cornwall:

I was sent off to one of those cottages that have no privacy at all. I entered straight from the road, through the open door, into the living room, and shall never forget the scene. Mrs. Polglaze, a cripple, was perched on a high chair in one corner of the tiny space. Seated on a couple of benches opposite her were seven or eight little children, mumbling aloud together, and laboriously pointing their fingers along what I supposed must be books. So black were these with use that no one could possibly read them, and the children must have been chanting from memory. Making my way through to Mrs.

Polglaze, I delivered [my aunt] Tony's pastries, fruit and butter, and was uncomfortable at her extreme gratitude. I returned to Tony full of questions.

"Yes, dear," said she, "tis a real school. Poor old Mrs. Polglaze gets a penny a week for each child she takes."

"But does she live on that?" I asked.

"Well, not entirely," replied Tony, pushing off to her work.[10]

There was, however, a genuine effort in many parishes, and especially in the Church of Scotland, to provide a real literacy for the sake of reading the Bible. Thomas Faed's *The Patron and Patroness's Visit to the Village School* (1851, fig. 7) shows the dominie or minister of the kirk dressed in black knee breeches, and his elegantly attired wife attended by their exotic liveried black page. They sit and listen to the youngest group of children, some dressed in pinafores, haltingly read their lesson while the school-master dances attendance upon the clergyman and his wife. The peculiar social position of schoolmasters, educated but still lower class, is suggested in his obsequiousness. Still, it is the schoolmaster's earnestness in his endeavors on behalf of the parish that suggests a real Scottish belief in the value of education. This is no old woman teaching the alphabet in her kitchen. Education here is, however amusingly, a matter of professional pride. Still, of all the boys in sight only one is actually engaged in study. The rest converse and beg for apples and whisper to each other.

An alternative to the parish or dame school was the so-called adventure school in which the proprietor/teacher ventured his own capital. These were run most often, according to the Argyll Commission (1867), by men who

had lost their other employment and fallen back on running a school as a last resort. . . . discarded servants or ruined tradesmen, who cannot do a sum of three; who would not be able to write a common letter, who do not know whether the earth is a cube or a sphere; and cannot tell whether Jerusalem is in Asia or America; whom no gentlemen would trust with the key of his cellar, and no tradesman would send on a message.[11]

This sort of entrepreneur was immortalized by Dickens in *Nicholas Nicolby* as Squeers of Dotheboys Hall.

William Mulready's *The Last In* (1835, fig. 8), which shows a school adjacent to the master's home, may be a less pernicious version of an adventure school. It is a crowded one-room school headed by a sarcastic master who bows elaborately to his tardy

Figure 7. Thomas Faed, *The Patron and Patroness's Visit to the Village School,* 1851. Courtesy of Dundee Art Gallery.

pupil. A short-handed birch broom, for cleanliness or discipline, leans below the desk, and in the immediate foreground is a boy who sits with his back to us, his left ankle chained to a log, a restraining device also found in Thomas Brook's *The Captured Truant* (1854, private collection). With its small-scale and unpretentious setting, Mulready's school is well within the picturesque myth of rural schooling acceptable to art market patrons.

The sight (and sound) of mass schooling for large, impersonal urban populations was not acceptable. One form of entrepreneurial education was Dr. Alexander Bell's "Madras System" of children teaching children. The system originated in the missionary schools in India and was adapted for use in England where its chief recommendation was that a single schoolmaster by using a monitorial system could dispense learning to hundreds of students through student monitors. Illustrations of the method show schoolrooms resembling warehouses with row upon row of desks, a few monitors taking questions at the end of the forms, and a single teacher far at the front of the class (fig. 9). These were used in the manufacturing districts to comply with the regulations

Figure 8. William Mulready, *The Last In*, 1835. Courtesy of Tate Gallery (Vernon Collection), London.

that required child laborers to attend some school. Rabid editorials against such schools objected to them on moral grounds:

> the very calling together of so many low-born children daily without some plan of moral guardianship over them justifies the assertion, that they are taught *immorality* and . . . *crime.* . . . a hundred boys at one time are taught to bawl out Lon-lon-don-don, London, with just a few more words, which leads them in the end to learn just enough of reading to peruse a two-penny Life of Turpin or Jonathan Wild. . . . their education completed, they being fully qualified to figure on the *pave* as pickpockets. . . . It is notorious that the *gigantic schools* provided for the humbler classes have done nothing but EVIL.[12]

The combination of large numbers of low-born children and reading of itself constituted a crime to this writer. Obviously from this viewpoint literacy, the simple task of learning to read was not the object of school. The Madras system was not

Figure 9. *Monitorial School,* **ca. 1839, engraving.**

church supervised nor was there direct supervision of the student by the authority figure of the teacher. It was purely utilitarian for minimal literacy, and the system died out in the forties.

A more appropriate school for the "humbler classes" can be seen in Webster's *The Joke* and *The Frown* (1841). Again this is a narrative of contrasts. Each painting is based on a quotation from that favorite Victorian literary source, Oliver Goldsmith's *The Deserted Village.* For *The Frown,* Webster inserted in the 1841 Royal Academy catalogue:

> Well had the boding tremblers learned to trace
> The day's disasters in his morning face,

and for *The Joke:*

> Full well they laughed with counterfeited glee
> At all his jokes, for many a joke had he.

The second picture is often referred to as "The Smile," implying that the teacher's attitude could cause pupils to quail or blossom, but the original quotes are much more revealing of just what was taught in school: careful attention to the attitudes and desires of one's superiors which would be, of course, laudable behavior in the social structure approved by nineteenth-century upper-class patrons of art. For this group from the British ruling class, education had little to do with content or progress. For them the real curriculum was a matter of learning one's place in the social hierarchy. The same idea is in force in Charles West Cope's *The Schoolmaster* (1842, City Art Gallery, Leicester), a subject also from Goldsmith's poem. In Cope's painting, the schoolmaster accosts two boys in the street who cringe and tremble in his presence while a younger brother, still in his pinafore, looks at the master's cane with innocent interest rather than fear.

The approved upper-class system of education was, of course, boarding school with Latin and Greek for content. The moral quality of these schools was questionable until Arnold's reforms, but they did teach dominant behavior toward one's inferiors, a difficult lesson for some boys. Webster's *Going to School* (1842) clearly demonstrates that going off to boarding school was an emotional ordeal for the children involved. The younger son openly bawls while his sister commiserates by weeping into her apron. The older brother, rather hollow eyed, stuffs one more homemade cake or muffin into his mouth as a last taste of home. The servants in the painting, the maid and the young footman, are shown kneeling. The maid packs the trunk and the boy helps the squire on with his boots for the journey. The lower-class members of the household are thus physically lower in the painting, embodying that sense of hierarchy which the boys' schooling will maintain.

The reviewer's reaction to Webster's obvious depiction of tears and despair is to comment on all the things being packed for them to take along: "The room is strewed with such items . . . as a fond mama provides for a darling of whom she is to lose sight for at least a quarter."[13] The implication is that these lads are spoiled mama's darlings. No mention is made of the emotions evident in the painting. Biographies and reminiscences suggest that sobbing farewells were not unusual. Lord Ashley always wept upon leaving home, and wept also at leaving school because his home life was so dreadful as well. An Edwardian reminiscence details a similar tearful departure:

It was that last home breakfast which did him in. He would come into the dining room pale but dry eyed, he turned his back to us

to lift the lids off the dishes, but when he came back to the table
tears were always pouring down his cheeks.[14]

Some of these tears and terrors might be in anticipation of the
bullying and harassment which could be found at any school.
Or, more immediately, it could have been the loss of home com-
forts including sausages and muffins. But there is the additional
possibility that some of this emotion sprang from the problems
of attachment. Many children were abruptly weaned according
to books of child management.[15] The early emotional development of middle- and upper-class children may have included
a series of attachments and losses of nurses and nannies which
might make them especially sensitive to this annual loss of parents
and siblings, trading home with its emotional investment for
school which constituted a peculiarly limited emotional environ-
ment. The preferred outcome, to the Victorian mind, was to
be detached, to be emotionally withdrawn in the face of oncoming
deprivation. This outcome can clearly be seen in *The Railway
Station* (1862) by William Powell Frith. The central scene in this
painting is of a mother kissing her younger son, perhaps aged
six or seven, farewell while her older son of ten or twelve stands
back with a faint smile on his face implying that he has risen
above such childish involvements and is now sufficiently a man
to be the detached observer.

In paintings of schoolboys operating within their own peer
group, Webster shows us the establishment of a local hierarchy
in *The Boy and Many Friends* (1841, fig. 10). The tallest lad in
the room fends off the importunate and maintains the right of
the small boy, who has received an ample hamper from home
to distribute his bounty as he wishes, presumably a reasonable
share going to his protector. Of this painting, the *Art Journal*
reviewer said:

> carefully drawn, ably coloured, and excellent as a composition; it
> is full of humour too, in no degree exaggerated; the expression of
> each member of the group is admirably true—calling forcibly to mind
> our schooldays, and sending the heart back half a century, to the
> joys and fear that have never been half so real as they were in boy-
> hood.[16]

The apparent appeal of such paintings was nostalgic. Still, the
use of the word "forcibly" has an interesting resonance with the
physical threat of the raised fist in the painting.

What is also interesting in the picture is the careful, knowledge-

Figure 10. Thomas Webster, *The Boy and Many Friends*, 1841. Courtesy of Bury Art Gallery and Museum.

able examination one boy by the hamper is giving to a corked black bottle of porter or port wine which Mama has sent her darling. Jonathan Gathorne-Hardy mentions that at this period, before the advent of C. J. Vaughan as headmaster, Harrow was "notorious for drunkenness" and the boys of Marlborough "used to invade the town, where they got drunk and infuriated the inhabitants, particularly the miller, who waged war on them (c. 1846–1852)."[17]

Bleeding the Freshman by James Collinson (1855, fig. 11) portrays an upperclassman taking shameless advantage of his inferior, the new arrival, by either trading a "fleam" or surgeon's blood letting knife for a sizable coin or, possibly, offering to provide minor surgery for a fee. Not only dominance, but a mercantile mentality is the point of the story and source of amusement here.

The value of games was not overlooked in the schoolboy experience. If Webster's paintings did not depict the complete social reality, they did present the kind of morality which Victorian art buyers appreciated as much as nostalgia or the reenforcement of class norms. Webster had been hailed as a moralist earlier

Figure 11. James Collinson, *Temptation* or *Bleeding the Freshman*, 1855. Courtesy of Edmund J. and Suzanne McCormick Collection.

by the *Art Union* reviewer of *Football* (1839), who gave a value-ladened interpretation of the game as Webster painted it:

> The whole scene is capital—the eager urchins rush forward in the very spirit of rivalry; each ardently struggles to get "the ball at his foot," as he will do for more important purposes in life.[18]

Lest this seem an exaggerated metaphor, one need only recall that the Duke of Wellington claimed that Waterloo was won on the playing fields of Eton, and it is that tradition including the knocks and jars of the game which Webster portrays. His painting follows the belief voiced a generation earlier that:

> The fascination of this gentle pastime is its mini war. . . . The play is played out by boys with that dogged determination to win, that endurance of pain, that bravery of combative spirit, by which the adult is trained to face the cannon ball with equal alacrity. . . . In independent out of door games . . . pluck, blood and bottom are best tested; and those lessons will long, we hope be taught, by which, in the words of the Duke, Waterloo was won.[19]

Small wonder games were considered such an important part of school life at Rugby and elsewhere.

There is a shift over a period of twenty years from 1830 to 1850 in the image of the school-aged child. The Romantic ideal of Collins's free-roaming child disappears. Children are more often painted in interiors than in landscape. Children's play begins to mimic adult behavior. And children, more and more, come under adult supervision in their play and schooling. The cost of literacy is control, symbolized most often by the schoolmaster's cane or occasionally by a log and chain. The image of the free and daring child becomes, by about midcentury, the image of a captive who, even in play, plays according to rules.

Notes

1. Roderick Floud and Donald McCloskey eds., *The Economic History of Britain* (Cambridge: Cambridge University Press, 1981), 223.

2. *Art Journal,* N.S. 1 (1862):138.

3. W. C. Taylor, "On the Cultivation of Taste in the Operative Classes," *Art Journal* 11 (1849):3.

4. Florence Thompson, *Larkrise to Candleford* (London: The Folio Society, 1979), 26.

5. John Lawson and Harold Silver, *A Social History of Education in England* (London: Metheun, 1973), 274–75.

6. John Howard Hinton, *A Plea for Liberty of Education* (London, 1843), 4, 35.

7. *Art Union* 7 (1845):187.

8. William Buchan, *Domestic Medicine* (Philadelphia: Dobson, 1809), 25.

9. Pamela Horne, *The Victorian Country Child* (Kineton: Hornwood Press, 1974), 26.

10. Mary Hughes, *A London Child of the 70's* (London: Oxford University Press, 1934), 140.

11. James Scotland, *A History of Scottish Education* (Mystic, Conn.: Verry, 1970), 264–65.

12. *Blackwood's Magazine* 35 (1834):232–33.

13. *Art Union* 4 (1842):251.

14. Joanna Smith, *Edwardian Children* (London: Hutchinson, 1983), 72.

15. For weaning practices, see Pye Henry Chavasse, *Advice to Mothers on the Rearing of Their Offspring* (New York: Appleton, 1844) and, of course, Mrs. Beeton. For nannies whose length of stay was subject very much to economic pressures, see Jonathan Gathorne-Hardy, *The Unnatural History of the Nanny* (New York: Dial Press, 1973).

16. *Art Journal* 1 (1855):294.

17. Jonathan Gathorne-Hardy, *The Public School Phenomenon* (London: Hodder & Slaighton, 1977), 79 and 103.

18. *Art Union* 1 (1839):67.

19. *Gentleman's Magazine* 145 (1829):334.

Squire, Parson, and Village School: Wragby 1830–1886

Michael J. G. Gray-Fow

Northwestern Military and Naval Academy

T HIS paper is about change in a world that saw itself as permanent and unchanging. It concerns an obscure Lincolnshire village, Wragby, but a village typical of many rural communities where the ancient patterns of deference, obligation, and function in a world dominated by the manor house and the vicarage were gradually transformed by the slow intrusion of outside agencies. The village schools were both the means and the focus of this social metamorphosis. Because of the schools the squire and the vicar invited in outside aid; through the accountability that went with that aid came the gradual erosion of ancient paternalist *dominium,* both secular and sacred. Alongside this, the village was inevitably affected by much broader political changes, changes reflecting the rapid transition of national power from an agrarian to an industrial base. Central government and national politics, hitherto distant forces, through a growing tide of legislation became matters of increasing local concern. Against this background of shifting power and influence was the usual time lag of rural life and, perhaps more importantly, a persisting traditionalist respect for the ancient order and those who represented it. The schools again illustrate both the old and the new, in this case the role of patrons and benefactors, and an increasing professionalism that owed another allegiance. The rural schoolmaster of mid-Victorian England was a man caught between two worlds: that of tenant and servant of his local masters, and that of accountable recipient of aid, advice, and regulations from external authorities themselves becoming increasingly conscious of

162

a role that supposedly transcended class structures and time-honored civilities.

The focus here, however, is not on the schoolmasters (though they will be taken into account) but on their ultimate patrons, the squires, particularly the way in which the Wragby squires, the Turnor family, both initiated and responded to the new order at the local level as it affected the schools. As a family the Turnors deserve a memorial in their own right. Over a number of generations they produced antiquarians and historians of merit, along with patrons of the arts. They were not simply fox hunters and Fieldingesque local magistrates. Their commitment to the land, the Church, the village, and their responsibilities was deep and sincere. In an age when paternalism is almost automatically an ugly word, we tend to scoff too easily at those who saw their duty and obligation in terms of helping those whom history and Providence had seemingly allotted to their care. Our story here is with one such local squire, Christopher Turnor, one such village, Wragby, and one such dimension of his concern, the schools.

For many rural landowners schools and education were a new dimension to traditional notions of patronage, but the Turnors of Wragby had longer experience in this area. An old Free Grammar School in the village, only barely subsisting on a meager endowment, had been helped and saved throughout the eighteenth century by the combined good offices of the squire and the vicar. In 1775 the then Turnor squire had even erected a new school building, though the cost was ultimately borne in part by the villagers. Without taking too romantic a view of them, the Turnors generally illustrate the better qualities of the old squirearchy. They were conscious of their position but also had a strong feeling about the duties that went with privilege. They were also, in their own way, a scholarly family. The sons traditionally went from Eton to Cambridge, and their aggregate interests suggest more than a collection of gentlemen's degrees. Younger sons usually went into the Church or into law, and the vicarage of All Saints, Wragby, was not infrequently the home of the reigning squire's brother or son. The old alliance between manor house and parsonage confirmed the squire's old monopoly of power and authority in the village. The world that Christopher Turnor inherited as squire in 1830 had an immemorial quality to it. Fielding and Parson Woodford would have felt at home in it; Jane Austen would have taken it all for granted. Yet by the time of Christopher Turnor's death in 1886 much of the foundation of his authority had been whittled away, while that of the Church had been reduced to a shadow. Yet both squire and vicar retained enormous local prestige and influence and continued to discharge through all the changes their old obligations as they saw them.

Christopher Turnor was born in 1809 and died in 1886. His youth belonged to the age of Regency bucks, and his old age almost reached Victoria's Golden Jubilee. A month short of his twentieth birthday he was called home from Cambridge by his father's death, and on reaching his majority a year later assumed the duties and privileges of the lord of the manor of Sandon in Wragby. He owned most of the village (that proprietorial *power* did not change), along with estates at Stoke Rochford in south Lincolnshire, and at Milton Ernys in Bedfordshire. A personable young man and popular with all classes, he was High Sheriff of Lincolnshire at twenty-three in the Reform Bill year of 1832, and subsequently Deputy Lord Lieutenant and a justice of the peace. Politically he was a traditionalist Tory, so much so that in 1837 he was acceptable as a son-in-law to that die-hard reactionary, the fifth earl of Nottingham. From 1841 to 1847 he sat in Parliament as the protectionist Tory member for South Lincolnshire, one of Disraeli's "Gentlemen of England" (though what he thought of Dizzy himself is unrecorded).[1] Christopher Turnor was a conservative without being a reactionary, and an agent of change without intending to reform. When he became squire, Wragby's links with the outside world were through the stage-coaches that converged on the Turnor Arms at Wragby and then diverged to their various destinations; when he died, Wragby was a minor stop on a railway system that knew little or nothing of Christopher Turnor.[2] In 1830 he was responsible for keeping the King's Peace, but by 1886 there was a village constable whose first duty was to the new county constabulary. In 1830 Christopher Turnor could feast and manipulate Wragby's few parliamentary voters at the Turnor Arms; three parliamentary Reform Acts and a Secret Ballot Act later, most of the villagers had the vote and their political allegiance was out of his control. In 1830 he could graciously indicate through the vicar of All Saints his continuing acquiescence in the mastership of the old Grammar School remaining with Richard Blundy, a man without any known academic qualifications; in 1886, and still working through the vicar, he had to acknowledge the opinions of diocesan inspectors of schools, government inspectors, and attendance officers. Alongside all of this, mandatory log books and registers implied increasing external rights of supervision. It was a gradual process of diminution of seignorial authority.

In 1830 education in Wragby was provided by a few temporary Dame schools, the old Hansard Free Grammar School, a Ladies' Academy (which went under about this time), and the two-year-old Church Sunday school—to which Christopher Turnor immediately added a lending library. The old Hansard School had long ceased to be a grammar school in anything but name, and, the Eldon judgment notwithstanding,[3] its curriculum was far more commercial than classical. Richard Blundy had been the master since before Christopher Turnor was born, combining the post with that of parish clerk and church organist. Supported by manor house and vicarage he had weathered Carlisle's survey of endowed schools in 1818, and a more critical visit from the Charity Commissioners in 1837.[4] He died in that last year, leaving the school without a master and his family without a support. Both problems concerned the squire and the vicar, whose joint solution was to appoint Blundy's eldest son to the mastership and help set up two of his daughters as proprietors of a new Ladies' Seminary.[5] Thomas Forster Blundy, about twenty-three years old, had even fewer qualifications than his father and proved a disaster. His sisters Martha and Caroline, however, turned their venture into a thriving business that lasted to 1917, though their own relations have a Brontëesque quality. Martha, the older sister, gave up her interest by marrying a tenant farmer in 1849. When the farmer died in the 1860s her sister Caroline took her back, but only as a teacher. Martha had her posthumous revenge; Caroline remained a spinster, and in her dotage the Ladies' Seminary was taken over by Martha's daughters.[6]

Long before this, in 1839, the village had acquired an entirely new school from the hands of the Turnors. It came about in a curious way. In the 1830s the Established Church suffered a number of setbacks. Its bishops had made themselves unpopular opposing parliamentary reform in 1832, and in 1835–36 a series of reforms pushed through Parliament created the ecclesiastical commissioners, secularized the registration of births and deaths, ended the monopoly of marriage ceremonies, and mandated the commutation of tithes. An additional worry was the increase in Nonconformist schools after the first government grant to the two religious societies in 1833. In 1839 the bishop of Lincoln set up a diocesan Board of Education to encourage and support the building of National Schools in the diocese. Its early subscribers included the new vicar of All Saints, Wragby, the Reverend Algernon Turnor, his brother the squire, Christopher Turnor (who was made a vice president of the board), and their brother and sister, John and Frances Turnor.[7] Their support was sincere, their prominence in the cause immediate, and the absence of a National School at Wragby suddenly noticeable. Before the year was out the squire had donated the land, and John and Frances Turnor had built the school. It bore the forbidding if unoriginal motto *disce aut discede* and was located next to the new All Saints Church, also erected with Turnor contributions. One year later Christopher Turnor added a house next to the school for the master. From the beginning the appointment of the master and the general oversight of the school was entrusted to the vicar of All Saints.

Wragby now had three recognized schools: the Hansard Free Grammar School (deteriorating rapidly under Thomas Foster Blundy), the new (mixed) National School, and the Ladies' Seminary. All three received either direct or indirect Turnor support (the Ladies' Seminary through the smallness of the rent charge), and all three were connected in one way or another with the Established Church. When Christopher Turnor left for Parliament in 1841 to defend the Corn Laws he did so as a Tory landowner with a creditable record of support for education in his home community.

Thomas Foster Blundy died in March 1842. Almost the last act of the Reverend Algernon Turnor before he too died in August was to appoint a Mr. Bellamy to run the Grammar School. Bellamy's incompetence finished the school. By March 1843 he was gone, and the new vicar of All Saints, George Yard, was obliged to admit in his advertisements for the post that no one should apply who could not guarantee to bring a supply of pupils with him.[8] We can assume that by this time most local children had already diverted to the National School, so the next step, though it presented problems, seemed an obvious one. After consulting with the squire, George Yard announced the merging of the old Grammar School and the National School. Yard later claimed that the decision was unavoidable,[9] but its object in part was to retain the Hansard endowment of £30 a year for a school in the village. This could only be done by maintaining the fiction that in some shadowy way the Hansard School continued to exist. Such a fiction was indeed kept up, with the connivance of all parties, until the school was redefined as a Foundation School in 1903. In the meantime, in 1843 the old Grammar School building became home to the Girls' National School (the National School had previously been mixed), while the new building near the new church became the Boys' National School. Both remained under the supervision of the vicar, and by a private arrangement the squire assumed responsibility for the fabric and appurtenances of both buildings, while the vicar took charge of their internal operations. The master of the Boys' School was appointed by the vicar (with the approval of the squire), and until 1864 the mistress of the Girls' School was usually the master's wife.

Backed by the squire and the vicar, education thrived in Wragby. The 1851 census revealed 92 percent of the children between the ages of five and thirteen registered as scholars, a figure that compares very favorably not only with neighboring townships but even with neighboring counties.[10] George Yard's return to an 1855 diocesan enquiry about schools in Wragby (there was a new bishop in Lincoln wanting to know these things) set forth the financial basis of the two National Schools, neither of which, oddly enough, was ever formally listed with the National Society. The annual income in 1855 totaled £112.30, comprising £30 from the original Hansard endowment, "School Pence" (fees by any other name, but very small in amount and waived for the really poor) amounting to £13.50 from the Boys and £9.50 from the Girls, an additional "Fuel Charge" yielding £2.50 from the Boys and £1.80 from the Girls, and two private subscriptions of £30 for the Boys' School and £25 for the Girls' School. We know that the extra £25 for the Girls' School almost certainly came from Christopher Turnor and can reasonably presume that so did the £30 for the Boys. Simple analysis of these figures yields £30 from the Hansard endowment, £27.30 from the parents, and £55 from the squire. In other words, almost 50 percent of the schools' annual income came directly from the manor house.[11]

In the year following the diocesan enquiry the squire and the vicar turned their attention to the education of adults. In the late eighteenth century the great debate had been about the wisdom of *any* kind of education for the poor, whether it was better to leave them in what was termed "natural" ignorance or to teach them at least to read so that they could read the Scriptures and worthy literature and thus be better equipped to resist the pernicious onslaughts of radicals and subversives. To some extent the debate rather resembles the current argument about sex education in schools; does information as such protect or subvert? Any first-year philosophy student knows that you cannot derive an "ought" from an "is"; that information of itself does not yield any concept of moral obligation. Historically, however, societies have tended to turn to education when worried about the young or the lower orders. In England by the 1840s and 1850s the great debate was over. Education was now seen as a necessary corrective to misinformation and misdirection by dubiously motivated groups and organizations (at least as so defined by the existing order). The children were being attended to in the schools with a wealth of private encouragement. In 1848 a Miss Humphreys published *Hymns for Little Children*. It included the hymn "All Things Bright and Beautiful" which contained (in those days) the immortal verse

> The Rich Man in his castle,
> The poor man at his gate,
> God made them, high or lowly,
> And ordered their estate.

and was no doubt sung with fervor at Wragby by both the children in the National School and the girls at the Ladies' Seminary. There still remained, in an age of Mechanics' Institutes, Cooperative Societies, and early (if inept) trades unions, the adults. To counteract the forces of disorder and dissension, even in rural Wragby, adults, even more than children, needed the *right* kind of information. Over and above all of this there had been alarmist voices raised at the Great Exhibition in 1851 suggesting that Britain's industrial lead could be imperilled by the educational system of foreign competitors.

Patriotic responses varied, but at Wragby in 1856 Christopher Turnor and George Yard took their own initiatives. In a building on the market square given rent-free by the squire, they organized a "Library and Reading Room for the Benefit of Working Men." It was well supported locally by subscriptions, and its finances were augmented by a small fee charged for winter lectures. Traveling lecturers (science was the preferred subject) were available enough and were the forerunners of university extension. The reading room received the main London and county newspapers, and the library had over a thousand volumes by 1868, and over fifteen hundred by 1889.[12] In the same year that he assisted adult education in Wragby, Christopher Turnor added to the local amenities by building a new water works for the village and a market house for the weekly markets and the two annual fairs. These, like the rebuilding of the almshouse back in 1840, were more traditional forms of patronage. Schools and library may have seemed the same but in fact were much more potent agents for social change.

One change came in 1860 with the coming of diocesan inspection of the schools. George Yard (with Turnor approval) had invited it in his reply to the 1855 Diocesan Enquiry, but five years passed before anything happened. The diocesan inspector in 1860 was the Reverend Charles Lloyd, rector at neighboring Rand, who continued in this role for many years. He was immensely sympathetic and proved so popular at the manor house and the vicarage that he was soon drafted onto the committee of school managers, an apparent conflict of interest which seems to have bothered no one. Diocesan inspection in this friendly form hardly seemed a major break with the past, yet a passing minor problem indicates an important breach in the old order. As inspector, Charles Lloyd required periodic reports from the Wragby schools. He had none from 1860 to 1863 (for which he had to make amends to the bishop), and the problem lay in the simple fact that neither managers, vicar, nor squire had any previous experience at having to explain or report to outside bodies. They adjusted in time, and their adjustment itself was an implicit recognition of changing times.[13]

The 1860s saw further changes. Despite the noncooperation of the Wragby managers over paperwork, in 1863 Charles Lloyd piloted a diocesan grant for a school monitor. The following year the wife of the National School master gave up running the Girls' School, and her successor was the first "certificated" Wragby teacher. From then on (with the odd exception) teachers in the Wragby National Schools had to meet more professional requirements than just being personally acceptable to the vicar and the squire. One of these figures had recently changed. In 1860 George Yard, for eighteen years Christopher Turnor's faithful adjutant with regard to schools, left All Saints, Wragby, and was followed as vicar by the Reverend William Knox Marshall. The new vicar marked his arrival by organizing a village savings bank, which was both popular and successful, and Knox Marshall rapidly established himself as a respected and powerful personality. In 1864 he and the squire approached their Lordships, the Committee of Council, requesting a government grant for the schools. This inevitably entailed state inspection, and it was no doubt a relief when the inspector appointed was none other than Charles Lloyd. Following Lloyd's inspection in his new capacity, a government grant was duly forthcoming.

The 1864 government inspection was carried out under Lowe's

Revised Code.[14] Over all, the children came out very well, with 91 percent of the highest Boys' School standard passing successfully, and 88 percent of the highest Girls' School standard. The two standards were not equivalent. The boys reached Standard VI, while the girls only reached Standard IV. This was no temporary accident but a reflection of how the respective educational needs of boys and girls were viewed in the village. Squire, vicar, inspectors, and villagers were at one on this. In any event, the examination was a success and Wragby schools received their first government grant in 1865.[15] The additional income was welcome but further complicated the exact status of the schools. Suffice it to say that the managers invoked whichever title was immediately apposite. For the purposes of drawing on the Hansard endowment, there still existed a Hansard Free Grammar School; to obtain diocesan funds reference was made to the Wragby National Schools or even the Wragby Church of England Schools; when applying to the state the reference was to the Wragby Free School or (by the end of the century) to the Wragby Elementary School.

By 1870 Christopher Turnor and William Knox Marshall, the squire and the vicar, had accepted that while they still ran the schools they were to a degree responsible for arrangements and performance to both the diocese of Lincoln and the state. That year, however, witnessed both an expression of the old way of things and the limitations already imposed upon it. In 1870 the Reverend Francis Cornish, who had succeeded Charles Lloyd as government inspector, was so disgusted with the current master's performance at the Boys' National School that the annual government grant was withheld.[16] Christopher Turnor and Knox Marshall promptly sacked the master, but in choosing his successor they were careful to select a man certificated under the new dispensation. In 1870 Christopher Turnor joined with other Lincolnshire landowners to resist the proposed Forster Education Act; there was even a great public meeting (we would call it a demonstration today) in Wragby itself. It was well reported locally but made no difference to the outcome. Power nationally was passing to a different base. Squires and vicars no longer counted for what they were. The Church saw the change most clearly. Tithes had been commuted in Wragby in 1847.[17] In 1864 the village Methodists, an increasing band, refounded their own Sunday school. They still sent their children during the week to the National Schools, but even here were biding their time. In 1868 church rate was abolished, which left the upkeep of

All Saints dependent on its actual membership, not on the entire parish.

Vicar and squire soldiered on. In 1871 Christopher Turnor's son Edmund Turnor, the current parliamentary member for South Lincolnshire, chaired a meeting of three parishes at Wragby that agreed on a new school rate for the parishes. The Wragby schools were important for more than just the village itself, and the measure was approved.[18] William Knox Marshall, meanwhile, carried out urgent reforms. The Girls' National School was suppressed and merged with the Boys' School to make a new mixed National School. The old Grammar School building became the Infants' School. To maintain Victorian proprieties at the new mixed school, a visiting supervisor was appointed for the girls only; this was none other than Caroline Blundy, sole proprietress and autocrat of the Ladies' Seminary. She seems to have confined her visits to an inspection of needlework, recorded in the National School log books, which date from 1868.

In the 1870s Christopher Turnor increasingly withdrew from active involvement in the Wragby schools. His interests and obligations were passed on to his son Edmund Turnor and his wife Lady Mary Turnor. Both were enormously popular and respected, apparently more receptive to change, and perhaps more resilient. They distributed prizes for the annual School Feast (dating from the 1870s), supported the new Wragby Floral and Agricultural Society from its founding in 1873 (Christopher Turnor was the official patron), and even gave a nominal nod in the direction of Wragby's own Temperance Society, set up in 1874.

The schools meanwhile went through their own ups and downs. Little has been said about the actual teachers, since our main concern is the manor house and patronage, but in a small community personalities are very important. From 1839 to 1868 the National Schools had a succession of able masters and mistresses, however uncertificated. Joseph Adams, the master from 1868 to 1870, was a disaster and brought about the temporary withholding of the government grant. His abrupt departure was followed by a shake-up of the managers. The new body still included William Knox Marshall and Charles Lloyd, but added three local laymen. Adams's successor, William Dodds, master of the mixed school from 1870 to 1881, was certificated, highly competent, imaginative, and respected. He adjusted, as did the squire and the vicar, to yet another incursion into the old rural domain, the coming of an attendance officer in 1877. This posed problems since Wragby, like most country districts, was accustomed to living with high absenteeism, whether partial or total, according to the seasonal demands of agriculture. Dodds and his successors had a little difficulty in explaining in the log book that boys were missing because the squire needed them to "beat" the coverts for game during the shooting season.

In the 1870s and 1880s the master of a village school was slowly transformed by circumstances into a *head*master, with a wide range of responsibilities for a growing hierarchy of assistants, pupil teachers, monitors, etcetera. He had to answer to an increasing body of external authorities, such as diocesan inspectors, government inspectors, attendance officers, and public health officials. He was still a part of the village, and a village still dominated by the squire and (to a lesser degree) the vicar or rector, so his performance necessarily involved a degree of deferential agility that has its modern counterparts but which we can easily underestimate.

At the same time, the traditional authorities in the village were also having to adjust, whatever their personal political persuasion, to a new age of outside interference and regulation. All of this meant the passing of the old monopoly of authority. How much actual influence and prestige remained depended on the families and individuals involved. At Wragby the Turnor squires displayed a remarkable adaptability and resilience to changing times. They may not have been aware of it as such, and they were by no means unique, but they illustrate very well the curious phenomenon of the conservative agents of change.

All that remains is to conclude this history of change. In 1881 Dodds was followed at the National School by an incompetent named Musgrave, who somehow survived until 1888. His survival was due in part to the fortuitous changes in local supervisors at every level. In 1883 there was a change in government inspectors, and in the same year William Knox Marshall resigned at All Saints to take another Turnor living at Holton Beckering. His successor at All Saints, Henry Bolland, was equally capable and able but took some time to find his feet. Finally, in March 1886 the old squire, Christopher Turnor, died at the age of seventy-seven. He had lived through a number of major changes at both the national and the local level. He had inherited a village that belonged to the days of Fielding and Parson Woodford and had presided over its gradual evolution into late-Victorian society. He had been from the beginning a staunch supporter of education and schooling and had learned to live with the growing fact that this very area was the one which more than any other laid open an avenue for the kind of outside interjection that gradually marked the passing of the old order he had known all his life. There were many Christopher Turnors in England in the nineteenth century, and we owe them, at the very least, our understanding and acknowledgment.

Notes

1. Robert Blake, *Disraeli* (New York: St. Martin's Press, 1967), 187.

2. W. White, *A History and Directory of Lincolnshire and Hull* (Lincoln: White, 1826), 204.

3. In 1805 Lord Chief Justice Eldon had ruled that in the light of their original endowment provisions grammar schools could teach *only* Greek and Latin.

4. Nicholas Carlisle, *A Concise Description of the Endowed Grammar Schools of England and Wales,* 2 vols. (London: Carlisle, 1818), 1:857; *Report of the Commissioners for (County of Lincoln) Inquiring Concerning Charities* (London, 1837), 724.

5. *Lincolnshire Chronicle,* 21 January 1841.

6. W. White, *A History and Directory of Lincolnshire* (Lincoln: White, 1842), 434; *Commercial Directory of the Market Towns of Lincolnshire* (Lincoln: Hagar, 1849), 350; *P. O. Directory of Lincolnshire* (Lincoln: Kelly, 1849); and census returns for Wragby and Binbrook for 1851, 1861, and 1871.

7. *Stamford Mercury,* 25 January 1839; Minute Book, Lincoln Diocesan Board of Education, 13 December 1838, Lincoln County Archives.

8. *Lincolnshire Chronicle,* 1 April 1842, 8 July 1842, 17 and 31 March 1843.

9. Diocesan Enquiry (1855), "Schools A. T. 492," Lincoln County Archives.

10. J. F. Phillips, *Town and Village* (Nottingham: Nottingham University Press, 1972), 80–81.

11. Diocesan Enquiry (1855).

12. *P.O. Directory of Lincolnshire* (Lincoln: Kelly, 1868), 346; W. White, *History, Gazeteer, and Directory of Lincolnshire* (Lincoln: White, 1882), 823–24.

13. Lloyd's letters to the Bishop, 4 January 1861 and 10 January 1863, Lincoln County Archives.

14. Under the Revised Code of 1862 government grants were made contingent on the success of pupils in examinations in basic skills, a system that came to be known as Payment by Results. The Code, universally unpopular with local schools, was not finally abrogated until 1897.

15. Examination Schedules, Numbers 24 and 25 (Form D), 6 December 1864, Lincoln County Archives.

16. *Report of the Committee of Council on Education* (London, 1871), 46; Wragby School Log Book (Number 1), 62. The Wragby school log books date from 1867. They exist in the form of two original notebooks (photocopies in the author's possession) and are retained by the current headmaster of Wragby Primary School.

17. Turnor Papers, Bundle 17, Lincoln County Archives.

18. Log Book (Number 1), 48–49, 56.

Student Tutoring and Economic Production: Nineteenth-Century British Parallels of Current American Practice

Myron Tuman

University of Alabama

A master teacher stands at the head of a large, open class-room presenting a lesson on some intricacy of grammar—today the differences between participles and absolutes—to dozens of advanced students who, despite their own youthful appearance, their own anxieties, and, in some cases, even their own lack of understanding of the lesson at hand, will soon be called on to teach other students only slightly younger than themselves. One professional teacher teaching dozens of advanced students who in turn will teach hundreds of junior students—a picture that many readers recognize as the cost-saving, assembly-line pedagogy of the monitorial system (or "the Mutual System") developed independently by Andrew Bell and Joseph Lancaster at the start of the nineteenth century. The scene I have in mind, however, comes not from Bell's school at Clapham, or Lancaster's at Southwark, or even Robert Owen's more famous, and more humane, educational experiment at New Lanark, but instead from a recent summer's training session for new graduate teaching assistants at the University of Alabama in Tuscaloosa—although it might just as easily have been the course meetings that I ran for undergraduates working as writing center tutors at West Virginia University in the early 1980s, or, for that matter, such seminars and training sessions held at campuses across the country where undergraduates are being trained to work as writing center tutors and where graduate students are being trained as instructors of freshman composition.

At first glance, such a comparison no doubt seems chimerical. The original purpose of the monitorial schools seems clear: to provide a cheap, limited education to the children of the thousands of workers who had left the scattered, obscure poverty of rural life for the more visible poverty of the new mill towns. At the basis of these schools was a mechanistic model of industrial production that allowed for the maximization of what was at the time, and remains today, a scarce resource—teachers: "The grand principle of Dr. Bell's system," wrote one contemporary observer, "is the division of labour applied to intellectual purposes. . . . The principle in schools *and manufactories* is the same."[1] Indeed, Jeremy Bentham, in drawing up his own scheme for education, what he coined his *Chrestomathia* (a neologism for "conducive to useful knowledge"), pushed the monitorial system to the very limit of unfettered industrial efficiency and monomaniacal bureaucratic planning. One of his provisions, the "Inspection principle," required a new kind of circular building, a Panopticon, constructed with the master in center (*"minimizing* the distance between the situation of the *remotest Scholar* and that of the *Master's eye"*), with the floors inclined ("prevent[ing] remoter objects from being *eclipsed* by nearer ones"), and with a series of screens that would allow the *"Master to see without being seen"*).[2] It was, alas, a building that could be used equally well as a school or as a prison. As a midnineteenth-century commentator notes, this emphasis on discipline built into the monitorial system further reduced the standing of the teacher "by requiring little else of him than an aptitude for enforcing discipline, an acquaintance with mechanical details for the preservation of order, and that sort of ascendancy in his school which a sergeant-major is required to exercise over a batch of raw recruits before they can pass muster on parade."[3]

Contemporary writing instruction, particularly as advocated by proponents of student tutoring, clearly has a different, indeed an opposite, model in mind—one that is decidedly decentralized, individualized, and labor-intensive, not hierarchical, regimented, and cost-effective; one that is holistic and nondirective, not intimidating and coercive. Indeed, at the center of much instructional practice today is the one-on-one conference, with its professionally nurtured concern for the well-being and inner feelings of the student-as-client, a concern that more traditional faculty, in examples like the following, might well find unduly solicitous, if not a bit overbearing:

> "That sentence is hard for me to read because it's so long. I need some pause markers to help me see the different parts. Punctuation would help. Where could you add some punctuation?"

> "I agree. Writing a conclusion to a description can be very difficult. What possibilities have you thought of so far? Even if they aren't the greatest, let's use what you've got as starters."[4]

Or the following example of a boorish tutor who abruptly and tactlessly challenges a student who has mistakenly placed the speaker in Matthew Arnold's "Dover Beach" in France: "You say the speaker is in France. Are you sure?" The authors then comment:

> The question, "Are you sure?" is rhetorical, just another way of saying, "You're wrong." The writer senses this and changes his position only because he has picked up the cue, not because he has thought the matter through. He says what he thinks the tutor wants him to say and does not question his original response. Instead the tutor could have said, "I can see why you think the speaker is at the window, but can you tell me why you think he's in France?"[5]

The implicit model for the competent teacher here is not a self-centered expert or other worldly professor but a counselor or therapist, someone trained to listen with care and sympathy, and then to be able to help people to achieve their own goals: "A student," writes Beverly Clark, author of *Talking about Writing*, "learns more if she is active rather than passive, doing rather than simply listening. Thus a tutor or teacher should not be dictating but helping a student to discover how to improve herself. Tutoring means sharing and guiding. It means coaching, catalyzing, collaborating."[6] Similarly, Muriel Harris in *Teaching One-to-One*, calls on writing teachers to "see themselves not as authority figures but as advisers, coaches, or helpers" (22). She continues: "The crucial distinction here is that the teacher is *not* the player but the person who stands on the sidelines watching and helping—not stepping in to make the field goal or sink the putt when the player is in trouble" (35).

What, if any, connection can we draw between these two cases, between the monitorial system as it developed in the first half of the nineteenth century and widespread contemporary interest in and practice of using student tutors and classroom instructors? An immediate response would be to look for a common economic origin—that is, we use students today, just as they were used in early nineteenth-century England—to save money. And the issue of funding can hardly be dismissed. It's apparent, for example, that throughout the nineteenth century in England the demand for education far outstripped the economic means of providing a professional class of teachers. The first state grant for elementary education, for example, was not made until 1833, and that for only £20,000. By midcentury, when the monitor system was finally replaced by a system of pupil-teachers (high-school age students who served a five-year apprenticeship in the elementary schools before going on to a teacher training college), there were still only 681 certificated teachers with over two million students attending day schools. Between 1849 and 1859, the number of certificated teachers grew to nearly 6,878[7] and the number of pupil-teachers from 3,580 to 15,224 (Tropp, 21). These pupil-teachers, unlike monitors, did receive a stipend, but one of only £10 their first year, increasing to £20 at the end of their fifth. Although one member of the Cross Commission of 1888 called the continued use of such pupil-teachers "the cheapest and very worst possible system of supply . . . [adding that] it should be abolished root and branch,"[8] the system itself remained largely in place until the Education Act of 1902.

So much for nineteenth-century economic crises—what about the situation in American higher education today? Surely, anyone concerned with administering an English department today must be aware of the many problems caused by chronic underfunding and the most widely implemented solution—the expansion of part-time faculty. According to the Fall 1988 *Association of Departments of English Bulletin,* the number of part-time English teachers between 1972 and 1983 has increased 69 percent in four-year institutions and 189 percent in junior colleges, while the increase in full-time faculty was a modest 21 and 29 percent respectively.[9] Nearly 40 percent of all English teachers in higher education today are part-time, and the problem is most severe in the two-year institutions where over half the students in the country now take freshman composition and where the average teaching load is 14.1 hours and the average class size is probably closer to the 27.1 average for all non-ADE departments (more than three-fourths of the two-year colleges fall into this category).[10] Is it any wonder, we might ask, that composition administrators and theorists (as opposed to traditional literature faculty) have taken the lead in elevating the status of students to teachers?

Yet matters are hardly that simple since, for one thing, students are serving as classroom instructors, not in junior colleges where the need is greatest, but in four-year graduate institutions where the need is least. Even more problematic is the distinction between the use of part-time instructors as a cost-saving strategy and the actual pedagogic practice that is being widely advocated— namely the increased reliance upon writing conferences and one-on-one teaching generally. Here a distinction needs to be drawn between two different contemporary approaches to student tutoring: on the one hand, the potential cost-saving approach offered by Emily Meyer and Louise Smith in *The Practical Tutor,* with its implicit image of the master writing teacher as the composition expert who compiles and teaches in an upper-division English course the wealth of practical material on tutoring writing that is their book; and on the other hand, the labor-intensive and thus more costly approach advocated by both Clark and Harris. What they want is more than better, more effective student tutors; they want everyone who teaches writing, students and faculty alike, committed to teaching writing in student-centered, labor-intensive (hence, costly) conferences.

What then of the original suggestion of a common economic motive behind the use of student tutors in the elementary schools of nineteenth-century England and American colleges and universities today? All that seems left in Clark and Harris is an obvious contrast: contemporary conferencing pedagogy seems to be the total antithesis of the bureaucratic efficiency at the center of the monitorial system. What seems to be most highly valued today is talk, not efficiency. But, we might ask, might there not be another parallel here, one beneath the surface that would help explain both the source and eventual wide acceptance of these two seemingly different methods of utilizing student tutors? After all, why should each age gravitate to such different modes of student tutoring and, just as importantly, with such fervor? Here from a letter of 1813, reprinted by Bentham in *Chrestomathia,* James Gray rhapsodizes on the advantages of the new system which ensures that "every boy [out of a class of one hundred] is employed every minute of the time he is in school, either in the acquisition or the communication of knowledge":

> The fifteen highest boys are monitors. The first thing to be done after the meeting of the class, is to see that they have their lessons distinctly. When this is ascertained, the whole class goes into divisions. In this way fifteen times as much work can be done in the same space, and, I can say with confidence, fifteen times better. From this contrivance, instead of the languor and restlessness that too frequently prevails, all is activity and energy. More noise, indeed, is heard; but the sounds are sweet, for they are the sounds of labour. Everyone studies, because by the exertion of his talents, he finds himself equal to every task; and his ignorance is more shameful, where the account is to be rendered to one of his own years, than to a man. [Bentham, 137]

Can one imagine a fairer, more harmonious picture of the self-regulation of society, a happier picture of laissez-faire economy where the natural expression of competing interests leads to the common good? Anne Digby and Peter Searby, two modern British historians of education, seem to miss this point in labeling English elementary schools in the first half of the nineteenth century "the focus of a powerful and impersonal attack on working-class values,"[11] stressing only the negative, what the schools were not. What the schools very much were, and what so inspired educational reformers, was the full and complete expression of the social, economic, and ideological forces that an emerging middle class saw as its primary means to a higher material standard of living. When this blind faith in free market economics died out later in the century, so too did the faith in the transformative powers of student tutors. The Cross Report of 1888, for example, concludes that, though imperfect, the use of pupil-teachers is the most "trustworthy source" available for securing prospective teachers with right moral qualifications" (Maclure, 132).

How striking then to find in composition specialists today an enthusiasm for student tutors and pedagogic practice generally equal to that found in Bentham and Gray. "Those of us who include conferences as a regular part of our teaching," writes Harris, "know from firsthand experience how effective and even essential the one-to-one interaction with the writer is. We tend to express not just enthusiasm but also a bit of evangelistic fervor for such teacher-student talk." Indeed, like Bentham, Harris sees the new curriculum as completely cost-effective, a "radical curriculum change," she calls it, "that costs nothing." Conferencing is recommended as the pedagogy of choice because it works best for the student on a case-by-case basis while at the same time seeming to invigorate the instructor. Indeed, Harris can offer the following description of a typical writing conference with her own unbounded, almost reckless, enthusiasm: "they are exhausting, the level of concentration is high, the intensity of the give-and-take can fry one's brain" (Harris, 4, 48, 27).

Her zeal here is equal to that of the English radicals in the early nineteenth century because, one might argue, its tie to an emerging mode of production is just as strong and direct. Instead of the factory, however, we have, mediated in the curriculum, the professional dialogue that is playing an increasingly important role in a postindustrial economy generally and, more importantly, in both the families and the working lives of that section of the American middle class from which college writing teachers (and many other professionals) are drawn. Whereas the English radicals directed us to the factory and the prison to learn the correct classroom practices, the new writing specialist has us draw upon "the literature of counselors and therapists . . . to guide us in conference strategies and goals" (Harris, 2). Teachers are here being asked to transform themselves into what for some of us is a startling new image of a coach: not the traditional American icon of the fierce competitor who will sacrifice everything, even his or her players' welfare, for final victory, not a tempestuous egomaniac like Billy Martin or Bobby Knight, or laconic taskmaster like Vince Lombardi or Bear Bryant—but instead a new type of coach, a human service facilitator whose nurturing, self-effacing presence has something of the effect of "new age" music in dissipating from our students the discord and anxiety of contemporary academic life.

"The better we understand society," wrote the French sociologist Emile Durkheim, "the better shall we be able to account for all that happens in that social microcosm that the school is." The origins of pedagogy, what Durkheim calls the "construction of a technique," lies "not in the individual, but in the collectivity,"[12] that is, in our ability to provide historical, not psychological, insight into the educational process. Where we need to look to find parallels between contemporary and nineteenth-century approaches to student tutoring, Durkheim tells us, is in the larger connections between schools and society, and between pedagogy and production. Behind the contemporary advocacy of student tutoring lies a broad, sustained critique of the very notion of the university professor as an expert engaged in ground-breaking research and only intermittently concerned with disseminating this knowledge to students, usually through lectures. And behind this critique of the professor-as-expert lies an even broader, albeit less explicit, critique of the model of economic production that sees wealth, progress, and, by extension, the common good all as coming from the large-scale applications of the insights and discoveries derived from the research of experts. Behind the new notion of teacher as tutor, in other words, lies the rejection of both an economy and a pedagogy that value products over process.

The contemporary critique of educational practice, therefore, is ultimately a critique of social life based upon the classical model of economic exchange that so excited Bentham and other early nineteenth-century British radicals and, as most of us well know, so angered Matthew Arnold, John Ruskin, and a host of other mid-Victorian critics. And while many of us would willingly join both our Victorian and contemporary colleagues in such an attack, we may also feel the need at certain times to rise above the fray in order to recognize the potential contradictions inherent in our position as both educators and critics: that is, that our critique may embody the very educational practice we are criticizing; that our common passion for certain pedagogic practices may itself be shaped by the critical distance, and hence relative protection, which our own mastery of academic discourse affords us. The same mastery of language that makes it so easy for us to criticize pedagogic practices based on unfavored modes of production—allowing us, for example, to expose the exploitative rationalizing at work in the nineteenth-century advocacy of classroom monitors and pupil-teachers—at times seems to blind us to the historical basis of our own critique and our own practice. Thus, what we can say finally is that we advocate using student tutors today for very much the same reasons Bentham and others advocated their use in the nineteenth century—namely, because of our implicit belief that the pedagogic practice we prescribe for student tutors and instructors will enhance both their own and their fellow students' standing in relation to what we feel to be a preferred mode of economic production.

Notes

This paper was presented to the Victorians Institute, University of South Carolina, Columbia, 15 October 1988.

1. Quoted in John William Adamson, *English Education, 1789–1902* (Cambridge: Cambridge University Press, 1964), 24.

2. Jeremy Bentham, *Chrestomathia*, ed. M. J. Smith and W. H. Burston (Oxford: Clarendon Press, 1983), 106. Hereafter Bentham, cited in the text.

3. Quoted in Asher Tropp, *The School Teachers: The Growth of the Teaching Profession in England and Wales from 1800 to the Present Day* (New York: Macmillan, 1957), 7. Hereafter Tropp, cited in the text.

4. Muriel Harris, *Teaching One-to-One: The Writing Conference* (Urbana, Ill.: National Council of the Teaching of English, 1986), 35. Hereafter Harris, cited in the text.

5. Emily Meyer and Louis Z. Smith, *The Practical Tutor* (New York: Oxford University Press, 1987), 36.

6. Beverly Lyon Clark, *Talking about Writing: A Guide for Tutor and Teacher Conferences* (Ann Arbor: University of Michigan Press, 1985), 1.

7. Michael Sanderson, *Education, Economic Change and Society in England: 1780–1870* (London: Macmillan, 1983), 20.

8. J. Stuart Maclure, ed., *Educational Documents: England and Wales, 1816 to the Present Day*, 5th ed. (New York: Methuen, 1986), 131. Hereafter Maclure, cited in the text.

9. Robert Denham, "From the Editor," *Association of Departments of English Bulletin* 90 (1988): 3.

10. Bettina Huber and Art Young, "Report on the 1983–84 Survey of the English Sample," *Association of Departments of English Bulletin* 84 (1986):40–61.

11. Anne Digby and Peter Searby, *Children, School and Society in Nineteenth-Century England* (London: Macmillan, 1981), 25.

12. Emile Durkheim, *Education and Sociology*, trans. Sherwood D. Fox (Glencoe, Ill.: Free Press, 1956), 131, 132.

Harriet Martineau's
Household Education:
Revising the Feminine
Tradition

Linda H. Peterson

Yale University

B EGINNING in 1846, Harriet Martineau published two series of articles in a short-lived magazine called *The People's
Journal:* one on travel called "Lake and Mountain Holidays," another on education under such unlikely titles as "The Natural
Possessions of Man," "How to Expect," and "The Golden Mean."[1]
Though *The People's Journal* (like many another radical scheme)
soon failed, its editor John Saunders encouraged Martineau to
finish her series on education, which she did in 1848, bringing
out the next year a volume called *Household Education*. In its day,
Household Education attracted much attention: Martineau wrote
to Fanny Wedgwood about its popularity among "the Workies"
and about the laudatory reviews it received in the British press.[2]
Both in Britain and America the volume was reprinted again
and again and gave a rise to Harriet Martineau's reputation,
not to say her bank account.

In our day, *Household Education* has excited little interest among
Victorian scholars or educational theorists: Vera Wheatley gives
it less than a page in her biography of Martineau, smiling at
the "quite unwitting humor, and . . . pedantic mode of writing";
Gillian Thomas dismisses it as educational theory, though she
finds it interesting as a "dress rehearsal for the more systematic
personal reminiscence of the *Autobiography*"; only R. K. Webb
devotes some serious attention to the volume, especially to its

expression of Martineau's radicalism and her "pseudo-scientific enthusiasms," including that love of "cleanliness and temperance," which were the "very religion of the materialist."[3] Martineau's *Household Education* is worth pursuing, however, as more than a nascent autobiography or an expression of pseudo-scientific obsessions. It is, as Webb points out, a radical document—radical in matters of religion, radical on issues of social rank. It is most radical, I believe, in its assumption of a *feminist* position on education and in its shrewd revision of an English *feminine* tradition of didactic writing on the subject of "female education."[4] Specifically, Martineau intends in *Household Education* to revise Hannah More's *Strictures on the Modern System of Female Education* (1799), a treatise that was a seminal influence on her thought and which dominated notions about women's education in the first half of the nineteenth century. By engaging More's ideas, Martineau enters that larger Victorian debate about women's intellectual capacities and social roles.

Martineau's literary relationship with Hannah More was a long and agonistic one. The Reverend Lant Carpenter, a Unitarian preacher and teacher under whose spell Martineau fell in adolescence, introduced her to More—not merely as a devotional guide but as a literary figure against which a woman writer might measure herself. In his own *Principles of Education,* Carpenter wrote:

> If any female writer should [hereafter] come forward to the public, possessing the clearness, simplicity, correctness, and well-stored understanding of an Edgeworth, the brilliant yet chaste imagination and "devotional taste" of a Barbauld, and the energy and high-toned and moral principle of a More, divested of bigotry, and founded upon genuine Christian theology, in the scale of utility she will probably stand unrivalled among her contemporaries. . . .[5]

That was a challenge to young Martineau: "to stand unrivalled among her contemporaries." As we know from a private memorandum, she vowed to become "a forceful and elegant writer on religious and moral subjects, so as to be useful to refined as well as unenlightened minds."[6] In fact, the female writers Carpenter praised provided the impetus for Martineau's career as a journalist. In 1822, as a girl of nineteen, Martineau sent to the *Monthly Repository* three articles surveying the intellectual and literary achievements of women: the first two, "Female Writers of Practical Divinity," covered Mrs. More, Mrs. Barbauld, and Elizabeth Smith; the third was titled simply "On Female Education," though from internal evidence it seems to be a review—and critique—of More's *Strictures on Female Education.*

This early review suggests that, however much she may have admired More, Martineau viewed her as a dragon at the gate, an obstacle to her own aspirations as a writer and, more generally, to women who aspired to achievements beyond the domestic sphere. Even in 1822, as a novice thinker and writer, Martineau challenges More's statements about women's capacities and e- vises her notions about female education. Martineau argues against three assumptions, all implicit in More, all common in nineteenth-century thinking, that hinder improvements in women's education: (1) that if women pursue knowledge, they will "neglect their appropriate duties and peculiar employments"; (2) "that the greatest advances that the female mind can make in knowledge, must still fall far short of the attainment of the other sex"; (3) that women are naturally so vain that "any degree of proficiency in knowledge" will make them forget "the subordi- nate station assigned them by law, natural and divine."[7]

Martineau's inclusion of the third issue gives away her hidden target in More's *Strictures on Female Education,* and not-so-hidden desire to counteract what she read there. More had included a long section on "The practical use of female knowledge, with a sketch of the female character, and a comparative view of the sexes," which emphasized (among other things) women's vanity and particularly the vanity of pretentious young girls who spend their time scribbling and aspiring to public authorship: "it will generally be found true," More suggests,

> that girls who take to scribble, are the least studious, the least reflect- ing, and the least rational. They early acquire a false confidence in their own unassisted powers: it becomes more gratifying to their natu- ral vanity to be always pouring out their minds on paper, than to be drawing into them fresh ideas from richer sources.[8]

These were hard words for a young woman who felt herself committed to authorship. In 1822, Martineau counteracts them by referring to principles of Christian humility that genuine edu- cation will inculcate and then, more shrewdly, by pointing out that if all women were better educated, none would have cause for vanity. "As the spread of information extend[s]," she argues, "there [will be] less cause for conceit."[9]

But the other two objections—that women lack the mental capacities of men and that their appropriate sphere is essentially different from men's—were more difficult to counter and would engage Martineau's attention throughout her career. In "On Female Education," she either skirts the issues or acquiesces in patriarchal notions about women's place. On the issue of women's mental capacities, she allows "that the acquirements of women can seldom equal those of men, and it is not desirable that they should"; she only wishes women "to be companions to men, instead of playthings or servants, one of which an ignorant woman commonly must be" (80). On the issue of women's proper sphere, she responds that women need education to carry out their designated duties, whether within the household or in "the wide field of charity" (78). In *Household Education*, however, written twenty-five years later and fifty years after More published *Strictures on Female Education*, Martineau takes up the issues of women's capacities and responsibilities more radically.

Overall, *Household Education* revises More's *Strictures* on a number of key points—not the least of which are religion and social rank. Whereas More proceeded strictly from Christian principles, it being her concern that modern prose literature had become far too secular, Martineau intended *Household Education*, as she later told a publisher, for "the Secularist order of parents"; if there was religion at all in it, it was the religion of the materialist—all cleanliness and temperance and self-control.[10] On matters of social rank, More and Martineau differed, too. Whereas More's *Strictures* addressed only women of the "higher class," those of "rank and fortune," as her subtitle puts it, Martineau aimed at the middle ranks, specifically the secure artisanal class that was sufficiently above poverty so as not to worry about everyday necessities, but sufficiently below inherited wealth so as to need both book learning and practical experience. The child of royalty, *Household Education* claims, can never be a truly educated man, never "approach to our idea of a perfect man, with an intellect fully exercised, affections thoroughly disciplined, and every faculty educated by those influences which arise only from equal intercourse with men at large."[11] Only those of the middle ranks can hope for such a liberal education.

Clearly, the shift from More's upper ranks to Martineau's middling sort shows a radical thinker at work, one who rejects rank as not only injurious to others, but injurious to the person him or herself. Even more radically, *Household Education* takes up a feminist position on women's abilities. Martineau is not to be persuaded that women's minds are different from men's—either in kind or degree. More had written that women's minds—like their bodies, *because* of their bodies—were inferior to men's: "Both in composition and action, they [women] excel in details; but they do not so much generalize their ideas as men, nor do their minds seize a great subject with so large a grasp":

> In summing up the evidence . . . of the different capacities of the sexes, one may venture, perhaps, to assert, that women have equal *parts,* but are inferior in *wholeness* of mind, in the integral understanding: that though a superior woman may possess single faculties in equal perfection, yet there is commonly a juster proportion in the mind of a superior man: that if women have in an equal degree the faculty of fancy which creates images, and the faculty of memory which collects and stores ideas, they seem not to possess in equal measure the faculty of comparing, combining, analysing, and separating these ideas; that deep and patient thinking which goes to the bottom of a subject; nor that power of arrangement which knows how to link a thousand connected ideas in one dependant [sic] train, without losing sight of the original idea out of which the rest grow, and on which they all hang. The female, too, wanting steadiness in her intellectual pursuits, is perpetually turned aside by her characteristic tastes and feelings. [More 1:367]

More's description of women's inferiority may derive from Hartleian associationist psychology, or it may, more broadly, represent late eighteenth- and much nineteenth-century "scientific" thinking about the correlation between brain size and intellectual capacity. As Stephen Jay Gould reminds us, anthropometry—and, more specifically, craniometry—were fashionable fields in the nineteenth century, and the data the body-and-brain measurers gathered were often used to demonstrate the intellectual inferiority of women. Little body, little brain, little intelligence. According to Paul Broca, greatest craniometrist of them all, "the relatively small size of the female brain depends in part upon her physical inferiority and in part upon her intellectual inferiority" (by which he meant the degenerative effect of centuries of underusage, due to the passive mental lives women lived).[12]

For all her pseudoscientific enthusiasms, Martineau shows no interest in craniometry or in any other system that links intellectual capacity to physical size. *Household Education* asserts the general principle that the aim of education should be "to bring out and strengthen and exercise all the powers given to every human being" (13), and it acknowledges no differences between the "powers" of the two sexes. Examples featuring both boys and girls illustrate the chapters on the development of the powers (will, hope, fear, patience, love, veneration, truthfulness, conscientiousness). Anecdotes using men and women, boys and girls, serve to make points in later sections on intellectual training (the perspective, conceptive, reasoning, and imaginative faculties) and on the development of good habits. Indeed, throughout the volume, Martineau uses the now-approved feminist technique of alternating masculine and feminine nouns and pronouns: a boy this, a girl that; she this, he that.[13]

What is most striking about *Household Education,* however, is its tacit assumption that one need not write different childrearing manuals or different educational theories about boys and girls— as More had done, as Rousseau had done, as Martineau's American contemporary Catharine Beecher chose to do.[14] Only when Martineau reaches chapter 21 (on the "reasoning faculties") does she treat the presumed differences—and then she dismisses them:

> I must declare that on no subject is more nonsense talked, (as it seems to me,) than on that of female education, when restriction is advocated. In works otherwise really good we find it taken for granted that girls are not to learn the dead languages and mathematics, because they are not to exercise professions where these attainments are wanted; and a little further on we find it said that the chief reason for boys and young men studying these things is to improve the quality of their minds. I suppose none of us will doubt that everything possible should be done to improve the quality of the mind of every human being.—If it is said that the female brain is incapable of studies of an abstract nature,—that is not true: for there are many instances of women who have been good mathematicians, and good classical scholars. The plea is indeed nonsense on the face of it; for the brain which will learn French will learn Greek; the brain which enjoys arithmetic is capable of mathematics. [*HE,* 155–56]

Continuing in this vein for two pages, in a series of logical deductions that sweep away all objections to women's acquisition of a "male" education, Martineau reasserts her initial principle: that "everything possible should be done to improve the quality of the mind of every human being," that "every human being is to be made as perfect as possible" (*HE,* 159).

In claiming that Martineau is "feminist" in her assertion of women's intellectual capacities and her advocacy of women's rights to equal education, I mean to suggest that she represents an early phase of the nineteenth-century "*protest* against [patriarchal] standards and values, and *advocacy* of minority rights and values."[15] Like Mary Wollstonecraft in *A Vindication of the Rights of Woman*, Martineau insists that the best educational system is one in which both sexes are educated together first in the family, then in day schools.[16] But Martineau's literary mode is not Wollstonecraftian, not what we usually associate with feminist protest and confrontation. In literary form and rhetorical style, *Household Education* inclines toward a masculine tradition of prose writing (though Martineau would have considered it universal). In form Martineau's work imitates neither Wollstonecraft's *Vindication* nor More's *Strictures*, but Carpenter's more general (and genderless) *Principles of Education*. Like Carpenter, Martineau handles issues of education under the broad classifications of "Intellectual, Moral, and Physical"; like Carpenter, she tends to minimize (or ignore) differences between the sexes. Moreover, Martineau's rhetorical style in *Household Education*, as in virtually all of her writing, is masculine—or, at least, is the product of what she considered a masculine education. In her chapter on the "reasoning faculties," she tells the story of her training in composition, a story she uses to illustrate the rational capacities of women. Martineau learned composition from a boy's school-master: a Presbyterian who turned Unitarian, lost his congregation and his pupils, and had it made up to him by local Unitarians who sent their daughters to his school. As one of those daughters, Harriet received a typical middle-class boy's education. She was trained in the conventions of masculine rhetoric, "taught the parts of a theme, as our master and many others approved and practised them": "the Proposition, the Reason, the Example, the Confirmation, and the Conclusion" (*HE*, 154). Martineau used this masculine rhetoric throughout her life in her journalism, as in *Household Education*. Her feminism in this book is thus a feminism based as much on a demonstration of a woman's achievements in a male literary style as it is on arguments for women's education in traditionally male subjects.

Yet if *Household Education* is "feminist" in its rhetoric and its position on formal education, it is "feminine" in its alignment with another didactic tradition, with treatises like More's that treat specifically the question of woman's sphere. Martineau was proud of her accomplishments in housewifery—quick to point out that she could make her living by the needle as well as the pen; quick to argue that the brightest women were the best housekeepers, the dumbest the worst; quick to ridicule pretentious bourgeois families who sent their daughters to finishing schools but gave them no "thorough practice in domestic occupations" (*HE*, 198).

Indeed, *Household Education* assumes that certain occupations (like sewing and cooking) are "natural" to women, that girls have a "natural desire and the natural facility for housewifery" (199). The illustrations in the chapters on "habits" show little boys doing carpentry and lock repairs at their workbench (198), with little girls "making beds, making fires, laying the cloth and washing up crockery, baking bread, preserving fruit, clear-starching and ironing" (199). Though Martineau seems to question religiously or biologically based arguments that women "are made for these domestic occupations" (156), she nevertheless accepts the tasks of housewifery with good humor, arguing that girls can manage the extra burdens and still keep up intellectually with their brothers.[17]

What Martineau does not accept, however, is the common "feminine" argument that women's proper sphere is the home, that education should train women to exert their influence within the domestic sphere so as to have it dispersed, via husbands, sons, and brothers, throughout the larger public sphere. This premise motivates More's *Strictures,* which begins with an "Address to women of rank and fortune, on the effects of their influence on society" (More 1:313). More emphatically denies that she is calling women to public action, "sounding an alarm to female warriors, or exciting female politicians"; rather, she wants women to exert influence "without departing from the refinement of their character, without derogating from the dignity of their rank, without blemishing the delicacy of their sex" (1:313)— without, we might translate, leaving hearth and home. The argument about feminine influence remained a tempting one in the nineteenth century. It was taken up in the United States, for instance, by Beecher, whose *Treatise on Domestic Economy* (1842) sets forth not only a theory of domestic management but also a theory of female education; as Jane Roland Martin has commented, the two are intertwined, since "in [this] view, female education constitutes a preparation for carrying out the domestic role."[18]

For all her interest in domestic things, Martineau adopts neither More's position on feminine influence, nor Beecher's on the feminine sphere. In *Society in America* (1837), she had attacked American men and women for failing to fulfill the implications of the U.S. constitution by failing to give women the vote or the right to function as citizens. In *Household Education* Martineau more quietly, but more shrewdly, handles this question of feminine influence. Rather than locate *feminine influence* within the domestic sphere, she more radically locates *education itself* within that sphere. She denies the central importance of the public school to human learning: in chapter 5 she dismisses the boarding school as a relatively insignificant aspect of English education, it being a place "where a few years are spent by a small number of the youth of our country" (*HE*, 27); in contrast, she points out that important citizens—Sir Issac Newton, Elizabeth Fry, even Queen Victoria herself—were educated at home. Indeed, the premise of *Household Education,* in contrast to that of More's *Strictures* or even Wollstonecraft's "On National Education," is that "every member of the family . . . must be a member of the domestic school of mutual instruction, and must know that he is so" (*HE*, 2). "The domestic school"—the phrase itself signals Martineau's departure from a position that equates formal schooling, whether in a public or private institution, with genuine education. As in her novel *Deerbrook* (1839), where the governess Maria Young complains she cannot really educate the Rowland children because the greater influence of their unfortunate home overwhelms her efforts, so in *Household Education* the home is the primary (and most significant) site of learning.

Having removed education from the public realm and relocated it within the domestic, Martineau undermines the authority of formal, male schooling. (She also means to undermine the authority of the upper classes, but that is another story.) This relocation makes it possible for girls and boys alike to learn, for men and women alike to teach. And, if her illustrations of learning in the early chapters feature boys and girls equally, so her illustrations of teaching throughout the volume feature mothers and fathers equally. The chapter on "Fear," for instance, shows both mother and father teaching their children courage through story and example (*HE*, 57–66). Sections on book learning illustrate Martineau's principles with both mothers and fathers reading after the day's labors are finished (*HE*, 31–33, 165). Such examples may not have reflected real Victorian life, but they reflect what Martineau thought should be.

The title *Household Education,* in other words, means more than meets the eye. It refers, obviously, to the learning that can and should occur within the average English household. It takes up, too, those social and domestic habits that shape the home, that make it possible (or impossible) for members to continue to develop from infancy to old age. But it most fully means to engage what is meant by education and to inquire where education best occurs.

Whether Martineau's approach is feasible (or even desirable) is another issue: it seems clear, for example, that she underestimates the influence of the public school on the shape of English culture, and she fails to explain how women are to be transformed from their current undereducated state to their imagined position of home-educators. Despite these and other omissions, Martineau does avoid two serious problems that plague other nineteenth-century theorists of women's education. As Martin notes, Wollstonecraft's arguments for women's access to formal education address the issues of rights and citizenship, but they fail to explain how the qualities traditionally associated with the feminine sphere are to be taught and learned.[19] Martineau solves this problem by embedding both "masculine" and "feminine" qualities (courage and patience, truthfulness and veneration) within the home and within the purview of all family members, male and female alike. Similarly, Martineau avoids a second problem which treatises like Beecher's create: by "professionalizing" women's role within the home and emphasizing the power of feminine influence, Beecher cuts women off from full participation in the public realm. Martineau avoids the professionalization of domestic responsibilities, assuming that tasks should be shared by family members and, more specifically, that when women pursue "professions," they will do so, as men do, in the public realm. *Household Education* stands, then, at the crossroads of Victorian debates about education and gender, but Martineau is not willing to follow a single path: not willing to stay within the feminine track of Hannah More and Catharine Beecher, nor yet willing to embrace a solely masculine tradition.

Notes

1. For these articles, see *The People's Journal*, ed. John Saunders (London: People's Journal Office, 1846), 2:128–30, 205–7, 274–76. Fourteen other articles, later collected in *Household Education*, appear in vols. 2–5. With vol. 6 the magazine became *The People's and Howitt's Journal*, with William Howitt taking control of the editorship and Martineau ceasing to contribute.

2. See letters of 3 August 1846 and 13 November 1851, in *Harriet Martineau's Letters to Fanny Wedgwood*, ed. Elisabeth Sanders Arbuckle (Stanford: Stanford University Press, 1983), 90–91, 119. See also R. K. Webb's discussion of the book's reception in *Harriet Martineau: A Radical Victorian* (London: Heinemann, 1960), 271.

3. Vera Wheatley, *The Life and Work of Harriet Martineau* (Fair Lawn, N.J.: Essential Books, 1957), 276; Gillian Thomas, *Harriet Martineau* (Boston: Twayne, 1985), 65; Webb, 269–72.

4. In distinguishing between "feminine" and "feminist," I follow Elaine Showalter's

terminology in *A Literature of Their Own* (Princeton: Princeton University Press, 1977), which uses the former to designate that phase in which women imitate "the prevailing modes of the dominant tradition and internal[ize] its standards" and the latter for women's "*protest* against [patriarchal] standards and values, and *advocacy* of minority rights and values" (13).

5. Lant Carpenter, *Principles of Education: Intellectual, Moral, and Physical* (London: Longman, Hurst, Rees, Orme, Brown, 1820), 41–42.

6. Harriet Martineau, "Private: A Writer's Resolutions," in *Harriet Martineau on Women*, ed. Gayle Graham Yates (New Brunswick, N.J.: Rutgers University Press, 1985), 33. Martineau wrote this resolution in June, 1829.

7. Harriet Martineau, "On Female Education," *Monthly Repository* 18 (1823):77–81. For Martineau's assessment of More's religious writings, see "Female Writers on Practical Divinity," *Monthly Repository* 17 (1822):593–96, 746–50.

8. *The Works of Hannah More* (New York: Harper, 1854), 1:364. Hereafter More, cited in the text.

9. Martineau, "On Female Education," 80.

10. Webb, *Harriet Martineau*, 270–71. See also John Reed's discussion of the differences between evangelical and rationalist writings on education, in "Learning to Punish," included in this issue of *Bucknell Review*.

11. Harriet Martineau, *Household Education* (Philadelphia: Lea & Blanchard, 1849), 29. Hereafter *HE*, cited in the text.

12. Stephen Jay Gould, *The Mismeasure of Man* (New York: Norton, 1981) 103–7, and "Women's Brains," in *The Panda's Thumb: More Reflections in Natural History* (New York: Norton, 1980), 152–59; the quotation from Broca appears on 154.

13. There may be more examples using "a young girl" because of the high proportion of autobiographical anecdotes; however, where Martineau does not record personal experience, she consistently balances references to the two sexes.

14. On Beecher's *A Treatise on Domestic Economy* (1842; reprint, New York: Schocken Books, 1977), see Jane Roland Martin, *Reclaiming a Conversation: The Ideal of the Educated Woman* (New Haven: Yale University Press, 1985), 103–38.

15. Showalter's phrase, n. 4. Showalter dates the "feminist" phase in English literature from 1880 to 1920, but I would include Martineau's work in *Household Education* as a pioneering example of that phase. Martineau anticipates what will later become a common protest against women's exclusion from "male" education.

16. See Mary Wollstonecraft, "On National Education," in *A Vindication of the Rights of Woman*, ed. Carol H. Poston (New York: Norton, 1988), 157–78. Though they take up similar positions on education, Martineau had little use for Wollstonecraft, calling her "a poor victim of passion, with no control over her own peace, and no calmness or content except when the needs of her individual nature were satisfied." Martineau disliked such proponents of women's rights, in that "their advocacy of Woman's cause becomes mere detriment, precisely in proportion to their personal reasons for unhappiness." In Harriet Martineau, *Autobiography* (1877; reprint, London: Virago, 1983), 1:400.

17. For such acquiescence in matters of housewifery, Deirdre David interprets Martineau's "attitude towards male cultural and social authority" as "undeniably ambiguous." See her *Intellectual Women and Victorian Patriarchy: Harriet Martineau, Elizabeth Barrett Browning, George Eliot* (Ithaca: Cornell University Press, 1987), 54–58. My interpretation of Martineau's acceptance of domestic duties would locate the ambiguity in two sometimes conflicting impulses of feminism: the impulse to attest the value of roles and duties that women have traditionally borne vs. the need to assert the rights of women to privileges and responsibilities that men claim.

18. Martin, *Reclaiming a Conversation*, 109. Though it is not certain that Martineau

knew the *Treatise on Domestic Economy*, Martineau had met Catharine Beecher, the sister of Harriet Beecher Stowe, in Cincinnati in 1835 during her tour of America; in *Household Education* she was probably responding to what she felt was a mistaken direction in American feminist thought. For Martineau's relations with American feminists, see Yates, ed., *Harriet Martineau on Women*, 127–60.

19. Martin, *Reclaiming a Conversation*, 91–102.

The Guidebook and the Museum: Imperialism, Education and Nationalism in the British Museum

Inderpal Grewal

"Do you mean to say, that the behaviour of the public, generally, is such as it ought to be in viewing the Museum?"

"Yes, the ignorant are brought into awe by what they see about them, and the better informed know, of course, how to conduct themselves. We have common policemen, soldiers, sailors, artillerymen, livery servants, and, of course, occasionally mechanics, but their good conduct I am very much pleased to see, and I think that the exhibition at the Museum will have a vast influence on the national character of Englishmen in general." [Evidence of Mr. Samouelle, assistant in the Department of Natural History][1]

SINCE the British Museum had been created by money raised by a state lottery and an act of Parliament, its accessibility to all members of the British public was a concern during the nineteenth century.[2] Government commissions such as the one questioning Mr. Samouelle were set up to make inquiries of museum officials regarding audience, admission practices, and the educational purposes of the museum. However, other ways to educate the public were also undertaken by publishers who printed guidebooks to the museum. These catered to the casual visitor and pointed out the highlights of the museum, leaving the specialized scholar to pore over the more detailed catalogues. A number of these general guidebooks were printed, some by the New Library of Useful Knowledge, one of the many societies for disseminating knowledge to the middle as well as working classes. For instance, there was *A Guide to the Beauties of the British Museum* (1826), (1838), and *The British Museum in Four Sections or How to View the Whole at Once* (1852). Many more of these guides were printed and some went through multiple editions.

The guidebooks did not merely teach; they also worked to sublimate the alienating practices of the museum, an institution formed by aristocratic contributions such as the Hamilton, Elgin, and Townley collections. Consequently, they assisted in the reduction of working-class radicalism which occurred by midnineteenth century. Since they mediated between those with "taste" and the "vulgar," they lay bare the role of aesthetics in the class conflicts of nineteenth-century England and express changing attitudes to working-class and public education. Moreover, they reveal the function of education and aesthetics in transformations that occurred in the nineteenth century: the rise of consumerism, nationalism, and imperialism.

It is in aesthetic and cultural productions, as Pierre Bourdieu suggests, that class divisions are reenforced precisely because they are concealed. As Bourdieu puts it, "art and cultural productions are predisposed, consciously and deliberately or not, to fulfill a social function of legitimating social difference."[3] The aesthetic methods by which class divisions were disguised in order to form a nationalist culture helped to create the nineteenth-century Englishman and Englishwoman to whom imperialism became acceptable, if not natural. Yet class division was not solely responsible for the colonizing dispositions of the English; the domestication of women, the division between private and public, between the home and the marketplace, were also part of the "habitus," as Bourdieu calls it,[4] in which the individual subject was formed and which replicated the divisions of race and gender that were the nexus of colonial power relations. Within the discursive formations that comprised Victorian culture, the colonies were "civilized" by a colonial venture that resulted in their commodification, while the British public was educated through a knowledge which involved their own commodification while it suggested their ability to reify the non-Western "other."

As an embodiment of such a taxonomic system, the British Museum exhibited and represented the world through certain objects to which the general guides directed the public. A very selective, dichotomized view of the world was thereby created, which presented not only a history of the whole world but also that of England, for it inculcated the opposition of self and other. Such an opposition generated class distinction as well as that of race and gender in both the colonies and England. It also encouraged a self-consciousness that nurtured national pride in English ability to gather knowledge and display the world in glass cases. The education of the public meant the dissemination by the museum's guidebooks and catalogues of a schematic aesthetic that inculcated class, gender, and racial difference.

I

In 1808 the first *Synopsis* of the contents of the British Museum was published by order of the trustees. Compiled by the museum staff, the *Synopsis* was the first official publication of the museum meant for the general public and could be bought for a few shillings. Other museum publications at this time were the detailed catalogues that were records and descriptions of the collections and which were often given away to trustees. These were expensive and not meant as guides for the casual visitor to the museum. The *Synopsis* was one of the very few publications of the museum that gave general descriptions, for it was not until the end of the century that the museum would publish a number of descriptive guides meant for the visiting public for most of its separate collections.

Yet it was clear that the *Synopsis* was not sufficient to fill the demand for guidebooks to the museum, for a number of publishers in London undertook to print books that would be of help to the public in seeing the museum. Such works, which were called "guides" or "guidebooks," shared their methods and intentions with travel guides, though guidebooks to libraries and museums had been published before 1836, when the first Murray's travel guide appeared. These works created a homogeneous discursive community where the user was treated as the perfect reader, receptive to the assumed transparency of a text which proposed to lay out an objective geography. To buy these was to follow in the footsteps of the writer in an actual physical space, without either straying into the dangerous territory of what was unknown or being allowed uncontrolled interpretation. The intention of museum guidebooks was the interpretation and description of the museum collection—in other words, the control of referentiality. Such a control was necessary since, in the collection, the object's removal from its use value, as Susan Stewart has suggested, enabled referentiality to become multivocal.[5]

One guidebook, published in 1826 by the firm of Thomas and George Underwood, was entitled *A Guide to the Beauties of the British Museum Being a Critical and Descriptive Account of the Principle Works of Art Contained in the Galleries of the Above National Collection*.[6] The price of the book was two shillings, and it therefore would not have been read by the working class. As Richard Altick points out, working-class readers, who often worked sixteen hours a day for two shillings or less, were only willing to spend a few pence at most for reading material; this guidebook would have been bought by a member of the middle class, or perhaps the lower spectrum of it such as the prosperous artisan or clerk, those termed by Altick the "modestly circumstanced booklover."[7]

Catering to a wider public, the 1826 *Guide* valorizes the discourse of labor which was so essential to nineteenth-century bourgeois, industrial culture.[8] The writer presents himself as replicating the endeavors of the travelers and collectors who obtained the artifacts in the first place, for he claims he searched assiduously in the museum for the beauties which he brings to the reader's notice. He hopes to "convey some of the impressions which he himself received, during a search, diligent at least, and often repeated, without which search the beauties here pointed out may have remained undiscovered" (preface). This labor of exploration within the museum mimics but also compensates for the labor of the collector whose work in creating the collection involves the obliteration of the use value of the objects and the substitution of aesthetic value. Stewart defines this as "the value of manipulation and positioning," and points out that the guidebook thus disguises the fact that the collection comes into being by the abstraction of labor within the cycle of exchange (164–66); it substitutes instead an aesthetic labor which masks the alienation of labor within social relations.

In addition, the writer of the Underwood *Guide* claims his search for the beauties in the museum was "often repeated," and thus invokes the process of verification that would give his text scientific objectivity (preface). The writer claims he has often repeated his search in the museum only to reach the same results and the same interpretation. Furthermore, such assumptions of transparency helped create a homogeneous discursive community which read objects with the same aesthetic suggested by the guidebook. Even though the guidebooks were texts that could themselves be interpreted, they worked by claiming a transparency that was taken for granted. Guidebooks were never interpreted; the logic of their functioning was the suggestion of value-neutral description.[9]

Though not a museum official, the writer of the 1826 guide is obviously a scholar/expert knowledgeable in aesthetics and taste, as well as in the needs of his public. Though the author's name is not provided, his credentials are: he is the author of *Beauties of the Dulwich Gallery* and *Beauties of the Fitzwilliam Gallery at Cambridge.* While claiming his expertise, he suggests there is no disparity between the author and the public, thereby creating what Jon Klancher has termed "the society of the text" with the "reciprocity of the reader and writer."[10] In this homogeneous society, the experience of a scholarly, upper-class "expert" (such as the writer of the guidebook) was replicated by middle-class readers in an actual geographic time and space experience.

Consequently, the writer of the 1826 *Guide* states that he will enable his audience to read the artifacts of the museum in the way that he himself has read them: "the writer of this guide would attempt to convey some of those impressions which he has himself received" (preface). By pointing out what the writer conceives to be the most striking and important objects, the guidebook attempted to control and direct responses to the artifacts in the museum, as well as to create a new context for the objects removed from their origins. The multivocal referentiality of the objects was controlled within the guidebooks through the replication of the writer's experience by the many readers who bought the guides and saw the museum through its lenses, suggesting the control and standardization of the museum's ability to generate meaning, and, consequently, of the museum-going public as well.

The 1826 *Guide* claimed that with its help even a one-day visit to the museum taught something. The guide is aimed, we are told, at those visitors who might leave "without gaining any permanent or distinct impression of what has been presented to them." It directs itself at "that numerous class of persons who have no time to seek out for themselves the peculiar beauties of this extensive collection" (preface). Like the traveler with the guidebook in a foreign country, the museum-goer was a new kind of visitor, one for whom time limited education and enjoyment. This new visitor absorbed alien histories and cultures within the historical context of his own history; his referent was, as Stewart puts it, the interiority of his own self (158).

This primacy of the self was further inculcated by the aesthetic that was disseminated by the guidebooks. Greek art, and the aesthetic of classicism, valorized through the museum guides, ultimately validated and inscribed English values. It participated in creating an ideal English subject, one who was receptive to a "moral" art, and who immediately recognized the "purity" of classical forms. Classicism was believed to be the apotheosis of all art forms, one that was seen as part of the European heritage. It stood as proof of the superiority of the West over the "barbaric" East; as such it laid the groundwork for the "civilization" of the East through European colonization.

Objects were therefore described and interpreted to a public which had no aesthetic education, while paradoxically suggesting such a transcendent aesthetic need not be taught. The audience was told how to read these objects, thereby influencing their taste, by means of guidebooks which had already laid down their aesthetic judgments and therefore eliminated the necessity to interpret; the subject was assumed to validate the guidebook.

Such interpretations often became moral lessons when, for instance, it was suggested that Greek art bespoke a rational control of sexual desire. Erotic or sensual interpretations were suggested and negated; what was stressed was the "purity" and the transcendent value of classical art. A binary aesthetic, positive purity versus negative sensuality, was offered. As was common with Victorian definitions of beauty, even those classical objects that, we are told, could be "sensual" created the "intellectual" effect. A statue of a drunken faun, mentioned in the 1826 *Guide*, even though "redolent of wine and woods," was believed to have "an ideal grossness and sensuality belonging to it, unmixed with anything that could be called low or vulgar" (17).

The *Guide* directed its readers and viewers to notice this cerebral quality of Greek sculpture:

> there is nothing more worthy of admiration, in the works of the Greek sculptors, than the exquisite purity and chasteness of their female forms. . . . The Greeks were in fact a people so wholly intellectual, that their idea of voluptuousness itself was an imagination rather than a sentiment. [13]

This conversion of what could be "sensuous" and "voluptuous" into the "intellectual" taught that having good taste meant seeing Greek sculpture with nothing but the predefined aesthetic of beauty, whose divinity excluded the erotic. The "sensual" was given prominence as well, but shown to be impure and problematic. Here the Romantic tendency to convert material objects into metaphors of the self extended into the Victorian practice of converting materiality, as the erotic element of the female body, into a representation of female purity that was aestheticized and consecrated. The white marble of the statues lent itself quite easily to this particular conversion, helping to elevate both the disciplined, "pure" female body and the sculpture of Greece. The fact that these statutes had been painted in their original state was ignored; the weathered historicity of the paintless, broken statutes was emphasized instead. Many Greek statues of nude figures were viewed through the same aesthetic transformation right through the nineteenth century. For instance, Hiram Powers's "The Slave Girl," which was exhibited in the Great Exhibition of 1851, was the statue of a naked Greek girl with chained wrists, implying that she was being sold into a Turkish harem. Elizabeth Barrett Browning wrote a sonnet praising its "passionless perfection."[11] Thus, aesthetic forms believed to be of the highest quality, such as statues from the Parthenon, were thought to exercise an effect of disciplinary purification; their aesthetic effect was also a moral education and it enabled the functioning of patriarchal fear and repression of female sexuality. Classicism thus participated in the nineteenth-century ideology of the division of women into the whore and the angel of the house.

In addition, such an aesthetic reveals the discourse of "orientalism," that formation which underlay colonial ventures and by which, as Edward Said discloses, the "West" represented the "East" to itself.[12] Yet such orientalism was created not only by representations of the East by itself, but by contrasting representations of East and West that replicated the aesthetic opposition of purity and eroticism. In the British Museum, Greek art functioned as a signifier of the former, while Egyptian art became that of the latter; thus contrasting values were given to them. Because it was believed to signify transcendent values, Greek art was thought to represent an "intrinsic" and divine aesthetic contained in the objects themselves, and thus immediately apparent, even to an uneducated viewer. Its excellence was believed, according to the 1826 *Guide*, to lie in its "intrinsic merit," which "speak[s] for itself" (38). Egyptian art, on the other hand, was suggested as being *given* value by the collector, a value emerging only because it was displayed. Implicitly, Greek art escaped the reifying practices of the collection, while Egyptian art did not.

Having display value and lacking intrinsic value, Egyptian

sculptures were not believed to have any elevating moral effect. They were, instead, signifiers of materiality. Egyptian statues were described as repositories of erotic, sexual, and animalistic qualities—qualities which were shown to be the opposite of the sexual normativity of Greek statuary. Figures of Egyptian sculpture were thought, according to the *Guide,* to represent "a phantasm and a dream" and not a reality, and were similar to those "which haunt us in that nervous affection called the nightmare" (30). Limited to the realm of nightmares, they became part of the unclaimed, unspeakable domain of abberant sexuality. Their lack of what was "human" prevented them from being ennobling or educational. According to the *Guide,* "We do not feel the least degree of human sympathy with the face [of an Egyptian statue], because there is nothing individualized about it"; instead of uplifting the viewer toward what is sublime, such art supposedly "exercises an almost painful and oppressive effect on the imagination" (33).

Egyptian characteristics, which included a barbaric, nightmarish sexuality, became alien quantities belonging to the "East" and thus were separated from those of the "West." Not surprisingly, the *Guide* suggested that England could itself be ancient Greece reborn. A statue of Acteon was described as having been executed "with great spirit and truth" (17). An ideal of human nature that was once "real" was conjured up as a contrast to life in the industrial age. As a result, an ideal classical form became conflated with and indistinguishable from what nineteenth-century England could and should be: classical art, the highest achievement of art, became an imitation of England. The virtues represented by classical sculpture were believed replicated in the people of England; the likenesses of the statues were the men and women of England. While Egyptian sculpture was believed to have nothing that could be called "natural," statues of Jupiter and Apollo were, says the guidebook, "actual likenesses of men and women that most of us have seen in the course of our own lives" (*Guide,* 13). Consequently, England was thought to embody this ideal and contain these "divine" forms; "classical" England was further differentiated from the "barbaric East."

Such a rebirth was part of the neoclassicism of the early nineteenth century. It soon was incorporated into the very body of the museum. The architecture of the museum, which was rebuilt by 1852, was in the classical style, according to a plan created in 1823 by the Tory architect, Sir Robert Smirke.[13]

II

Yet even during the height of nineteenth-century neoclassicism, the education of the working class was of great concern. The fear of the mob, aroused by the French Revolution, was augmented by the rise of working-class radicalism. The education provided by the museum was believed to be part of the process of "civilizing" the mob, though there were many in English society who opposed the policy of civilizing through education. However, despite Tory fear that the literate and educated masses might, armed with the weapon of knowledge, rebel against the upper classes, education was increasingly seen as an agent of pacification. Middle-class groups such as the Society for the Diffusion of Useful Knowledge (SDUK), which published some museum guidebooks, believed that knowledge would provide "the means of content to those who, for the most part, must necessarily remain in that station which requires great self-denial and great endurance."[14]

It was not surprising, in light of exacerbated class tensions and the aims of the SDUK, that working-class radicals were suspicious of the educational policies of the government and the SDUK. Thomas Hodgskin wrote in *Mechanics Magazine* in 1823, that "men had better be without education, than be educated by their rulers; for their education is but the mere breaking in of the steer of the yoke." He argued that the government merely wished "to control the thoughts and fashion even the minds of its subjects," in order to continue that "most pernicious practice . . . of allowing one or a few men to direct the actions and control the conduct of millions."[15] Thus the concept of "radical education" came into being, by which radicalism developed its own agenda of "really useful education," one that separated itself from education provided by the state and focused instead on political knowledge, socialist principles, and labor economics.[16] Consequently, even though many working men's improvement societies were set up in the 1820s and 1830s to promote "rational recreation," with libraries and lectures as the means for learning,[17] not all working men remained part of such institutes. Many were alienated by the absence of democratic management and the emerging rigid censorship of discussion and reading.

Working-class distrust of the education offered by the societies extended to a distrust of their institutions as well. Thus Richard Cobbett, member of Parliament for Oldham, argued in 1833 that money requested from Parliament for the running of the British

Museum, especially the one thousand pounds set aside for cases of dead insects, could better be spent on starving weavers.[18] The other Cobbett, William, was equally against public money being given to the museum. That same year he spoke in the House of Commons questioning which class of people the museum served: "Why should tradesmen and farmers be called upon to pay for the support of a place which was intended only for the amusement of the curious and the rich, and not for the benefit or for the instruction of the poor?"[19]

Despite radical distrust of state institutions such as the museum, there were some who were interested in what it offered. The secretary of the London Working Men's Association presented a petition for the Sunday opening of museums, arguing, as had the middle-class societies, that "the best remedy for drunkenness is to divert and inform the mind."[20] There were accounts of working-class visitors to the museum, even though many of these accounts deplored the presence of such visitors. Yet museum guidebooks reveal that what the radicals had feared in state education was indeed correct: the aesthetic education provided inscribed class difference and taught the power and superiority of the aristocracy that could collect artifacts through various means from all parts of the world.

Admission to the museum had become far easier than it had been in the eighteenth century when it could only be obtained by tickets applied for in advance with references.[21] By the year 1810, when the second edition of the *Synopsis* for the public was published, admission had become open to all persons on Mondays, Wednesdays, and Fridays. In 1835, when the House of Commons ordered a committee of inquiry into the museum, the principal librarian was still resistant to the committee's recommendations to open the museum for public holidays and more days during the week. The librarian, Sir Henry Ellis, opposed having more public days, for he believed that the museum should also cater to the men of rank and to scholars, who should not mingle with the working classes. He was against the opening of the museum on Easter, for then "the most mischievous portion of the population" could enter the museum (*Minutes*, 99). He did not believe that the collections would educate the public. As a Tory, his concern was the upper classes. He claimed that

> people of a higher grade would hardly wish to come to the Museum at the same time with sailors from the dockyards and girls whom they might bring with them. I do not think that such people would

gain any improvement from the sight of our collections. [*Minutes*, 100]

His successor, Josiah Forshall, who was Ellis's assistant at the time of the inquiry, was also resistant to policies that would make the museum more accessible to the general public. When asked if, in a free country, was not the public the encourager of literature and science, Forshall replied, "Certainly, including in the word public those very persons of rank and wealth to whom I allude" (*Minutes*, 81).

Though for Forshall and Ellis, the "public" which mattered comprised the men of rank and wealth who they believed were most fitted to visit the museum, the committee (and presumably the House of Commons which had created the committee) had another definition for the word "public." Their interest was the working class, for they questioned Forshall on his views regarding the museum as a means for improving the "vulgar class," as he had termed it. Thus, while the museum officials and its trustees believed their public to be the men of "rank and wealth," the committee presumed it to include the "vulgar class." Consequently, at the same time that the House of Commons was interested in bringing the working class into a museum that was being supported, in large part, by parliamentary grants, the officials of the museum were interested in making it a more exclusive institution.

Such a contradiction was apparent in the guidebooks written by the museum officials and published by the SDUK, which, while claiming their audience was the section of the society that needed to be educated, created a culture in which the aristocracy and the wealthy collector became increasingly idealized. Thus, even though the power of the English bourgeoisie in the nineteenth century cannot be denied, the aristocracy still was powerful in the values of collecting and capitalism that it represented. "Men of rank and wealth," as Forshall called them, were enshrined as preservers of culture and as persons who placed national interest and national education before their personal needs. Thus the cultural hegemony of the aristocracy was suggested within the discourse of education, and during a period of the increasing fluidity of class distinctions. For instance, the guide to Egyptian antiquities in the British Museum, written by a G. Long, and published in 1832 by the SDUK, presented the world in imperialist terms as a storehouse which supplied an "inexhaustible" number of collectible objects for those capable of obtaining them.[22]

Even though the names of the collections in the British Museum proclaimed that only the very rich could do so, the guidebook suggested the possibility of collecting and of erasing the distinction between the collector and the viewer. While the British Museum was believed to contain the whole world, it also came to embody the power of Britain as a nation able to bring about this containment with the help of its wealthy collectors. Aristocratic power became collapsed into that of the imperial collector.

The SDUK published, as part of its Library of Entertaining Knowledge, two museum guidebooks written by Henry Ellis. One of these, describing the Elgin Marbles, sold ten thousand copies. This was the same Ellis who had, in his evidence before the 1835 House of Commons Committee on the British Museum, shown his disdain for working-class visitors to the museum. The SDUK guides, then, were no different from those published by the museum, to which Ellis also contributed. These guides created a culture that was produced by the scholars and the museum officials who saw themselves as guardians of culture and art, but which was consumed by the middle class and its less affluent sections as well as the better off working class. Though this reading public suggested the growing fluidity of class lines in the first half of the nineteenth century, the population excluded from this consolidation of a growing "cultured" class that looked toward the aristocracy for knowledge on taste were the very poor. These were the consumers of the radical press and of the "penny dreadfuls," and they did not spend their money on "rational recreation" or improving knowledge.[23]

By 1845, though the SDUK had lost the audience to which it had originally directed its efforts, it had not failed in its purpose of education, for it had participated in the growing separation of the better off sections of the working class from their poorer compatriots and united them with a middle class that was rapidly growing and anxious to improve itself educationally and financially. It was to this increasingly powerful middle-class public that the SDUK directed its New Library of Entertaining Knowledge, a series of books on topics such as the biographies of great men and the lives of Hindus and Egyptians. These narratives of self-improvement and orientalism were combined with the museum guidebooks' presentation of the upper classes as the preservers of excellence; imperialist knowledge was constituted as knowledge for improvement and given by the upper classes to the lower.

In this culture, men of taste, i.e., the collectors, along with the scholars and explorers they helped to fund, formed the aristocracy, more acceptable because it did not seem to be founded on rigid class lines. Instead it seemed founded on national lines, with patrons collecting not to improve their own collections but that of the nation.[24] The power of this new aristocracy is visible in the SDUK's guides written by Henry Ellis, one on the Elgin marbles (1846) and the other on the Townley marbles (1848).[25] For Ellis, the museum could educate only because of the power and generosity of the wealthy, implying that the education of the public, and the idea of a "national" art and a "national" repository, could occur only because of the aristocracy. By midnineteenth century, therefore, class distinction became, paradoxically, the method for the removal of class differences. Ellis's guides made apparent the contradiction at the heart of the museum collection: the recuperation of class distinctions in the very process of removing them.

Both these books begin with their first chapters devoted to accounts of Lord Elgin and Charles Townley bringing their collections to England. In the *Elgin and Phigaleian Marbles*, Ellis discusses the controversy surrounding the obtaining of the marbles, suggesting that Elgin did so because of his concern that England had no classical models for its artists and students. He points out that Elgin had also obtained the marbles out of his concern for their preservation, since he had heard of the "almost daily injury which the originals were suffering from the violent hands of the Turks" (3). Ellis claims that since the Turks had no consideration for Greek statues, were "even in the habit of shooting at them" Elgin, as a lover of art, had no recourse but to save them (4). Thus, while representing the Turks as barbaric people without any knowledge of aesthetic value or taste, Ellis exonerates Elgin from blame for taking the statues from Greece and describes him as the savior of art, one who ventures stratagems and money in order to save the marbles for the education of the English. Ellis ends the chapter by saying that Elgin's perseverance and taste have helped establish England's reputation as a repository of art: "The possession of this collection has established a national school of sculpture in our country, founded on the noblest models which human art has ever produced" (10). The aristocratic collector of the seventeenth and eighteenth centuries is here recast as a patriot, one who collects not for his own power but for the power of the state and for the disinterested improvement of art and taste in its population. National pride becomes pride in the power of the aristocracy and, as a result, class difference is valorized.

Ellis's *Townley Marbles* is also a testimony to the cultural power and aesthetic taste of the aristocracy which can, in England, reproduce the classical world even when faced with increasing industrialization and the growing strength of the middle classes. It opens with an account of the lineage of Charles Townley. Townley, the reader is told, is a descendant of the Duke of Norfolk and belongs to a family which "had been seated at Townley for many successive generations" (1). When he brought his collection to England, Townley established, according to Ellis, a house for his collections in which the furnishings and decorations suggested that "the interior of a Roman villa might be suspected in our own metropolis" (6). The recreation of a Roman interior in England seemed valuable to Ellis because it became a setting that combined wealth and scholarship, taste and rank.

For Ellis, such a world was the one for which and by which the museum had been constituted. In the hearings by the House of Commons committee in 1836, when asked why men of literature and science were not trustees of the museum instead of the men of "high rank and station" who comprised both the official and the nonofficial trustees, Ellis had replied that he saw no advantage to making men of science trustees since a "well-educated gentleman knows science and literature in sufficient quantity to make him a good trustee (*Minutes,* 9). For Ellis, Townley was this model gentleman; that such a belief had other supporters is apparent in the fact that Townley was elected a trustee in 1791 and remained so until his death.

In the guidebook, Ellis praises Townley not only for the setting in which he placed his marbles, but also for the "select few" that he invited to dinner. Townley's dining room is described as having walls with fake prophyry, with valuable statues placed among lamps that were positioned so as to increase the illusion of the Roman setting. Awed and impressed by the room, by the society of the "select few," Ellis revels in the recreation of ancient Rome in England, just as the Underwood guidebook of 1826 had suggested that ancient Greece had been recuperated in England. In contrast to the Underwood guide, however, the recreation of the classical world occurs only at Townley's aristocratic table. The Townley guide is written by a staunch Tory seeing in 1848 that the museum was becoming more and more open to every kind of person, poor or rich, so that it seemed even more important to reclaim the world of art and culture as an aristocratic realm. At a time when bourgeois values were gaining dominance, aristocratic values became idealized.[26]

The renewal of the classical world is, for Ellis, made possible by the wealth of the collector. In its didactic valorization of classicism as the most essential part of an aesthetic education, the *Elgin Marbles* is addressed to teachers of the classics and to those wishing to read and understand the classics. From the classical world they are to learn "how infinite in variety are simplicity and truth" and to "pay a tribute of thanks to the nobleman [Elgin] to whose exertions the nation is indebted for it" (215).

In the museum the importance of the wealthy collector was further illustrated by the titles given to exhibits: the Townley Marbles, the Elgin Marbles, the Payne-Knight Collection, the Christy Collection, the Sloane Collection. Each object in the museum came to be a mark of those who funded the travelers and collected the objects.

The committee of 1835 had been aware of the problematic importance of the aristocratic collector, for they asked Ellis why portraits of the trustees and of benefactors were hung in the museum. In 1850, at the hearings of another parliamentary commission on the British Museum, the keeper of the Department of Antiquities, Sir Charles Fellowes, commented that the Elgin collection would perhaps be better called the Athenian collection, and that collections would be better named chronologically or geographically than by the name of their patrons. Despite Fellowes's suggestion, the museum continued to give prominence to its collectors, reminding visitors of the distance between the visitor and the collector.

III

In the first half of the nineteenth century, therefore, the museum furthered the consolidation of a "cultured" middle class while it also deepened a sense of class distinction. England was a nation constructed by class differences but also conscious of the possibility of self-improvement and of individuals moving into a higher class and of living without class antagonisms—as a nation.

Yet it was still the upper classes which were shown to be responsible for this happy unity. Matthew Arnold, writing in 1867, believed that the upper classes could uplift the lower by teaching them culture and inculcating in them aristocratic qualities. Culture will develop, according to Arnold, the national spirit that will pacify the masses and make England "a great nation."[27] He believed that education would, above all, teach the culture of nationalism, which, as aesthetic education, implied the perfection of both individual and state.

Though Arnold had suggested that the availability of culture signified the democratization of England, what it effectively concealed was the social reality in which a large number of the working class had no part in such a culture. The possession of cultural capital in the hands of the dominant classes was presented as a disinterested and gratuitous sharing of national wealth. This "misrecognition" of class divisions, as Bourdieu puts it, was necessary for the operation of the sphere of symbolic and cultural goods.[28]

While there is no clear evidence of how many working-class visitors went to the museum. it is well-known that they flocked in large numbers to collections such as the world fairs, which exhibited objects and goods from many countries.[29] The number of visitors to the British Museum increased rapidly in 1851, the year of the Great Exhibition, when almost two million people visited it, more than the entire residential population of central London.[30]

The Museums Act of 1845 and the Public Libraries Act of 1850 enabled local authorities to build libraries and museums out of the public rates. Whereas in 1800 there had been less than a dozen museums, by 1850 there were nearly sixty and by 1887 there were at least 240.[31] The British Museum had grown immensely as well, both in its buildings and in its collections. A new reading room had to be added in 1857, and the White Wing opened in 1882. Between 1880 and 1883 the natural history collections were removed to South Kensington.

Advances in public participation in libraries, fairs, and museums occurred within the context of the decline of working-class radicalism after 1850. Richard Johnson has suggested that after 1850 the alternative system of working-class "really useful education" supported by radicals such as Cobbett, and by the Owenites and the Chartists, was replaced by working-class demands for education provided by the state. Whereas many radicals had opposed state education on the Godwinian grounds of opposition to authoritative education,[32] the acceptance and even the demand for state education signaled that the incorporation and the pacification of the working class had begun. After 1851, all classes were visiting the British Museum, though the numbers did not reach the peak of almost two million a year that occurred during the Great Exhibition.

To claim the necessity and the success of the museum and library laws, the Select Committee on Public Libraries was told in 1849 that the character of the workingman had improved in recent years both "in a moral and literacy point of view." By 1852, it was believed that the British Museum had become successful in educating the public. The preface to an 1852 guidebook to the museum, published by the New Library of Useful Knowledge, another series of books aimed at educating the middle and lower classes, begins with an enthusiastic counting of the steady increase in the number of visitors to the museum, a counting that inscribed the participation of the working class in the dominant culture.[33] It is "wonderful" that 53,912 people came to the museum in one week; what is even more a matter of wonder and jubilation is their "perfect propriety and decorum," which is "highly creditable to their good taste and feeling" (13). It was felt that the "mob" had been disciplined by seeing and acquiring knowledge and information. To indicate the success of the museum the guidebook of 1852 continues:

> formerly the English populace was a mere mob—a mischievous assemblage, incapable of appreciating the beautiful or the good, or of behaving with common decency in public places; and upon this plea they were virtually excluded from inspecting not only the mansions of the nobility . . . but our noblest national treasure.[13][34]

While suggesting that it was merely a lack of proper behavior that prevented the "mob" from participation in the glories of the nation, the writer states also that increased participation can come about now that the lower classes have shown civilized behavior in the Crystal Palace during the Great Exhibition of 1851. The "mob" has behaved with propriety in viewing the "houses of the aristocracy, several of which have been liberally thrown open to their admission" (preface).

It comes as no surprise, therefore, that the guidebook of 1852 concludes happily: "Verily this is an age of progress, and the conviction of this truth . . . that the sympathies of the rich and the poor are identical. . . . That we are all of one common nature, let us still further show (by acting on) the maxim of universal love" (13). Thus the union of rich and poor is believed to have taken place by means of institutions such as the museum, and therefore only through the much greater wealth, learning, and condescension of the wealthy.

The guidebook suggests, furthermore, that with its help, the objects in the museum are now accessible to all visitors. The guidebook proposes to give visitors "a general idea of the nature and amount of the treasures that lie within their reach" (5). It points to a world of objects, "within the reach" of the visitor, proposing the possibility of ownership even when the separation of viewer from artifacts kept in glass cases, of visitor from the collector whose name was enshrined in the museum displays, denied that such a possibility existed. The objects were only "at a glance," for they could be viewed, but not really within reach, for they could not be bought or owned by the many thousands of museum visitors. The museum displayed realms of knowledge that had earlier been hidden from the general public and provided the proximity of valuable objects that without any possibility of possession aroused the pride of national ownership. The viewing public felt pride in the collections, without realizing that they were looking upon objects that exemplified their own alienation, for the products included in the collection would be property created by the division of the worker from the product of his labor. The guidebook of 1852, by pointing out the harmony and unity in the nation, collapsed the difference between capital and labor, seeming to reunite the workers with the product of their labor. Yet the reconciliation was proposed through the promise of ownership, which, though national, was a relation very different from the reconciliation of labor value with use value wished for by early nineteenth-century radicals. This new form of ownership promised, to all visitors to the museum and to the greatly increasing audience which included the working class, the breakdown of class divisions through the creation of a new homogenous class: the consumer.[35] The consumer suggested a new homogeneity and a unity by promising a breakdown of class differences, for everyone could consume faced with a world that was shown to be consumable.

The consumer was a product of the collection because, as Stewart argues, the consuming self constituted not by the production but the consumption of goods is the result of alienation. This alienation emerges from the abstraction of labor from the process of production of the collection.[36] The separation of labor from product, and of object from production, resulted in the creation of a self that could only overcome alienation by consumption.

The existence of the public collection, in which objects seemed to be produced magically, signified the subject who was not the producer but the "inheritor" of value. And because the discourse of the consumer was the nonlabor of "magic" and not the labor of production, the collection came to signal the economy of consumption. Such a relation is suggested in the 1852 guidebook, marking the decline of working-class agitation and the rise of state education as well as the increased commodification of social relations which signals the emergence of the consumer. While guidebooks before 1850 carefully included narratives of the labor of collecting and writing to mediate the radical disjunction of the object from its origin and production, even though what was produced was not use value but display value, the guidebook of 1852 contains no such narrative.

What it provides instead is a narrative of magic and transformation, which, in the case of artifacts from Asia and Africa, depicts colonial penetration as aesthetic transformation in the service of bringing artifacts to the consumer. There are no accounts of the acquisition of objects, as in Ellis's guides. What is mentioned is that when objects arrived at the museum—and we are not told how they arrived there since the writer merely quotes from the most current edition of the *Synopsis*—the museum had to be made bigger. If a narrative is given, and this occurs in the description of the Lycian room, it is one of accident and chance and not of labor or hard work. Sir Charles Fellowes, we are told, made the "discovery" as a "result of mere accident," for while traveling in Asia Minor he "happened to alight upon the ruins of an ancient city." Being "struck with the beauty of the sculptured remains" he made drawings of these and took them back to England. There it became "immediately apparent" that these were the ruins of the ancient capital of Lycia (27). In contrast to earlier narratives of learning and acquisition, all of Fellowes's responses are represented as being unpremeditated, easy, not sought or worked for. Collecting is presented as discovery without labor. The Lycian collection thus becomes a narrative of chance, of a magical transformation of ruins (stumbled onto by chance) into beautiful remains that have value.

The narrative of transformation becomes also the narrative of the process by which the museum educates. The education does not occur by the conscious mental labor of the viewer but by the effect of the proximity of objects. With a visit to the museum, says the 1852 guidebook, "the mind of the visitor will become gradually the recipient of an invaluable variety of information and knowledge, and will find itself qualified, in a superior degree, for historical, artistic and antiquarian pursuits, should inclination and circumstance prove favorable" (5). The public would be "civilized" simply by viewing the objects in the museum, objects that suggested its own commodification.

The education of the working class by means of state institutions such as the British Museum and the concomitant emergence of the consumer thus furthered the rise of imperialism, for it presented the world as a storehouse of consumable goods that could be brought back to England. Furthermore, the British subject, alienated and made into a consumer by his own commodification, saw other races and other peoples also as commodities. The British Museum had shown the world to be full of collectible and consumable objects; imperialism and the acquisition of artifacts for the museum became synonymous processes.

When late nineteenth-century guidebooks mention objects acquired through military conquest, they elide the labor and cost of acquisition by suggesting its ease. Again, it is not the labor of production but the discourse of magic which is suggested here. The preface of the 1899 museum catalogue, for instance, describing antiquities from Benin, presents them as obtained by "a recent successful expedition sent to Benin to punish the natives of that city for a treacherous massacre of a peaceful English mission."[37] The destruction of Benin city, the reader is told, "made accessible to students of ethnography the interesting works of native art which form the subject of the following pages."[38] The cost of the acquisition in human lives, time, and money is not mentioned. In these catalogues the military might of a colonial power is given credit for enabling the collection and preservation of objects. Since display value in the collection comes from the transformation of goods into artifacts and art, military conquest becomes a source of aesthetic value, one that is easily converted into economic value. The history of the museum can be seen as the history of colonization.

Yet finally, not only were the guidebooks to the British Museum implicated in the commodification of the world and of the English public, but the museum itself inscribed this process. It was an imperial project because it embodied a love of order, what Walter Pater described as the "element of classicism." The world was reassembled in the museum as an ordered construct. The love of variety, that function of the power of capital through the acquisition of goods, was the aesthetic of the imperialist collector; it enabled the collecting of objects that could be put in order within a familiar taxonomy. Gaston Bachelard, in *The Poetics of Space*, mentions that Robinson Crusoe reconstructs a world from objects that he transforms magically.[39] The British Museum did the same. It collected objects that were believed to have obtained value only by being placed in the museum collections. Taken out of circulation in their original economic spheres where they had use value, they were placed in another economy in a different form. However, what was suggested was that they had been transformed into use when they were made objects of knowledge; without this new use value they were merely the dirt that awaits transformation into gold.[40] Thus the British Museum constructed a world that showed what was unknown and alien as being constructable and which could be temporally as well as spatially frozen into artifacts within the museum.[41]

The museum also provided a discourse of communication with the rest of the world. Like Jules Verne's traveler in *Around the World in 80 Days,* whose house was filled with speaking tubes and clocks, communication as well as movement in time and space was proclaimed by the collection of objects in the museum. The unmoving, frozen spoils of travel showed the mobility of the English collectors. The visitor who perambulated through the museum, past the atemporalized, stilled artifacts, replicated with incredible ease the journeys of the intrepid British travelers. A visit to the museum was like a guided journey to foreign lands.[42] Here lay the ivories from many "dark" places; the spoils of travel, like the novel, the travelogue, narrativized the "other." The "rescue" of personal fragments, which for Walter Benjamin gave the private collection its ability to provide rebirth and renewal, was, on a public and national level, an imperial ordering.[43]

Notes

1. From the *Minutes of Evidence taken before the Select Committee on the Condition, Management and Affairs of the British Museum,* 1835. Hereafter *Minutes,* cited in the text.

2. Sir Hans Sloane willed his collection to the British government. When George II refused to buy it, Sloane's trustees petitioned the House of Commons, and by means of a state lottery and an act of Parliament, the British Museum was created.

3. Pierre Bourdieu, *Distinction,* trans. Richard Nice (Cambridge: Harvard University Press, 1984), 7.

4. Pierre Bourdieu, *Outline of a Theory of Practice* (Cambridge: Cambridge University Press, 1977), 85.

5. Susan Stewart. *On Longing: Narratives of the Miniature, the Gigantic, the Souvenir, the Collection* (Baltimore: Johns Hopkins University Press, 1984), 164.

6. *A Guide to the Beauties of the British Museum* (London: Underwood, 1826). Hereafter *Guide,* cited in the text.

7. Richard Altick, *The English Common Reader* (Chicago: University of Chicago Press, 1957), 266.

8. John Barrell, *The Dark Side of the Landscape* (Cambridge: Cambridge University Press, 1980). Barrell shows how this discourse of labor functioned in the depiction of the rural poor in English painting from 1730–1840.

9. It is still taken to be value-free. There are very few analyses of guidebooks in current scholarship. Stewart's *On Longing,* which is so useful on the collection, has very little to say about the catalogue or the museum guide. More useful is Roland Barthes's very brief piece on "The Blue Guide" in *Mythologies.*

10. Jon Klancher, *The Making of English Reading Audiences* (Madison: University of Wisconsin Press, 1987), 22.

11. Fani-Maria Tsigakou, *The Rediscovery of Greece* (London: Thames & Hudson, 1981), 77.

12. Edward Said, *Orientalism* (New York: Vintage Books, 1979).

13. Joseph Mordaunt Crook, *The British Museum* (London: Lane, 1972).

14. Charles Knight, *The Old Printer and the Modern Press* (London: Murray, 1854), 307.

15. Patricia Hollis, *Class and Conflict in Nineteenth-Century England* (London: Routledge & Kegan Paul, 1973), 336.

16. Richard Johnson, "Really Useful Knowledge: Radical Education and Working-class Culture," in *Working-class Culture,* ed. J. Clarke, C. Critchen, and Richard Johnson (New York: St. Martin's Press, 1979), 76–88.

17. J. M. Golby and A. W. Purdue, *The Civilization of the Crowd* (London: Batsford Academic and Educational Press, 1984), 93.

18. Marjorie Caygill, *The Story of the British Museum* (London: British Museum Publications, 1981), 25.

19. W. H. Boulton, *The Romance of the British Museum* (London: Low, Marston, 1931), 12.

20. B. Harrison, "Teetotal Chartism," *History* 58 (1973): 197.

21. Kenneth Hudson, *A Social History of Museums* (London: Macmillan, 1975), 10.

22. G. Long, *The British Museum: Egyptian Antiquities* (London: Knight, 1832), 5.

23. Altick, *English Common Reader,* 192.

24. Though I include the explorers with the collectors, the latter were generally the patrons of the former. For instance, Giovanni Belzoni, who was responsible for the excavations of the Pyramids at Giza, was funded by Sir Henry Salt, the English consul general in Egypt, who then became the owner of the artifacts that Belzoni discovered. Many of the collectors were the men of rank who, like Sir William Hamilton, had enough money to make their own classical collections and were in influential government positions abroad where they could obtain local artifacts.

25. Henry Ellis, *Elgin and Phigaleian Marbles of Classical Ages* (London: Knight, 1846). Henry Ellis, *The Townley Marbles* (London: Knight, 1848); further references cited in the text.

26. Juliet Mitchell, *Women's Estate* (New York: Vintage Books, 1973).

27. Matthew Arnold, "Education and the State," *On the Study of Celtic Literature and Other Essays* (London: Everyman's Library, 1976), 187.

28. Bourdieu, *Distinction,* 477.

29. See Edmund Swinglehurst, *The Romantic Journey* (New York: Harper & Row, 1974). Swinglehurst mentions that excursion clubs were set up to take the less affluent to these fairs. James Cook took 165,000 people to the Great Exhibition through the creation of excursion clubs in which people could save up for trips. Swinglehurst comments that

this tour fulfilled James Cook's best ambitions: "to bring travel to people, to stimulate desire for learning and to make them aware of the glorious future which the Great Exhibition presaged" (35).

30. Crook, *The British Museum*, 196.

31. Ibid., 90.

32. Johnson, *Working-class Culture*, 95.

33. *The British Museum in Four Sections or How to View the Whole at Once* (London: Cradock, 1852); further references cited in the text.

34. The 1985 BBC series (also an exhibition at the National Gallery in London) called "The Treasure Houses of Britain," does exactly the reverse. It reeducates the British public about the glories of the English aristocracy by taking the viewers back into the houses of the wealthy and showing them the art and artifacts within.

35. See forthcoming work by David Lloyd regarding the connection between the rise of the consumer and the incorporation of the English working class in the nineteenth century.

36. Stewart, *On Longing*, 156.

37. Charles Hercules Read and Ormonde Maddock Dalton, *Antiquities from the City of Benin* (London: British Museum, 1899), 4.

38. Ibid., 4.

39. Gaston Bachelard, *The Poetics of Space* (Boston: Beacon Press, 1969).

40. In a contemporary example of this attitude, John Russell (chief art critic of the *New York Times*) writes in the *New York Times Magazine*, 2 June 1985, that "art is everywhere in India, if we know how to look." Rejecting any Indian idea of art or beauty, Russell appreciates India in moments of epiphany when he can see "a private India, a confidential India and an alternative India." Proving that he still thinks he can turn dust to gold, Russell writes that art "is just there [in India], in the air, on the ground, all over the place, for the taking, and no name attached to it." Russell reveals that colonial discourse is still alive in speaking of what is called the "Third World."

41. The Victoria and Albert Museum even at the present time functions as a reminder of the glories of England's imperial past.

42. The British Museum is now a journey into the past of all the cultures of the world. As one popular guidebook (*Lets Go: The Budget Guide to Britain and Ireland*, 1985) says: "it is the closest thing this planet has to a complete record of its civilizations" (115).

43. Walter Benjamin, "Unpacking My Library," in *Illuminations*, trans. Harry Zohn (New York: Schocken Books, 1969), 59–67.

English Studies and the Cultural Construction of Nationality: The Newbolt Report Reexamined

Patrick Scott

University of South Carolina

> An education based upon the English language and literature would have important social, as well personal, results; it would have a unifying tendency. . . . pride in the national language would be a bond of union between classes, and would beget the right kind of national pride. Even more certainly should pride and joy in the national literature serve as such a bond. . . . through all social differences, human nature and its strongest affections are fundamentally the same. . . .
>
> Literature, in fact, seems to be classed by a large number of thinking working men with antimacassars, fish-knives and other unintelligible and futile trivialities of "middle class" culture, and, as a subject of instruction, is suspect as an attempt "to sidetrack the working-class movement.". . . We were told . . . working men felt any attempt to teach them literature or art was an attempt to impose on them the culture of another class. [Newbolt Report, 1921][1]

O NE of the most important and divisive current debates concerns the relation between nationality and education. In the West, generally, critics have for some time been emphasizing the arbitrariness of national cultures and stressing the value of multicultural education for multiethnic societies; indeed, in the United States, the educational foregrounding of ethnic- or gender-based cultural diversity often seems a way of maintaining official blindness to the more intransigent social disjunctions of economic class. In other parts of the world, in Africa for instance, or in the submerged nations of the Eastern bloc, writers and

218

activists stress the importance of centering school curricula on unified national cultures, both to promote national cohesion and to resist the cultural and economic hegemony of the neocolonial powers.[2] The debate has been sharpened in Britain by the Conservative government proposals for a national curriculum and in America by such alarmist critiques as William Bennett's *To Reclaim a Legacy* (1984) or E. D. Hirsch's technically derived argument for monocultural schooling in his bestseller *Cultural Literacy: What Every American Needs to Know* (1987). More theoretical cultural analysts worldwide repeatedly and disdainfully expose the hidden interests of class, race, and gender that lie behind even the most liberal-seeming and well-intentioned of national educational programs.

Yet these issues are not new, and our accommodation to them can be helped by looking at previous attempts to resolve them. In Britain, the complexities, motivations, and self-deceptions of modern cultural nationalism are most fully anticipated by a single document, the Newbolt Report on *The Teaching of English in England,* published late in 1921. This, above all others, was the means through which, after centuries of classical dominance over English schooling, vernacular culture and the national literature were given curricular centrality. For anyone involved in the current debates, the arguments of the Newbolt Report still make fascinating reading. Aside from organized sport, the idea of an English-based liberal education may well have been Victorian England's longest-lived legacy to the twentieth century—where is Victorian industry? where the railways? where the Empire? where is Victorian belief? where, even, Victorian doubt? yet "English" still remains, to traditionalists and reformers alike, whether as "Great Books" or as "Textual Studies," the apparently inevitable site of much that matters most in the educational experience. The Newbolt Report picks up themes treated in several earlier essays in this volume, and, indeed, it poses something of a test case for current modes of cultural inquiry.

There can have been very few government reports that have ever sold as well or been discussed as widely. The Report was presented as the formal findings of a departmental committee of the national Board of Education "to inquire into the position of English in the educational system of England," but its broad humanistic approach and its readable style soon set it apart from most such official publications. It became widely used as a teacher-training manual and as the blueprint from which school textbooks and curricula were planned.[3] In its firm renunciation of the classics and in its argument that instead English language and literature "form the only basis possible for a national education" (NR, 14), the Newbolt Report marks a major British cultural shift.

During much of the past seventy years, the Report has been taken as a step forward in educational history. It was not deeply original; its general approach derived from Arnold, and many of its specific recommendations had been anticipated during the preceding decade in the board's own circulars to teachers.[4] But it summed up and made official the new claim that a liberal education in English should be the center of the school curriculum, and it risked exploring what this might mean, not just in the abstract but in specific educational institutions. In addition to having all the right names from contemporary educational discussion, the list of the committee's members and witnesses reads like a Who's Who of literary scholarship—Quiller-Couch, Dover Wilson, Caroline Spurgeon, F. S. Boas, George Saintsbury, E. K. *and* R. W. Chambers, Helen Darbishire, Israel Gollancz, W. W. Greg, Herbert Grierson, W. P. Ker, Edith Morley, Walter Raleigh, Ernest de Selincourt, and Sir Sidney Lee. Though W. P. Ker is said to have burnt the published report in the courtyard of University College (he found it antiphilological), for a long time the Newbolt Report stood as a model of how a well-run government committee could move events forward and create public and professional consensus.[5]

The consensus supported a surprisingly idealistic and pluralist idea of what a national education might be. It certainly did not involve the imposition of a single centrally promulgated traditional curriculum nor of relentlessly utilitarian goals (NR, 12). For one thing, influenced by the experience of the Great War, Newbolt asserted that national education must be socially inclusive; "English" was accessible to all classes, while classically based education necessarily excluded "the general mass of any modern nation" (NR, 13). Second, national education must be liberal, rather than merely functional or vocational (NR, 12); even the chapter on "English in Commercial and Industrial Life" used questionnaire responses from forty "prominent English firms" to make a case that "schools would best serve the 'needs of business' by developing to the utmost the intellect and imagination of those about to enter the business world" (NR, 129; the quote marks around the 'needs of business' paradoxically both foreground and put under erasure the phrase that best justifies the chapter's existence and which the chapter most needs to counteract). Third, the Report placed extraordinary emphasis on educational channels outside ordinary primary and secondary schooling—"continuation" and technical schools, evening classes, the university extension movement, the Workers' Education Association, and so on (see especially NR, 252–77); there are special sections on public libraries, community theater, and the influence of publishing and bookselling developments in the national culture (NR, 328–34). Fourth, the Report argues for the centrality of students' own writing, endorsing witnesses' claims that

> in teaching Composition they are concerned directly and immediately with the growth of mind. . . . the teaching of Composition develops individuality . . . it has, indeed, a transforming influence on the children, on their whole outlook, on their whole judgment, on their sense of responsibility. [NR, 72]

In composition teaching, the Report recommends emphasis on "positive, not negative methods," on frequent brief assignments, on oral preparation for writing, and on "the intermediate steps" by which a longer composition can be approached, while explicitly condemning "the teacher who limits his teaching to correction" (NR, 74–75). And on almost every other litmus test of English teaching for the last half century, the Report comes down on the liberal side—against grammatical prescriptivism and formal grammar instruction (NR, 11, 292–93), for classroom drama (NR, 316), against puritanical censorship of school texts or libraries (NR, 335–40), for examinations that reflect long-term educational goals rater than simply the cramming of set texts (NR, 303–8), against compulsory university Anglo-Saxon (NR, 227), and for connecting advanced literary study with philosophy and history (NR, 206–7). Even though considerable stress is placed on the social utility of "correct" spoken English, there is also repeated acknowledgment of the social and literary value of regional dialect (NR, 144, 260, 275, 277, 317); indeed, the Report comes out strongly against any "suppression of dialect," and even against any idea that standard English is socially superior, suggesting instead the encouragement of bidialectalism (NR, 67). The Report has its quainter passages and some preemptive concessions to more traditionalist viewpoints, but, even after sixty years, on most issues its specific conclusions, if not its emphasis on great literature, would cause little surprise if reissued by such contemporary educationist lobby groups as the Association of Departments of English, the English Coalition, or the National

Council of Teachers of English.

Recently, however, at least within Britain, the Newbolt Report has come to be considered in a different and more sinister light. Increasingly, critical theorists have turned their attention from literary interpretation itself to the social and educational institutions through which literary ideas have been generated and mediated; to the young turks of the new cultural studies, the Report has presented a very easy target. The committee's eponymous chairman, Sir Henry Newbolt himself, is remembered almost solely as an 1890s imperialist balladeer. Probably his most recognized poem remains "*Vitai Lampada,*" about how the game of cricket prepared public schoolboys to "Play up! play up! and play the game" in the afterlife of colonial warfare.[6] To the cultural analysts, little further research must have seemed necessary before Newbolt's Report could be reinterpreted to prove that literary study was an upper-class conspiracy, a false substitute for critical and class consciousness. "It is no accident," asserts Terry Eagleton, that "the most influential Government report" on English teaching was written by "a minor jingoist poet."[7] Chris Baldick's slightly less throwaway analysis sardonically highlights Newbolt's hope in a speech some years later that "English" could create "a national fellowship in which it shall be possible for everyone to forget the existence of classes."[8] The political ambiguity of such a hope is neatly encapsulated in the Report's prediction, quoted in the epigraph to this essay, that "pride and joy in the national literature" would serve as a "bond" between classes (NR, 22): who, the cultural analysts would ask, is in bondage to whom?[9] From this perspective,"English" was (and by implication still is) being prescribed, if not as the dream-inducing opium, then as the tranquilizing Valium of classes and masses alike, fostering false consciousness in the interest of traditional class hegemony.

Of course, such a portrayal of canonical high culture now seems standard enough, and the cultural analysts paint (or perhaps smear) with a pretty broad brush, but in this instance more detailed knowledge only adds plausibility to the standard cultural-studies analysis. For all the star-studded list of witnesses, the Report was very much an inside job, produced to a predetermined agenda. The big-name scholars might give evidence or decorate the masthead (Quiller-Couch attended only one meeting, W. P. Ker uttered only one sentence),[10] but the committee's working members were nearly all known to each other, and included a preponderance of Board of Education staff, His

Majesty's Inspectors and London County Council inspectors, with a shared and well-developed point of view. Indeed, Dover Wilson, himself then employed by the Board, described Newbolt's group as "largely . . . the Executive Committee of the English Association" meeting under a different name,[11] and the Report preface noted that the committee had "not thought it necessary to invite evidence from witnesses representing" the association, because their views were already well represented (NR, 3). Newbolt's own attitudes were firmly fixed from the very beginning (of course, that was why he had been chosen as chairman):

> [Gilbert Murray] and I had lunch together yesterday . . . he's in a pessimistic mood about Greek: says that in a few years there won't be a Professor in England to lecture on Milton with any knowledge of Greek or Latin. Even now in the North they are teaching English who only English know—as in America. I don't think I regret this quite as much as he does, and certainly I don't *dread* it so much. . . . As a language English has more *magic* than Greek, and more power of expression. I feel sure of that, and if anyone says "Yes, for an *Englishman*" that does not interfere with my argument, obviously.[12]

But the committee not only shared a common fund of ideas; it also showed a remarkable homogeneity of social background, as Newbolt's memoirs happily and innocently underscore. Newbolt had become involved with the committee through a casual conversation at a long-established private dining group, The Club (founded by Dr. Johnson), where he had been priming Hal Fisher, the president of the education board, for a speech on the topic "what makes a nation?" (LL, 263). Before the first committee meeting, he lunched with Fisher at the Athenaeum, and at that first meeting he noticed a surprising fact about its membership: "I found them a very pleasant lot. . . . Odd that out of eight men four were Old Cliftonians and one a Clifton master: none of them proposed by me" (LL, 264). This would not, of course, have seemed odd to Eagleton ("It is no accident"), but more revealing, perhaps, than the predominance of a single Old School Tie on a committee largely concerned with state-funded education is the fact that Newbolt misrecorded the size of his own committee: there were fourteen members, not eight, for in his alumnal bemusement he conveniently forgets the six women.[13] And Dover Wilson's reminiscence of the subcommittee that actually drafted the Report chapter by chapter reduces the active participants still further, to a mere six names, all male, all educated at public schools, and sixty-six per cent Cliftonian.[14]

This class-dominated English educational policy group would soon extend its influence into colonial education; in 1927 Newbolt was invited to the Colonial Office (for tea) and found himself coopted onto another government committee for (in his own unlovely but revealing phrase) "making Niggers into Noble Natives on the principles of the Newbolt Report" (*LL*, 350). It surprises me, a little, that neither Eagleton nor Baldick make capital out of the economic implications of the Report for Newbolt's own future cultural production. Immediately the Report came out, with private encouragement from Fisher, and at the suggestion of his war-time friend John Buchan (also a fellow member of The Club), Newbolt became general editor of Thomas Nelson's bestselling series of school anthologies; a whole new area of publishing enterprise was opened up by the Report, and, like a modern composition theorist who publishes a process textbook, Newbolt reaped a substantial financial reward from the curricular changes he was promoting.[15] Even without resorting to paranoid political conspiracy theory, and dragging in accusatory mention of Newbolt's connections in naval intelligence, or Quiller-Couch's enthusiastic wartime training of Cambridge officer recruits, or Dover Wilson's suspicious information-gathering activities among the Russian social revolutionary underground in prewar Finland,[16] there is no evading the Report's extraordinary enmeshment in the contemporary politico-economic power nexus.

Indeed, the new cultural analysts' case is almost too easy to make, because most of the sociopolitical motivations that are now being put forward as the disgraceful origin of English studies were stated quite explicitly in the Report itself, as arguments to support its curricular changes. First, the Report argues explicitly that education is a top-down process, and that the great texts of the national canon teach unitary and stable social and moral values that the recipients of government-funded education would not develop unprompted:

> Just as the physicist or mathematician show us deeper aspects of matter or of space, which in the life of every day we should never have discovered for ourselves, so poets, philosophers, and historians have the power of revealing new values, relations of thought, feeling, and act, by which the dull and superficial sight of the multitude is illuminated and helped to penetrate in the direction of reality. [NR, 17]

Second, the Report attempts quite openly to give education a new urgency, because of postwar fears that the war had damaged traditional British patterns of social stability and deference. It quotes an army chaplain (Tubby Clayton, the founder of the veterans' organization Toc H) in evidence that British soldiers had been unsettled by discovering the better educational standard of their fellows from the Dominions:

> The overseas man, with his freedom from tradition, his wide outlook on life, his intolerance of vested interests and his contempt for distinction based on birth rather than on worth, has stirred in the minds of many [British soldiers] a comparison between the son of the bondwoman and the son of the free. [NR, 17]

The Report warned that the "alienation" of "the working classes" from the dominant culture "points to a morbid condition in the body politic which if not taken in hand may be followed by lamentable consequences" (NR, 252), and it specifically drew the parallel between British working-class attitudes and "the hostility towards 'the culture of capitalism' now prevalent in Bolshevist Russia" (NR, 254). The Report itself argues that in England it was the divergences of language and culture that created and maintained dangerous class polarization (educational diversity "went far to make of us, not one nation, but two," NR, 22). It is the Report itself that nominates the teaching of English as the government's best panacea for these social divisions, forming "a new element of national unity, linking together the mental life of all classes" (NR, 15). In modern historicist analysis, according to Maureen Quilligan, "the assumption necessarily is that the text does not, at the surface level, want said what the critic finds in it to say,"[17] but it hardly takes sophisticated cultural analysis to find social motivations in a Report that never tried to hide them. Though one might discount these passages as audience-controlled, as a conscious use of politically directed arguments to ensure government support for a new educational initiative, there remains an interpretative problem in the very earnestness, the innocence, with which the Report puts forward a case now widely seen as at best morally ambivalent.

Yet in any event the standard British cultural-materialist exposé, uncovering selfish class interests behind a selected cultural phenomenon, very soon becomes curiously unsatisfying, and the less satisfying the more often one sees it done. The defamiliarization reveals only the familiarly diagrammatic. It is like un-

packing a set of Chinese boxes or Russian dolls and discovering
that the art work becomes less, rather than more, realistic the
further one gets inside.

If, however, one makes the alternative move within the cultural-
studies model, and shifts the focus of analysis from content or
class attitude to the genres and codes through which the Report
is written, even the social attitudes of the text become more complex and more interesting. Most commentary on the Newbolt
Report has read it as a kind of officially sponsored *Culture and
Anarchy,* an essay on education, the unified voice of its class and
culture. It is noteworthy, too, how often the more stringent analysts of the Report look for their most damning quotations not
to the Report itself, but to a contemporary single-author work
by one of the committee members, George Sampson's polemic
little book *English for the English.*[18] The Newbolt Report had to
be put together within a quite different textual tradition, that
of the government bluebook. Like the rather grander select com-
mittees or royal commissions, Newbolt's departmental committee
was generically bound to incorporate within its single discourse
the actual words, the voices, of a multiplicity of viewpoints and
witnesses. The Report both accepts and overwrites these generic
expectations. It includes verbatim evidence from experts but sub-
merges the quoted material within its own syntax and paragraph-
ing; indeed, it seldom quotes directly evidence with which the
Committee disagreed, usually preferring indirect speech and
nameless sources, while clearly attributed direct quotation is reserved for contemporary allies or historical sources. Typographically, too, the Report resists the visual distinctions of type size
and the crammed pages of tabular information that had been
conventional in early Victorian bluebooks; typographically, aside
from the section numbering, it could be a single-author text,
and Newbolt's own graceful introduction is a classic deployment
of the Victorian periodical essay form.[19] The Report could be
read, then, as the overwriting of a genre that imaged fact and
multiplicity, the early Victorian bluebook, by a genre that scorned
fact and that kept pluralistic awareness subordinate to a single
dominant literary voice, the late-Victorian cultural essay. In its
interplay between different generic expectations, the Report re-
peats the social tensions and political stance already discussed
on the basis of content.

But one might choose instead to read the Report against
discourse codes selected not from prior categorization but on

chronological grounds, cutting against conventional generic comparisons by New Historicist cross-sectioning. One of the new discourse forms of these postwar years was the official military history (which indeed provided Newbolt's other main employment through the mid-1920s). Here also full quotation from participant documents (signals, dispatches, and the like) had to be firmly subordinated to official narrative interpretation. Revealingly, the divergent stories of the documents could cause writers more trouble than the official overview; as Newbolt commented while at work for the Admiralty on the *History of Naval Operations,* "I am well and buzzing along but weighed on by tons of Official Secrets—horrible corpses which are just now heaving up the mounds and seem likely to burst their coffins" (*LL,* 350). This last image evokes a rather more startling cross-sectional intertext from the early 1920s; those still rooted in high culture might read the Newbolt Report against *The Waste Land* (and vice versa).[20] Both texts are fascinated and disturbed by the social variety of postwar Britain, both control their disturbance through close editing of the "different voices" they appear to let speak for themselves, and both attempt to use religio-literary allusion to soften this newly recognized cultural fragmentation.

To use Eliot as intertext is to realize just how heavily (and self-consciously) the Report has relied on religious imagery for its readability and textual coherence. It was not wholly as a sop to traditionalist diocesan education boards that the Report recommended reading aloud the King James Version, in English classes, as "the one great piece of literature which for centuries gave something of a common form, a common dignity, to the thought and speech of the people" (NR, 342). Baldick has drawn an interesting contrast between the kind of religious imagery in the Report itself and that in Sampson's book: where Sampson sees literature evangelically as a source of spiritual revelation and portrays English teachers as the savers of lost uncultured souls, the Report usually prefers the language of institutional religion and of the church establishment, seeing literature as a kind of liturgical text, creating social harmony through familiar verbal patterns.[21] Baldick does not, however, draw out the full implication of this contrast, that Sampson was insisting literary culture gave access to unitary spiritual values, while the committee Report looked to literary culture only for a harmony of surface signs, verbal deferences, of a kind that, like the established Church of England and its Common Prayer, or the reading aloud of the King James Version for its sentence patterns, allowed an almost infinite multiplicity in ideas about what exactly was being signified.

Even the Report's more fanciful (and more easily mocked) religious flourishes often reveal an ironic, almost parodic, detachment that Newbolt's political critics seem not to have recognized. What cultural analyst could resist quoting, for instance, the Report's description of volunteer adult education lecturers as "a fraternity of itinerant preachers on English literature" (NR, 25), but which has pointed out what the Establishment might think about itinerant preachers? Or what critique could ever omit the Report's admonition to redbrick professors in industrial towns?

> The Professor of Literature in a University should be . . . a missionary in a more real and active sense than any of his colleagues. He has obligations, not merely to the students who come to him to read for a degree, but still more towards the teeming population outside the University walls, most of whom have not so much as "heard whether there be any Holy Ghost." The fulfilment of these obligations means propaganda work, organisation and the building up of a staff of assistant missionaries. But, first and foremost, it means a right attitude of mind. [NR, 259]

Quite apart from its implied Arnoldian distrust of machinery, the imagery overturns the usual cultural-studies interpretation of the Report as complacently monocultural, for "missionaries" are, by definition, moving between cultures, moving beyond the secure boundaries of their cultural origin.

Similar uncertainties about the nation's central cultural tradition might be read out of the Report's other images, yet the cultural-studies critiques seem curiously reluctant to discuss this linguistic complexity. Take, for instance, the Report's much-quoted statement that "the rise of modern Universities has accredited an ambassador of poetry to every important capital of industrialism in the country" (NR, 259). Rather than traditional culture being a dominant imperial power toward which the industrial towns had a colonial relationship, the image here surely implies that there really were two nations, two or more independent cultures demanding mutual political recognition, and that industrialism was a major, perhaps even dominant, power, one with which poetry would do well to make terms, or which it must, at the least, treat diplomatically. The point is spelt out explicitly a little later in the same chapter, in a critique of Arnold's cultural elitism, this time linking the diplomatic imagery with the religious:

> The ambassadors of poetry must be humble, they must learn to call nothing common or unclean, not even the local dialect, the clatter of the factory, or the smoky pall of our industrial centres. [NR, 260]

The "not even" might suggest a less-than-total cultural decentering, but the sentence's core image (from the Acts of the Apostles, chapter 10, as interpreted by Henry Sidgwick) is about Jewish attitudes toward Gentile customs in the Early Church, and it surely leaves industrialism free from judgment by a traditional culture that the biblical pretext stigmatizes as Pharasaic.

On close examination, therefore, many of the very passages educed to illustrate the Newbolt Committee's cultural naiveté and its traditionalist assumptions show instead an ironic awareness of just how diverse English society was by the early 1920s, and of how marginal, even alien, the high-cultural literary canon would be to most English people. To a degree unimaginable in more recent educational literature, the Report, duty bound as it was to discuss the educational machinery of schools and teachers and curricula, still maintained a surprisingly clear-eyed understanding of the limitations of formal educational policy, recognizing that its particular recommendations must be set against the complexity and intractability of wider social developments.

Through reexamination of the Newbolt Report, we may perhaps defamiliarize the debates in our own time over national curricula and the construction of national cultures. Different observers will draw different lessons, but three, at least, may be drawn, based on the three main sections of the foregoing analysis. First, even the best, most influential, most progressive opinions of our time may, in due course, come to seem simply instances of social or psychological manipulation; the idea of English studies as the benign cultural formation, indeed cultural liberation, of free individuals remains the dominant ethos of our profession, and in light of the similarities between Newbolt's pedagogic outlook and that of our modern professional organizations, we might well reflect on how benign, or how manipulative, current pedagogy really is. Second, we might reflect, in light of the social origins of the Newbolt Report, on our own motives and investments as purveyors of culture, and on the inevitable narrowness of the social networks through which educational manifestoes are developed; yet we might also note, as cultural historians our-selves, how two-dimensional and self-validating is much cultural-materialist analysis, and so keep in mind the heuristic benefits of deferring closure on our political judgment when undertaking cultural-historical research. And, third, we might note the special hazards risked by those cultural educators who see and make explicit the social context and values of their work; paradoxically, if the Newbolt Committee had been less politically conscious, and less explicit about the social goals it hoped to accomplish, the Report would have been much less vulnerable to subsequent political criticism, but it would also have been much less signifi-cant. We should perhaps have a special respect for contemporary educators who discuss openly the political implications of their educational recommendations, even if some of us, or even most of us, are in political disagreement with their conclusions.

Questions about culture, social diversity, and national cohesion are surely both legitimate and important within educational de-bate, and if we commit ourselves too strongly to a (political) her-meneutic of suspicion, we may drive underground precisely the kind of questioning contemporary educators most need seriously to address. For me, the cultural-materialist analysis of Newbolt (and of his contemporary counterpart E. D. Hirsch) has been exercising that kind of counterproductive hegemonic pressure. What remains for me most impressive in the Newbolt Report is not its rhetoric about the noble tradition of English culture, nor its rather dated post-Great War-apocalyptic sense that tradi-tional culture, like traditional social hierarchy, was doomed, but its attempt to set a curricular change (the institutionalization of English studies) against the broadest of social contexts (industrial-ization, social conflict, regional and linguistic diversity). In this respect, at least, the Newbolt Report may serve not just as a warning but as a model.

Notes

1. *The Teaching of English in England, Being the Report of the Departmental Committee Appointed by the President of the Board of Education to Inquire into the Position of English in the Educational System of England* (London: His Majesty's Stationery Office, 1921; New York: Harcourt Brace, 1922), 21–23 and 252. Hereafter referred to as the Newbolt Re-port, cited in the text as NR.

2. See, e.g., Ngugi wa Thiong'o, *Decolonizing the Mind: The Politics of Language in African Literature* (London: Currey, 1986); Ernest Gellner, *Culture, Identity, and Politics* (Cambridge:

Cambridge University Press, 1987), 1–28; and, from a contrary perspective, John Trimbur, "Cultural literacy and cultural anxiety: E. D. Hirsch's Discourse of Crisis," Journal of Teaching and Writing 6 (Fall/Winter 1987):343–55.

3. For a good survey of reception, see Noel King, "'The Teacher must exist before the Pupil': The Newbolt Report on the Teaching of English in England, 1921," *Literature and History* 13 (1987):14–37, esp. 15–24.

4. See Derek Shayer, *The Teaching of English in Schools, 1900–1970* (London: Routledge & Kegan Paul, 1972), chap. 3, esp. 68, 72.

5. For the Ker incident, see John Dover Wilson, *Milestones on the Dover Road* (London: Faber & Faber, 1969), 98; on the Report's importance, see Margaret Mathieson, *The Preachers of Culture: A Study of English and Its Teachers* (London: Allen & Unwin, 1975), 69–81.

6. *Selected Poems of Henry Newbolt,* ed. Patric Dickinson (London: Hodder & Stoughton, 1981), 38. See Patrick Howarth's discussion of *homo newboltiensis,* the representative public school product, in his *Play Up and Play the Game: The Heroes of Popular Fiction* (London: Methuen, 1973), 1–14, 171–75.

7. Terry Eagleton, *Literary Theory: An Introduction* (Minneapolis: University of Minnesota Press, 1983), 28.

8. Chris Baldick, *The Social Mission of English Criticism, 1848–1932* (Oxford: Clarendon Press, 1983), 104, quoting Newbolt's *The Idea of an English Association* (London: The English Association, 1928), 13; see also NR, 15.

9. Other recent (and more circumstantial) analyses of the Newbolt Report, within the general cultural studies perspective, have been offered by: Brian Doyle, "The Hidden History of English Studies," in Peter Widdowson, ed., *Re-Reading English* (London: Methuen, 1982), 17–31; Janet Batsleer, Tony Davies, Rebecca O'Rourke, and Chris Weedon, *Rewriting English: Cultural Politics of Gender and Class* (London: Methuen, 1985), 13–40; Brian Doyle, "The Invention of English," in Robert Colls and Philip Dodd, eds., *Englishness: Politics and Culture, 1880–1920* (London: Croom Helm, 1986), 89–115; and King, "The Teacher."

10. Dover Wilson, *Milestones,* 96.

11. Ibid.

12. Margaret Newbolt, ed., *The Later Life and Letters of Sir Henry Newbolt* (London: Faber & Faber, 1942), 265. Hereafter LL, cited in the text.

13. Because the main focus of this essay is on questions of interclass cultural recognition, I have not explored the question of the Report's gender attitudes, though quite clearly the development of English studies, which became established much earlier in girls' secondary schools than boys' classics-dominated public schools, and which at the college level attracted far more women undergraduates than men, raises complex questions of self-definition for a male-dominated committee. The Report includes rather ambivalent discussions of girls' secondary schools (at NR, 99–102), of the superior qualifications of women English teachers (at NR, 125), and of the pioneering role of adult education classes in circumventing traditional gender barriers (at NR, 268), but it recommends authors "whose view of life is deepest and most virile" (at NR, 338), and the extensive quoted material from Quiller-Couch, a lecture addressing the audience as "Gentlemen," treats English prose tradition in terms of its effect on "men" and the memory of "your fathers;" on gender in Quiller-Couch's lectures, see Eagleton, 28, though note that in the Report, Q's attitudes are bracketed out as formal quotation.

14. Dover Wilson, *Milestones,* 99.

15. The official biography is peculiarly reticent about Newbolt's work for Nelson's (the textbook series appears only in a couple of footnotes, and even the index prefers to reference those footnotes, not under Nelson, but under the more idealistic heading

of *The Teaching of English;* LL, 421, 424). A similar reticence governs the memoirs of his close friend and publisher at Nelson's, who manages several pages about Newbolt without mentioning that they had produced books together: John Buchan, *Memory Hold-the-door* (London: Hodder & Stoughton, 1940), 178, 218–19. Yet in a letter of 1931, Newbolt acknowledged that, as his poetry became less profitable after the war, he and his family had been economically dependent on his educational publications (*LL*, 311).

16. For Dover Wilson's Finnish years, see *Milestones,* 47–63, and Baldick, *Social Mission,* 98–100.

17. Quoted in Edward Pechter, "The New Historicism and Its Discontents," *PMLA* 102 (May 1987):299.

18. George Sampson, *English for the English: A Chapter on National Education* (1921; reprint, Cambridge: Cambridge University Press, 1970). In the preface to his 1925 edition, Sampson asserted (in a formulation that cries out for gender analysis): "Deny to working-class children any common share in the immaterial, and presently they will grow into the men who demand with menaces a communism of the material" (quoted in Mathieson, *Preachers of Culture,* 74–75).

19. For evidence that Newbolt negotiated with the Report's publisher, His Majesty's Stationery Office, to alter conventional government printing styles in the direction of commercial book publication, see King, "The Teacher," 15.

20. Newbolt was to include Eliot, along with Ezra Pound, Herbert Read, Harold Monro, and Robert Graves, in his influential anthology *New Paths on Helicon* (London: Nelson, 1927), 101–6, chosing, "The Hollow Men" over the better-known "Prufrock" (and see Newbolt's acutely ambivalent editorial note, 401–3).

21. Baldick, *Social Mission,* 101.